Mindless Psychoanalysis
Selfless Self Psychology
and Further Explorations

Mindless Psychoanalysis, Selfless Self Psychology

and Further Explorations

Robert L. Bergman

The Alliance Press, Seattle

© 2008 by Robert L. Bergman, M.D.

Published by The Alliance Press, P.O. Box 798, Seattle, WA 98111. The Alliance Press is the publishing arm of the Northwest Alliance for Psychoanalytic Study. The goal of the Alliance is to make psychoanalytic knowledge available and useful to interested professionals and to the community at large in the Pacific Northwest.

Designed by Dennis Martin

Printed in the United States of America

ISBN 0-615-23602-5

To the many people who have taught me, especially my family and the people who come and have come to see me professionally.

Contents

Preface

WHEN THE NORTHWEST ALLIANCE FOR PSYCHO-analytic Study decided to venture into book publishing as a way of introducing some of our community's distinctive thinkers to a larger readership, we didn't have to look far for our first title. Robert Bergman's essays have been a vibrant and thought-provoking part of the Alliance's annual conference for many years. His yearly presentations are deceptively simple and jargon-free, but are theoretically sophisticated explorations of topics that matter to students of the human psyche and the healing arts. This collection of essays will, we hope, please those who are familiar with Bergman's work but have not yet had an opportunity to collect it in written form and will allow others to experience a new perspective on complex psychoanalytic topics, such as the interplay of subjective and interpersonal worlds in everyday life.

In creating these essays, Bergman is informed by his career as a psychiatrist and professor at the Universities of Washington and New Mexico, his years as the chief of Mental Health Programs in the Indian Health Services, and his long and ongoing career as a supervising and training analyst at Seattle Psychoanalytic Society and Institute. He also draws on his poet's heart, creating lyrical and moving reflections on his connection to his profession and to those whom he credits with having taught him not simply theory, but its human underpinnings.

Often deeply personal, these essays reflect a life of hard work and stringent study with a remarkable cadre of teachers. Bergman's mentors include such notable and diverse figures as Heinz Kohut, Bruno Bettelheim, and the Navajo medicine men who adopted him as a brother and fellow healer. He also credits, with gratitude and respect, his "customers," those who have come to him for help over the years and who, he reminds us, give as well as receive in the therapeutic relationship.

Bergman writes the way he speaks, plainly and with questions whose answers sometimes go unknown, but are nonetheless approached with curiosity and, to use a word he favors, enthusiasm. The papers are presented here, with one exception, in the order in which they were originally presented. In this volume, Bergman offers a brief introductory note for each paper on how he came to write it.

We at the Alliance hope that this collection of essays gives its readers what Bergman's writings have given us: the pleasure of encountering a truly original and down-to-earth synthesis of psychoanalytic thought and practice.

— *The editors of the Alliance Press: Ginger Harstad Glawe and Kris Wheeler, cochairs; Susan DeMattos, Kathy Knowlton, Rebecca Meredith, Bev Osband, Helen Palisin, Carol Poole, and Marcia Robbins*

Acknowledgments

I AM GRATEFUL TO REBECCA MEREDITH, BEV OSBAND, Helen Palisin and Carol Poole who have seen it through; to Michael Allison, Jordan Engel, Ginger Harstad Glawe, Kathy Knowlton, Dennis Martin, and Kris Wheeler, who helped in important ways; to the Philosophy Club, a study group in the University of Washington Department of Psychiatry, who read and discussed much of the book and gave me the idea of being a mindless psychoanalyst; and to the Northwest Alliance for Psychoanalytic Study, who have made the book and so many other good things possible for me.

Introduction

I AM A MINDLESS PSYCHOANALYST—HAVE BEEN SINCE about 1990. I decided that was what I wanted to be while taking part in a mind–body study group founded by Gary Tucker and Mark Sullivan in the Department of Behavioral Science of the University of Washington School of Medicine. The group included psychiatrists and psychologists of various persuasions, neurobiologists, philosophers and a psychoanalyst or two. We used to joke about how biologists think that psychologists are brainless, and that psychologists think biologists are mindless. As we tried out various ideas of how the brain produces consciousness and other mental phenomena, I decided to dispense with the whole idea of mind, and turned the joke around to think about mindlessness.

During the years when I was learning the elaborate quasi-anatomy and physiology of the structural model as developed by ego-psychology, as well as the geography of the alleged inner world of object relations, I came to doubt the usefulness of these metaphors. It seems to me that the concept of mind as a thing is needless, confusing and tautological. I believe that we can think more simply and clearly if we regard the mind as an activity of the physical beings we are. I have been trying to show that instead of thinking of models of the mind, we can say all that we have been saying, and a little more, by thinking in terms of the models of the world that everyone is constantly making in collaboration with the people around her or him. I have found that the mindless version is congenial with both the guilt psychologies of Freud and his followers, and with the shame psychologies of Adler, Sullivan, Kohut and others. It seems to me that the leading characteristic of mindlessness is its complete dependence on the notion that reality is a construct constantly negotiated with our fellows. These deliberations go on in the actual interaction of real people, but more of the time in imaginary interaction—what we call thought and feeling. In this system, emotions are seen as instinctively given means of influencing each other.

My first efforts to discuss mindlessness out loud and in writing were centered in the mind–body study group, but for the past decade and a half Seattle's Alliance (the Northwest Alliance for Psychoanalytic Study), a diverse but wonderfully cohesive and energetic group of several hundred clinicians and academics who are interested in psychoanalysis, has given me the opportunity to think through a reformulation of basic concepts. My first paper along these lines was given at a meeting sponsored by the Alliance, and most of the rest have been given at their annual conference on theory and practice. Over the years, others have appeared in the Alliance newsletter, the *Forum*. Both have given me a friendly audience, which I have been addressing in reality about once a year and in fantasy all the time. Colleagues whose reactions I can imagine are the people on whom I try out my ideas, and in the process I have learned what I think and have been able to get my ideas as straight as I can. By now I have made a fairly complete statement of what I think of as mindlessness. I think it is useful in working and thinking psychoanalytically, and yet preserves most of the concepts that used to be called metapsychology—the account of human nature and human life.

Over the years, I have focused on theoretical concepts such as affect and motivation, on clinical topics such as how to work with fragile and explosive people, current events such as terrorist attacks and aspects of everyday life such as marital conflict and crime and punishment.

I am grateful that, in addition to giving me the opportunity to make these papers public, the Alliance has now published them in this form. Few of the ideas I present are original, but I think the means of presentation are, and the radical constructivism I have accustomed myself to has changed me as a clinician.

I have become ever more devoted to the idea that conventional interpretations, especially of criticism or anger are defensive and damaging, and that thinking and talking with my customers about who each of us believes the other is and looking for agreement as to what is true is more helpful than talking about how their supposed inner worlds distort their alleged outer worlds.

Mindless Psychoanalysis, Selfless Self Psychology

and Further Explorations

Audience

This paper is not the earliest one collected in this volume, but I suggested that it be first because the idea that we all need an audience in order to think is essential to most of the others. In addition, it seems a good way to introduce myself to you the reader, who are an unexpected but greatly welcome addition to the friends in the study group and at the Alliance Forum who were the people I was experiencing when I wrote it.

The impulse to write this piece arose one day when I was working with a particularly embattled couple who themselves knew that their main complaint against one another was that they were such terrible audiences for each other. Thinking about their distress and my own experience revealed to me more vividly than ever before how much we need each other's attention and response.

AUDIENCES, VISIBLE OR INVISIBLE, ARE CONSTANTLY with us. As I sit at the computer writing this, you, my audience, are here—particularly vividly so because I dreamt of you last night. Actually, there are at least two of you audiences with me, you to whom I hope to be speaking at the Alliance meeting, and you the study group. Differences between you are giving me a little trouble at the moment because I want to make my ideas as clear and convincing to you as I can, and what seems likely to be suitable for one of you seems a little different for the other. If the differences were great, I would be so perturbed by them that I would have a hard time writing at all, let alone clearly and convincingly. It is that kind of perturbation, especially as it affects an analyst or therapist, that interests me the most, but I am getting ahead of myself in order to explain why we should think more about a somewhat unfamiliar topic.

4

I think that *audience* is not a common psychoanalytic term because privacy is one of the most important conditions for our work. We tend to deny the presence and the effect of an audience, even if one is present on the other side of one-way glass. That unusual situation is not so different as it might seem from the one in our offices. When we see an analysand whom we are presenting to a conference, study group, consultant or supervisor, those other people are there with us, and affect our feelings and our actions. Occasionally, the analysand knows it, too. Some years ago I took part in a continuous case conference in which the analysand, who had been told that control cases were sometimes presented, said, "There, tell that to the big boys down at the institute!"

Even in situations where there is only one audience—this is a hypothetical construct and probably is never more than approximated—the nature of that audience has profound effects on the performer. Of course, my experience of you is formed from a combination of what I sense of your communications to me and various audience experiences of the past. Right now, as I write in an optimistic mood, I form my impression of you using a large dose of my mother who, when I was a toddler, found what I said so charming that she took notes. If, as I go along writing, I have a change of mood—most likely caused by some awkwardness in my sentences or contradiction in my theories—or if, when I am reading this to you, you look bored or disappointed, my mother will vanish like the children that used to go back in the little house of certain barometers when the pressure fell, to be replaced by the low pressure, bad weather witch—my bad mother, who never could be satisfied by my piano playing no matter how hard I tried. The disappearance of my ideas then will be like the protective reaction of the Little Lame Prince's magic cloak, which he could use to fly anywhere in the world when he was alone. When a hostile person came on the scene, it would shrivel up into a small dirty old rag so that no one would notice it.

The effects of audience are most spoken about in sports, where it is taken for granted that home field advantage is important. The relationship between athletic teams and their fans is particularly illustrative. The fans' sense of themselves is enhanced by the success of their team and they make themselves part of it. "We're number one!" they gloat, even though the players are strangers who work for a business enterprise whose success has no practical benefit to the fans. The effect on the players (or on me at this moment) depends on how the audience takes them into themselves—a group self. Sigmund Freud, Janine Chasseguet-Smirgel and Heinz Kohut, among many others, have worked out the details of how and why such things happen. Being included by fans in a mutually congratulatory group confirms the players' best version of themselves. Like everyone, they have various versions that consist of relationships to others. If the others confirm the hoped-for versions they are enhanced in many ways, but if the others deny them they are shamed, and suffer damage that may be crippling. They hope they are the fans' heroes, and the cheers show that they are. On the other hand, home field advantage is no advantage at all if the fans boo—a much worse situation than being booed by the other team's fans when away from home. The boos of the enemy are almost as confirming as the cheers of friends, but being booed at home dashes players' expectations and hopes, and performance is likely to suffer, leading to louder boos, leading to worse performance, in a vicious circle.

The theater, the concert hall, and especially the political stage demand more direct attention to the audience than does the athletic field, because the performer relates more overtly to the audience and aims to please by something more specific and complex than winning the game.

A person I know is a particularly skillful public speaker. His audiences routinely are moved to tears and seem to be changed by hearing him. I believe that one of the secrets of his success is that he is exceptionally attached to the people he addresses. He loves them, and is quick to sense who they are, what they are worried about, what they want, and what kind of language is natural to them. He never reads a speech, because doing so would handcuff his ability to relate directly and precisely to who his audience is at the moment. They can tell that he is talking to them and cares about their reaction. If his remarks are sentimental and dramatic, as they often are, the sentimentality and drama are their sentiment and their drama, and he shares it. His identification with the audience is apparent. His approach to them is genuine and free-flowing because he wants to be part of them and they are part of him. His speeches are more effective than the run-of-the-mill politician's because he is a lover, not a seducer.

I believe his love of his audience is common among successful performers. I once traveled with a famous politician and was dismayed by being greeted at every stop by excited hordes of people who looked a bit carnivorous to me, but the politician always happily went to the center, shaking every hand he could and saying over and over, "Glad to see you. Thanks for coming." I realized after a while that he really meant it. He loved these people and was really glad they were there.

Public, large group phenomena are clear examples of the effects of audience, but are not the most common or important instances. Very small audiences, especially audiences of one in intimate performances, have major effects on how we feel. Kohut wrote that he and his wife joked that marital trouble arose from couples' not mirroring one another well. Painful experience, clinical and otherwise, easily shows that it is true and no joke at all. Yesterday, someone told me that his wife's response to a dozen roses was, "Two of the stems are broken and one is wilted." He had something quite different in mind and felt disappointment and shame, as I presume his wife did, too. She had expected a better bunch of flowers. He wanted a more positively responsive wife and she wanted a more careful, thoughtful husband who would love her so much that he would make sure the flowers he brought her were good ones.

Once a couple is fighting, invisible audiences often become as important as the two audiences that are present. A man I know has been able to realize that his tenacious sticking to his guns in arguments with his wife gets him only trouble. He is capable of seeing her point of view, but for the most part he refuses to tell her so. "I just feel as though something awful will happen to me if I admit she's right in any way." Part of the trouble is that, in his eyes, the ghost of his cold, domineering mother is inhabiting his wife at those moments, and he feels as if giving an inch will result in her taking a mile and enslaving him. In addition, I and the ghost of his father are there, too, and he can't bear to give up a position that he feels would, or at least should, prove to us that he is right and that we should help him.

I think that the most important audience reaction is the parents' response to the infant's smile. Something from the instinctual center of the baby is answered by an equally central pleasure of the parents. The interplay of gaze, funny noises, pleased surprise and laughter establishes the new person and confirms the old ones. If all is well in the life of the family, the particular things that come natural to the particular child are seen and appreciated. The process supplies a lifelong sense of being someone whose nature makes sense to others and will be well received. My mother's note-taking caused me some trouble in the long run. I had to learn painfully that not everyone thought I was that cute, but it established the persistent optimism that allows me to write a paper and read it in public. My optimism allows me to risk saying things that have occurred to me and to think they may be valuable to someone else.

A woman I know can force herself occasionally to say a few words to an audience, and she says them well, but it is agony for her to do it and she believes afterwards that she did poorly. Her greatest comfort and her greatest skill are in drawing others out. People love to talk to her because she is such a good listener. Being a good listener is a role that she likes because she is successful at it, and also because it can guide what little she says. She has found out what the other person is interested in. To be in analysis is agonizing for her because she has to do the talking, and for the most part she has to go without her usual way of being at all secure: finding out what I would like to hear about and supplying that. Her mother not only didn't take notes, she usually told her daughter to be quiet and not to bother her. The mother is someone who especially appreciates a good audience for herself, and she doesn't like the daughter stealing the show to any degree.

In that, she differs from most parents, who want the children to be part of their show. The trouble is that many parents need to write the script and to direct, and so their fantasies and not the children's are enacted, because what the children might do spontaneously is not necessarily what will be favorably responded to or demanded.

Ideally, parents continue to be charmed by what their children say and do without having dictated the behavior themselves. Even so, the behavior is shaped by the parents' response. The parents unconsciously reinforce the utterance of the phonemes of their language and not ones that they can't hear, and the child's sound production conforms. The same kind of process affects the child's entire behavior. Not everything that comes naturally will be pleasing and noticed; but for the most part, even though it develops within cultural and familial boundaries, the recurrent features of behavior that make up much of personality are individual and experienced by the young people as their own. This kind of direction is qualitatively different from the parents' demand for performance before their own audience. The essential difference is in how many audiences are present. Ideally, the parents are the child's audience, and vice versa. It is the presence of a third audience—the parents' audience—that screws things up.

The characteristics of a good parent-child relationship are similar to some found in any good relationship. The people involved are (among other things) good performers and audiences for each other. What they do is genuine and straightforward, and the response is, too. The people involved relate primarily to one another, and the impressions they have of the others approximate the impressions each has of him- or herself. Where there are disparities they can be negotiated primarily with reference to the ideas and experience of each. When things don't work this well, it is often because invisible people intrude, leading to a breakdown of someone's ability to be genuine and directly responsive.

In psychoanalysis we are familiar with the intrusions of people from the past who inhabit and distort our perceptions of people in the present and what we want and fear from them. In addition, invisible audiences from the past are ready to condemn us for enjoying or hurting the people we are with in the present. But these are relatively gross interferences. Subtler problems—problems with genuineness, spontaneity and flexibility—are often caused by the presence of an invisible audience consisting of a group from the present day that demands concrete literal adherence to some kind of loyalty. A Communist or a Republican or a psychoanalyst should see things certain ways—sacred dogmas must be preserved.

I am caricaturing—not that caricatures don't commonly occur—in order to illustrate the kind of trouble I mean. Just as good relationships are similar to the earliest good relationship, this kind of trouble resembles and derives from one of the problems in early child-parent interactions.

Kohut distinguished two ways that people can be grandiose. One is the direct continuation of the situation in which doting parents treat babies as if they are not only unique but also uniquely wonderful. In infancy the exaggeration is desirable, and if all goes well it will gradually be toned down to the point that the person has a strong sense of individuality but has ambitions gradually worn down by experience so as to be just a little beyond what is possible. Manageable disappointments in oneself and in the response of one's audience lead to modifications in the fantasy of greatness, and strictly personal greatness is supplemented by an extension of the sense of self to include idealized parents, idealized other people, and ultimately abstract ideals. Interruptions in this line of development occur when disappointment is too sudden and too great to bear or when there is overindulgence. Then fixations result in conflict between the grandiose ambitions and fear of shame if they should be revealed. The defense against the emergence of infantile grandiosity is primarily repression—Kohut's horizontal split. The unrealistic fantasies and the ambitions that power them are below the level of ordinary experience, but at the heart of one's being.

The other form of grandiosity, that which is vertically split-off, has a more complicated history and a defensive boundary that is harder to describe and understand.

The intrusion of other audiences into the situation of baby and parent is crucial. Over the years, one of the complaints about parents that I have heard most frequently is that they never seemed pleased with what one did except when overheard bragging about it to others. Naturally and desirably, our children are part of ourselves. We experience their successes and failures as our own. Trouble arises when a parent is so concerned about her or his appearance to others that the small child has to be shaped toward some ideal or ambition of the parent's, regardless of whether it comes natural to the child. The need can be so intense that parents exert rigid control of children's whole presentations of themselves, including not only the demand for performance of the parents' fantasies but also the prohibition of the independent performance of anything else. Sometimes this results in the ritualization of life seen in some of the intensely connected parent-child couples that we call symbiotic.

Fifty years ago, a young mother, deserted by her husband when her daughter was less than a year old, went through terrible hardships. The failure of her marriage and of some of her efforts to keep things together caused her intense shame, for which she compensated by elaborating and constantly enacting a myth of success, joy and of harmony between her and her child. Constant and effusive declarations of love and admiration between them as well as various falsifications of their history formed an ornate, invariable and highly detailed way of life from which neither could depart. About fifteen years ago, analysis had freed the daughter from some of these shackles. One day her mother called and asked, "How are you?" The daughter replied with a matter-of-fact "Fine," and the mother responded with a panicked and enraged, "What's wrong?" "Fine" was not the right answer.

The daughter, when I first met her, was more than a little self-important and demanding, but she was quite unaware of being so. Unlike the grandiosity that is beneath the horizontal split, this egoism was not only in consciousness but it was frequently acted upon. It wasn't repressed but it was disavowed. She thought she was acting naturally and properly. She was living the way her mother had made it clear she had to live. Disavowal of grandiosity only works for the person doing the disavowing.

The best example I know is of Frank Lloyd Wright testifying in court. When asked to state his occupation, he said, "World's Greatest Architect," and later when his wife reproached him he answered, "But, my dear, I was under oath." My analysand's conviction that she was not at all self-important was further supported by her feeling that the person she portrayed was false and that it somehow wasn't hers. It was her mother's.

Vertically split-off grandiosity is the home of inauthenticity and a sense of hollowness. Probably all people experience these unpleasant feelings at least mildly and occasionally, and some people suffer from them intensely and all the time. We also sense a lack of genuineness in others, usually, I think, in agreement with their sense of themselves, but not always. I am using Kohut's formulation, but this area of personality theory is a point of convergence of many points of view. D. W. Winnicott's False Self, Melanie Klein's splitting and her manic defense, Janine Chasseguet-Smirgel's ego ideal, and Jacques Lacan's desire of the Other are also accounts of the same phenomena.

Margaret Mahler's separation-individuation, the idea of triangulation as an aid to separation, and Heinz Kohut's second chance via the establishment of an idealized parent imago are descriptions of the prevention or the cure. There will be less need for false structures if the parents remain available and encouraging of much of what the child spontaneously is, and if, when they must, they frustrate without trauma the child's demands for independence. If one parent is experienced as too controlling, a resort to relationship to the other can provide a way out.

That escape can be especially important to girls because boys have the natural advantage of being differentiated from mother by gender. Plenty of mothers pressure their sons into being something great so that the mother can feel great vicariously, but that can happen to girls, too, and in addition they are likely to be the recipients of considerable pressure not to have a will that is distinguishable from Mother's. I think that what most crucially separates and individuates is will, one's sense of being one's own decisionmaker. In particular, what is common is an insistence that the daughter not embarrass the mother by not being a nice lady. Ladies are nice to one another, do not compete with each other overtly, do not contradict one another or do things just because they want to. I have heard many women and almost no men say, "I don't need that," as a reason to not have it. Mothers commonly reprove their daughters, but seldom their sons, by saying, "You don't need that."

I think the pressure to be ladylike is less common today than it was, but we and our analysands were born in an even more sexist time. I believe that the rise of women's athletic teams is a good thing for, among other reasons, the usefulness of providing a channel for the tomboyishness that has saved the independence of many a girl, only to have it dashed by the conventions of adolescence.

The conventions of adolescence can also provide for an escape. Especially then, but as Harry Stack Sullivan pointed out, even earlier, the establishment of intimacy with friends or a special friend can have the effect of rescuing someone from being, as Sullivan said about himself, a clothes horse for his mother's illusions. Unfortunately, such alliances are not a sure-fire escape from being trapped in false self and inauthentic relationship. The rigid conformity of many peer associations is a solution by countervailing power—the peers' concreteness against the parents' concreteness. In the more favorable case, the new relationship is like the baby smiling and the parents responding. The interactions come from what is central, spontaneous and real, and new ways of being evolve. In the unfavorable case, stylized behavior elicits stylized response. Freedom and genuineness are sacrificed so that false security can be shored up. People's cracking veneer is patched. The center feels as empty as ever but the facade is in better shape.

Since these are connections between false selves, they could be called *falseselfobjects*. The distinction is between them and *selfobjects*, which are other people or things or ideas that are cherished as part of one's sense of self. A false self is one that is manufactured to give an appearance of group membership. A sense of hollowness and falsity is, in large part, a sense of not really belonging with crucial others. Selfobject relations ameliorate that awful feeling by providing experiences in which what feels central, spontaneous and most intimately personal is responded to by someone else. Falseselfobjects are those things and people with whom one colludes to reassure each other of group membership. Most of the time this kind of membership depends on symbols used concretely, and with false reverence, to establish that each person who supposedly believes and acts correctly is a member.

It seems to me that this kind of interaction is best portrayed by Gogol in *Dead Souls*. The father of a young woman demands that her fiancé demonstrate that he is a person of substance by the ownership of a large number of serfs. Each landowner is recorded as officially owning as many people as he did at the last census, even if some have died. If the fiancé, Tchichikov, can persuade rich landowners to sell him dead souls at a price, he can afford and record them as his property and he will be able to qualify as a husband.

The layers of falsity that will contribute to this supposed substance are only part of Gogol's playing with soul deadness. Tchichikov's conversations with the landowners, bureaucrats and others are *tours de force* of empty conventionality. Each person repeats the formulas of group belief and custom that demand formulaic response. The manipulation of cardboard slogans results in a cardboard transaction of, "I'm okay, you're okay. We are both people of substance who deserve respect." Nothing is happening except in the world of empty appearance. The narrating voice constantly praises these fine people and their wonderful performances, and this irony too is many-layered. Scorn for the protagonist's vacuity, pity for his desperation and love, and admiration for his persistence even in absurdity, are all indistinguishably mixed.

I believe that this kind of irony, one of the main cultural themes of the modern sensibility (and even of the postmodern, as in the photograph, "Piss Christ"), was a partial solution to the need for artistic escape from the constricting falseselfobjects of the nineteenth century.

Artists, even more acutely than the rest of us, need to speak directly and genuinely to their audience. Clinical experience with artists whom I have been lucky enough to know has convinced me that one of the main things that will stop them from working, or will spoil what they are doing, is self-consciousness. Their concentration on what they are doing for the audience that they imagine is interrupted by awareness of another, their knowing friends, or other hostile critics. The fear that the primary audience will not like the work is bad, but what is worse is the thought that a secondary audience will say something like, "We know, and that isn't how it's done." Or worse yet, "You are a member of our group and we don't do that."

In chopping up the idols of the past, artists from the Fauve Period on have made an escape into the freedom to play, and that play is usually ironic. Irony has the advantage of being too inconsistent and indistinct to be pinned to any concrete meaning, and falseselfobjects have to be concrete. For something to serve as a badge of membership in a self-congratulatory group, it has to be easily recognized and responded to simply and rigidly. Ideals such as freedom for the individual in the midst of majority rule are complicated and slippery. Reverence for the American flag is simple and, as a falseselfobject, has to be taken with utmost literalness—no burning.

The artistic movements of the early twentieth century took themselves seriously, and also didn't. "I am an idiot. I am president of Dada. You are all idiots. You all deserve to be president of Dada." Architectural ornamentation was given up, especially ornamentation that was a reference to past works that were falseselfobjects of the falseselfgroup, those who know good architecture. The diatonic scale was abolished. Realism was no longer a goal, or at least not simple, literal realism. If, in a Mahler symphony, a corny brass band is always marching in at the tenderest moments, isn't that more like real life than pure tenderness? Is it tender? Is it corny? Is it satirical? Yes to all three.

It seems to me that the fullest development of irony is camp. Things are so bad they're good. "I love the pink flamingo in my yard. Isn't it wonderful?" How can such statements be understood? Do they mean what they say, or the opposite? Both. And we do love the old times when people in less confusing circumstances simply cherished their lawn ornaments, yet we don't want to be bound by allegiance to those times and their values. Anti-conventional self-presentation can serve to expand the space for individual play. Did Mae West represent an ideal of the feminine, or a caricature? In the space carved out by the uncertainty, she could be supremely independent.

One of the catches is that irony too—like anything—can become a rigid demand for the false. A side benefit of being ironic is that you never have to take a stand on anything. No one can pin you down to saying that this or that is what you believe and so it can become a hedge against ever being wrong or out of it. Coolness, which was an escape from meaningless sentimentality in music, among other things, can become hip caution. If you're too cool to applaud, you won't be caught applauding a performance that turns out not to be approved by the group. One meaning of *postmodern* is that it is a rebellion against the tyranny of coolness. My word use is confusing here because part of relatively recent changes in everyday speech, as I hear it, is a reversion to an earlier meaning of the word *cool* as a definite, quite uncool approbation. One way or another we struggle against the third audience. You and I can express whatever we want (more or less) unless a third invisible audience is there to keep us loyal to its idols.

This struggle, as I was saying earlier, is at its height in adolescence. Then, especially, kids are often partly real and partly false with each other. High school sweethearts may each serve the other as a new and real power to oppose the vertical split parent. The families of the couple can also serve this function—a paradox, because the acceptance of each by the other's parents can be a wedge to free them from their own parents. Real-life cases are complex and mixed. I know a couple who got together in adolescence because the father of each died. Both mothers were opinionated and controlling, and both the boy and the girl had benefited from being on good and intimate terms with their more flexible and responsive fathers. When the girl heard that her father had incurable cancer, she changed her mind about the boy's pursuit of her. She knew that his father had recently died, and without full recognition of why this was important, it made all the difference. Each became the father of the other, which worked well for a fairly long time, but because their way of being together was not just itself but also a bulwark against the intrusion of the mothers' ambitions, it had to be defensive as well as free, and the defensiveness gradually eroded the freedom. Ideas and customs that had spontaneously and playfully evolved had to be adhered to rigidly, thus deadening large portions of the interaction.

The kind of deadness I mean is phenomenologically the same as that described especially by members of the British Object Relations school (e.g., Thomas Ogden) but my conception of its development and significance is different. I agree that there is much anger at the heart of the deadness, but I see that anger as secondary to disruptions in the false relating, and the falseness as the primary deadening condition.

In the case of this couple, what Kohut called the idealized parent imago played a complex role and underwent an unfortunate transformation. Both people idealized their fathers and accepted the father's ideals. If the fathers had survived, the children probably would have been able to become more realistic about them and to have substituted ideals for the idealized actual people. The deaths were at too early an age for the children to grieve effectively, and their substitution of each other for the fathers, which was facilitated by the ideals of the two men being similar, kept them stuck with idealized, fallible people instead of immutable ideals. The saving idealized parent became the enslaving parent of the vertical split.

The reverse can also happen. The outstanding public speaker I mentioned earlier first consulted me because he felt desperately driven to perform superbly and effectively for everyone all the time. He doubted his motives for everything. Was he only trying to impress? It didn't feel like it, and yet he was obsessed with the need to make the right impression at all times. His parents had also been prominent performers and obsessed with their prominence. Neither was much interested in their children except as audience for themselves or as part of the act.

Their child, my analysand, was shy and socially unskilled until much later. He had little nutriment for his true grandiosity, which remained stuck at a relatively primitive and demanding level, but his idealization of his parents worked a little better. They were easy to admire, but the trouble was that they weren't often available. They didn't help him feel that he was part of them and their greatness. In large part, they became the parents of the vertical split by only attending to what he did that fit into their performances. But when he succeeded at that, they were rewarding. In addition, he was able to identify with certain social ideals that they and other people important to him cherished. The result was in part that he felt a combined push from his grandiose ambitions and from his conviction that he would only be acceptable to his parents if he, too, were a great performer. Many horrible troubles in early adulthood led to his joining a group whose ideals he adopted with zeal. This adoption helped to channel some of the intense pressure into successful leadership.

In analysis, the development and working through of an idealizing transference produced a change in his experience of external demand for success. He became convinced that his connection to me wasn't as crucial as it initially felt and that it would remain intact even if he didn't impress me with his skill. He was left much freer to love his audiences without constantly looking over his shoulder to see if another audience was satisfied yet.

I believe that this path of development—usually without benefit of treatment—has been historically quite important. The lives of many world leaders (Winston Churchill and Harry S. Truman, for example) have been shaped by overly involved, controlling mothers—often not like my analysand's mother in being prominent themselves, and usually much more attentive to their sons than she. The sons' success was a result of their talents and of their conviction that their mothers would reject them if they didn't succeed. Their real successes probably couldn't have been achieved had they remained controlled by the real or imagined presence of their mothers.

I think the escape for some of them has been by way of loyalty to a real group—as big a one as a nation—and its ideals which gradually replaced the controlling figure that drove them from birth to early adulthood. As leaders (and of course public speakers) they can combine the pursuit of their ideals with the fulfillment of their grandiose ambitions by moving great numbers of people to cherish, protect and even die for their ideals.

The work with my public figure analysand depended on my living up to his ideas of me most of the time and failing only to a degree that he could stand. He particularly needed me to be honest and genuine, and he had a keen sense for the kind of fakery that was most crucial to him, pretended intimacy with him that would be really for the purpose of self aggrandizement—being vicariously great by knowing him. He needed to know that I was primarily interested in what happened between us and not in what would happen between me and my various audiences because I knew him and heard inside dope about other famous people from him.

The hardest part for me was to avoid pretending I wasn't interested. When I did, I could see or hear him notice it and be disappointed because I was pretending. Being interested in his success and its trappings was natural, but I needed to be more interested in him. One thing that made it easier was that I didn't have to say much. He did most of the talking. Other patients' needs are harder to meet because they do require more activity; they are equally keen bullshit detectors, and they react disastrously to it. These folks occupy points on a spectrum between those who react to fakery with disintegration and rage and those who react with disintegration and depression. My countertransference problem with the former is anxiety and defensiveness, and with the latter, depression and defensiveness. In a certain way, it is more accurate to say that the anxiety and depression are not problems, whether the other person knows about them or not. The various forms of defensiveness are the problem.

Most forms of it include my conjuring up an invisible audience—oddly, pretty much the audience I am now writing for. I imagine you reassuring me that I did nothing to be ashamed of. You say that anyone would have done the same as I, that it was the analysand who made me do it and besides, the person's anger at me is a sign of how crazy he or she really was. Something has happened that I interpret as evidence that I am inadequate, not a real analyst, and if I am desperate and ready to fool myself, I resort to falseselfobjects. I tell myself no jury—at least no jury of my analytic peers—would convict me. I think of various theoretical shared beliefs and rules of technique that prove that I am really a member of the analytic world and the other person in the room not only is not a member, but is to be pitied as being a lesser kind.

This is one of the most dangerous forms of this kind of defensiveness, what Erik Erikson (in another context) called *pseudospeciation*. The members of the analytic tribe are the real humans. Nonmembers are something not as good, and can permissibly be treated as enemies. In this case, like many others, they are only treated as enemies for their own good. My actual behavior that results from this awful transformation from real to false is various. It could be silent withdrawal when saying something would be natural and helpful, or it could be pomposity, condescension, needless instruction, or countless other ways of harming the relationship, and probably the other person, that derive from my paying attention to an audience other than the one that I can see and hear there and then.

It is equally unfortunate if I don't conjure you guys up, but instead treat the other person as a false audience by becoming compliant without conviction. In this case, I attempt to shore up my false analytic self by being what the other seems to want me to be. If it works, that is if it works as a countertransference, a maladaptive defense, not as therapy, the other people may at least seem to feel better. The ones that don't are better off, and they are good supervisors. "Now you're treating me as if I'm fragile," one of them used to yell at me. If the reaction is seemingly for the better, what has happened is collusion. We are now putting on an as-if performance of psychoanalysis. I fear that whole analyses are conducted on this basis.

It bothers me a lot that I often hear this kind of false compliance referred to as empathy. Despite the fact that self psychology is one of my important real and false selfobjects, I have tried for the last few years to eliminate the words *empathy* and *narcissism* from my active vocabulary because they have come to be almost exclusively falseselfobjects. I hear people say that they are being empathic when they mean that they are being nice to the other person, and that the other is narcissistic when they mean that the other person isn't quite as good or fully human as they and those they are addressing.

I believe that the currency of the word *empathy* derives from Kohut's work, and I am sure that he didn't mean being nice to someone. I think that he meant to name the way that he thought we actually understand each other by using all our responses to another to preconsciously form a model of the other's experience. In making that model, we use all that we know about the world that is relevant to the other person, and that certainly includes our clinical experience and our theories of personality and behavior. But Kohut was speaking of empathy distinct from the use of theory or logic or anything else not connected to a commonsense apprehension of immediate experience. His insistence on treating the experience of both parties to an analysis as the *sine qua non* of interpretive knowledge foreshadowed the full development of the intersubjective point of view, and offered psychoanalysis a transition from logical positivism to more reasonable, defensible epistemologies. He was arguing against the admission into the office of a group self that knew better than the analysand. When we do invite such a group self in, we have a horrible resemblance to some adolescent men who rely on the opinion of their peers and therefore know that it doesn't mean anything when women say no to their sexual advances.

If I am not in good working order, I will sometimes rely on falseselfobject truths, such as, anyone prominent in a dream besides the dreamer is me, the emotional truth of any statement can be arrived at by removing the person spoken of and substituting myself, discussion of problems with others is a defense against talking about problems with me, regardless of circumstances missing an analytic hour is motivated by some sort of wish to avoid self-knowledge, or reporting a personal achievement is a request for an infantile gratification that must be frustrated in order to promote thought, insight and growth. All of those beliefs are sometimes correct, but their blanket application without much consideration of the whole of the immediate experience, and without the realization that the other person's point of view is as likely to be correct as your own, will lead to interpretations that will probably be heard as dicta from a member of the elite rather than as part of an evolving shared view of what is going on. I believe that a good analyst is what Lionel Blitzten liked to call himself, the Apostle of the Obvious. When things are going well, the analyst says what has been becoming obvious to both people, though one or both of them has been trying to ignore it.

Describing my ideal of the analytic situation that way again worries me about the question of empathy and niceness. Some years ago, toward the end of a fairly long analysis, I was alarmed by my analysand's embarking on a destructive extramarital affair. I thought that one of his motives was to see if I cared more about his hurting himself than his father had seemed to. I said so repeatedly, but not much changed. One day, he came in and told me that he had just had intercourse with his friend without wearing a condom. She had herpes and he did not. He then told me a dream about a walrus. He knew that I, like him, had spent time in Alaska. I said, "You may not have a bone in your penis, but you have rocks in your head." He laughed, though with some pain, and said he knew I was right. He didn't catch anything, and he did stop the affair.

Telling you that makes me anxious. I can all too readily hear various criticisms you might make, the mildest of which is, "That may have been good therapy, but it wasn't analysis," at which imaginary remark I bristle and reply by referring to my favorite definition of analysis, from Samuel Lipton: Analysis is what analysts do. I don't think he meant that just anything we do is analytic or otherwise valid. I think he meant that what we do on the basis of our best analytic understanding is analytic.

I use that idea to counteract a particular kind of intrusion of an invisible audience into my office. It is quite different from the intrusions I promote to reassure myself—what might be called intrusions of an ego ideal kind. This kind of intrusion is of an audience of a superego kind and it is just as maladaptive, and even more uncomfortable. I do not mean to say that all such audiences are harmful. If I need any help in behaving myself ethically, the appeal to your opinion, should some ethical failure be known, can help me to hold on. I don't mean only gross ethical violations such as sexual ones, but also the trickier little failures of confidentiality or, even trickier, of self-indulgence—storytelling, for example. As must be more than clear by now, I love to tell stories. I do not think that it is necessarily a mistake to tell one to an analysand, but if I did it as often as the impulse occurs my analysands would never get a word in. Spontaneity is necessary, but so is restraint. What I have learned to do is to listen to the story in my head as fully as I can while still listening to the other person, and then try to extract the moral I had in mind in thinking of telling it. Nine times out of ten, the moral is something the other is already well aware of. If not, I usually say the moral as an interpretation. Sometimes, I tell the story.

The times when the appearance of a superego-type audience is not a help are when it interferes with my ability to be genuine and immediately present. I try to hear as much of what is going on as I can, and ultimately make the latent parts of it overt. In doing so, I have to be a member of my profession as well as a member of the little group of two, but I want to use my professional self as a listening device and a guide to how to talk about our interaction. There is a constant tension between what I sense going on and my ideas of human nature and good analytic functioning. The particulars of any real situation strain the oversimplifications that make up my personal theories, and they may move me toward some idea of what is happening that contradicts some cherished belief. Under those circumstances, various other people individually or in groups appear to me and admonish me to be loyal to how we think and what sorts of things we say.

Part of the problem is that psychoanalysis is now several generations old and has followed the path that I think all great discoveries or revelations take. An unusual, iconoclastic leader breaks with the established views of his time and shows the world a new way of looking at things. In the early stages of the development of his work he has many enemies (he may get crucified) and some loyal friends. The new ideas are used to free people from the tyranny of the old. A psychoanalyst at this stage (ninety years ago) telling a patient about the existence of infantile sexuality, the Oedipus complex and the pervasiveness of sex and aggression was providing a breath of fresh air and a new and exhilarating experience for them as they explored together the personal workings out of these new insights.

What always goes wrong is that, in the next generation or two, the supporters of the movement, whether scientific, political or religious, are people like the old enemies. They like to know the established truth and protect it. What was a new discovery becomes dogma. Believing the ideas that once got you kicked out of decent society now are shibboleths one must believe in order to stay in. Infantile sexuality, and so forth, remain important, but lots of people already know about them and have been variously affected by their becoming part of universal intellectual parlance. Mechanically and loyally pointing them out may be a breath of stale air when some other aspect of life, now more of a problem, needs to be addressed. At other times a dogmatic interpretation may simply make no sense, but I may feel I have to make it to remain a member in good standing.

I am sure that such things occur in any profession, but they are particularly dangerous to psychoanalysts. Not only is it essential that we be free to see what is and not what we think should be, but we have a ready-made rationalization for asserting the existence of what we think should exist but doesn't: the unconscious. I am an authority on the unconscious, and so if I convince myself of something that I know the other person will reject, the rejection is simply based on the fact that what I say is in the other person's unconscious. Furthermore, it is unconscious because being aware of it will cause anxiety, and so naturally the person resists being conscious of it. Similarly, the poor, benighted, infantile analysands don't realize that the rules of analysis are for their own good. For example, if they want to borrow a magazine from the waiting room and I interpret the transference meaning of the request and never say it's okay with me or it's not, and they get mad, it's because of their resistance to being shown the unconscious primitive wishes they want to act out. If I persist in my view, the other person is likely to be angry indefinitely, and I can conjure up plenty of group support for self-congratulation on giving the patient a chance to experience previously unconscious rage.

Would that this were caricature. It is not only a daily reality, but also it is one of the greatest problems for our profession. The alternative is not at all easy to state, but I believe the essence of it is situating myself as entirely as I can in the room alone with the other person and listening to her or his version of things as being as authentic as my own. I believe that there are powerful, even inexorable unconscious wishes and fears motivating both of us and, given the chance, they will become evident to us without the knowledge being imposed by my authority. Forcefulness in that imposition is usually not necessary. Unfortunately, many people long for just such an imposition for various reasons, most of them having to do with patching up a false self.

A long time ago, I used to hypnotize lots of people. Most of them were patients. The others were at my seminars on hypnosis: participants, or my secretary whom I used in demonstrations. She was a wonderful subject, especially after she had lots of practice. One day she came to work with a nasty cold sore. She asked if hypnosis would cure it. I didn't know, but thought it would be worth trying. After the session, she was delighted with the cure. The bad part was that only she thought I had succeeded. The lesion looked at least as bad as ever and for days she insisted on showing anyone who would look. "He cured me," she told them. They must have thought that if this were a success they would hate to see a failure. It would be good to think that there are not psychoanalytic versions of the same thing, but we all know better.

Since it is impossible to know what is conscious or is not in anyone but ourselves, I do not know if she had any awareness of what was going on. For all I know, she was consciously getting even with me for what in some ways was exploitation. I think she was doing exactly that, but unconsciously. I am convinced that many people are conscious that their as-if psychoanalytic treatment and its as-if results are inauthentic, but they don't let on. I think that it is like the Emperor's New Clothes. The supposed results may not be very real, but claiming that they are qualifies the claimant as one of the enlightened. Thirty years ago, many psychoanalysts believed in the vaginal orgasm. It was better than the clitoral orgasm. Any fixated woman could have a clitoral orgasm, but only a well-analyzed one who had fully accepted her normal female receptiveness and passivity could experience the fulfillment of the vaginal orgasm. Lots of analysands, including especially analysts, attested to this truth. All was well until Masters and Johnson actually looked at what goes on anatomically and physiologically, and found that there wasn't such a thing as a vaginal orgasm.

Besides establishing oneself as one of the cognoscenti, analytic compliance may be motivated by a wish to protect the analyst or to protect oneself from the analyst's wrath. It is bad enough to damage someone's selfobjects, but hell hath no fury like someone whose falseselfobjects are scorned.

If someone tells me that they think analysis is no more valid than phrenology it disturbs me, but not much. Analysis as a theory, a point of view, a kind of therapy and an intellectual movement is an ideal or set of ideals that form a major part of who I am, and I am secure about it. Analysis is part of who I am, not part of my pretensions.

On the other hand, if someone suggests that the Seattle Psycho-analytic Society and Institute give up being an affiliate institute of the American Psychoanalytic Institute, I am likely to get serious, pompous and longwinded in explaining the importance of the connection and of the American in tedious detail. I have various offices and other positions which are not central to my sense of self, but do buoy me up at moments of self-doubt, and they are based on membership in groups that I can use to try to convince myself of my importance. To make matters worse, I have my doubts about the very question raised and I would likely feel the need to shout them down. Some of the people I see in therapy are partic-ularly considerate about such things—to our detriment. They tend to be people whose parents relied on certain signs and symbols used concretely to feel secure. In any event, I will sometimes notice and sometimes they will when they are bending over backwards to see things my way, or they may just get awfully worried when they don't do me the favor of forming a part of a false self relationship with me.

As undesirable as such relationships are, they beat the false distinc-tions that I sometimes make between myself and my patients. These pseudospeciations occur when I feel insecure and they depend on my bringing other people into the room to feel superior along with me. Case conferences, supervisors and friends are the usual third audiences. Re-alizing this has made me worry about talking about cases—especially talking casually and humorously.

A woman I work with has contributed to the worry. She is the daughter and sister of psychoanalysts, and is infuriated as an analysand to hear them talking reassuringly or self-congratulatorily about their pa-tients. She has a point. When people are dissatisfied with my work with them and forceful in expressing their dissatisfaction, I find it tempting to make jokes to friends or family about how unreasonable patients can be, but I have noticed that doing so, particularly if the audience for my joking is sympathetic, is likely to promote my taking some sort of distant and superior position when I am next with the dissatisfied person.

Consultation should be better, and sometimes is, but not always. Years ago, I consulted a colleague I admire about a woman who had been giving me a very hard time for years and showed no sign of relent-ing. The colleague was sympathetic; so much so that he suggested that I consider ending the treatment on the grounds that either the person was impossible to help or that it was just too hard to be worth taking all the abuse. What I did was not what he suggested, a careful consideration with the patient of the possibility that we should stop, and maybe that is what I should have done, but I didn't think so then or now. But it was trying work, and one day when she was berating me for not understanding her and for thinking I was better than she because I was more intellectual, and added, as usual, that really she ought to be able to find a better therapist, I thought that my colleague knew how I was suffering. I thought it was excessive and I impulsively said, "Maybe you're right. Maybe you should look for someone else." She was badly wounded. She said, correctly I believe, that I had betrayed her. I had given her every reason to believe that she was free to say whatever she wanted to me and that I wouldn't retaliate, and now I had retaliated in the cruelest way. We worked it out, and the therapy ended fairly well, but it took years to work that incident through.

Since I consult, supervise, conduct case conferences and occasionally give papers in which I include case examples, I have had to think quite a lot about how these activities can be done to minimize my apparition in the offices of others and their apparition in mine. It seems to me that, like all problems in analysis, the solution is to think and talk about it as fully and carefully as possible, but beyond that I try to keep in mind how limited my knowledge and authority are and I try to express opinions labeled as such. I try not to convince myself or anyone that I know what is happening between two people when I'm not there, or that I know what the analyst or therapist should do. Especially I try not to promote false assurance and dogmatic belief in the insignia of our craft guilds. In talking about the people I work with, I try to say only what I could feel relatively comfortable having them hear me say. If I don't exclude them when they aren't there, I think I am less likely to exclude them when they are. If we keep our discussions free, playful, honest and genuine, we are likely to support each other in being that way in our offices.

Mindless Psychoanalysis, Selfless Self Psychology, and the Elusiveness of Reality

This talk is the earliest written. At the time, I had been working on the mindless idea for several years but had just thought of the name for it. I feel like someone who climbs up to the roof and then kicks the ladder away so that he will look like he flew up, because I have forgotten what friend it was who called one day and asked me to give an Alliance lecture and invited me to name a topic. To my surprise the ungainly title tumbled out of my mouth, and the whole thing more or less jelled in that instant—one of the only times that has ever happened to me.

I BELIEVE THAT PSYCHOANALYSIS IS GRADUALLY MOVING toward the abandonment of its most basic concept: the mind. This process may never be complete because the idea of the mind is so pervasive in our culture.

Some cultures do without it. In Navajo there are words for thinking, for thoughts, and even for unconscious thoughts. These are activities of people, not of some abstract part of them. There is no distinction between people and their bodies because "the body" is not a Navajo concept either. Arms and pancreases are parts of people, not parts of "the body." In the years when I worked psychotherapeutically almost exclusively with Navajo people, I found that their lack of Cartesian dualism, the mind–body split, was a great help to me. For one thing, it came naturally to them to think that cognition and affect could make a person sick, and that sickness affected cognition and affect. Another advantage was that in discussing psychology with Navajo mental health paraprofessionals and with medicine people, I was forced to talk and therefore to think in terms of what people wanted and what they feared, and so on, instead of in abstract terms. I discovered that some of my usual thinking was tautological or otherwise confused.

Some of that confusion was built into analysis, because analysis was born in the heyday of Cartesian dualism, and it (and other psychological disciplines) increased the confusion by introducing another split. Earlier, the mind had been a person's experience and its locus. Then psychoanalysis and other psychological disciplines gave it more (metaphorical) substance. The topographic model of the mind includes as its largest part the unconscious, which was unexperienceable, and in the structural model it has anatomy and physiology like a second body. The result was an unacknowledged tripartite division. Where there had been two realms, experience and the body, there were now three: experience; the mind, whose structure and function gave rise to experience; and the body, which was related to the mind in only partially specified ways.

In the 1930s, Harry Stack Sullivan was aware of the drawbacks of building a theory of the mind and avoided them by making relationship the basic unit of his study. Though his work has few of the problems I am discussing, he failed to account for some of the phenomena that classical analysis explains well. However, he did influence some mainstream analysts to recognize the problems of thinking in terms of drive and structure. The Neo-Freudians, such as Karen Horney, who broke away (or were kicked out), as well as mainstream ones, especially Hartmann and his collaborators, emphasized and developed the adaptational point of view as a way of giving the interpersonal realm greater importance than was natural to a psychology based on the individual mind. Heinz Hartmann, Ernst Kris, and Kurt Loewenstein also improved the structural model by elaborating the idea of the conflict-free zone of the mind and its moving forces, the neutralized drives.

At about the same time, Erik Erikson beautifully described the importance of a cultural view of identity and its development in interpersonal experience. I don't think he cared much that identity had no clear place in the mind as analysis conceived of it, but David Rapaport did care, and engaged in even more elaborate mind description to fit it in. I think it was at this point that the theory began to collapse from its own ponderous complexity. Such things as the varieties of cathexis and counter-cathexis and the many states of drives—fused, defused, sublimated and neutralized—were hard to understand, implausible and very far removed from real life.

The theory was quite inclusive, and Rapaport and others suggested it could become a general psychology, but its answers to many basic questions were clumsy. How did the tripartite mind develop? What was the origin of guilt before the oedipal period? If perception was accomplished by an apparatus of the ego, how did the id have such free and immediate access to the occurrence of temptations or provocations?

There were answers to these questions, but they tended to complicate the model further and to make it hard for most of us to think about both it and ordinary human feelings at the same time. In 1971, Heinz Kohut said that the proper point of view for an analyst was within the mental apparatus and equidistant from its structures. I think he meant it as a way of being especially in tune with, and responsive to, the analysand's whole experience. But it was also a description of empathy that could have meaning only for people who, like him, were especially talented in thinking abstractly and concretely at the same time, and who had used the structural model so much that it had become second nature.

It is hard to say exactly what happened to the theory—that tightly specified, complicated mind that was an analogy to human anatomy and physiology. Thirty years ago it was almost psychoanalytic dogma. Now it is not, but it has not been replaced. It withered away. There was no revolution, though Joseph Sandler says that now it is time for one. Various iconoclasts like G. Klein and Roy Schafer have argued that there was a clinical theory of psychoanalysis that was independent of metapsychology, and that metapsychology should simply be abandoned.

I think that Schafer's work epitomizes the process that has taken place. In the mid-1960s, he wrote *Aspects of Internalization*, a neat, precise, elegantly reasoned and complex description of the origin and fate of objects within the psychic apparatus. In the process he neatened and tightened and cleared up ambiguity. He also was at pains to be clear that the apparatus itself was not a real thing but a way of thinking. Within a few years, however, he appears to have given up the struggle, and he became one of the most eloquent advocates of thinking and talking in terms of what people do instead of what they are made of.

At the same time that the structural model was losing authority and prominence, object relations theories were gaining them. The object relations point of view has the advantage of being more flexible, and particularly more suited to seeing people as existing in families and other social milieus. Jay Greenberg and Stephen Mitchell have argued that the structural model with its highly determined drives does not allow for the influence of actual experience in the development of objects—that the drive determines the form of the object—while object relations theories give due prominence to actual interpersonal life. I think this is a great exaggeration, but only an exaggeration. Though Melanie Klein, as much as any theorizer, seemed to see the object as formed by the nature of the drive, many of her successors, especially D. W. Winnicott, paid superb attention to the parent-child interaction and its effects. Object relations theories are numerous and diverse. To the extent that they account for human experience and behavior in terms of motives rather than mental contents, such as internal objects and object representations, they seem to me to be a move in the right direction.

Heinz Kohut was another major figure whose work moved from dependence on a highly structured mind toward "mindless" theory. His early theoretical work included a sophisticated refinement of the structural model, but in 1966 he turned in a different direction. I don't think he recognized just how different it was, but even in his first paper on narcissism he provided a new theoretical approach that accounts for the great diversity and changeableness of who we most basically are. In that paper, "Forms and Transformations of Narcissism," he was still very much embedded in the old concept of mind, but he planted one of the main seeds of its destruction. Unfortunately, in subsequent work he relied on a new, easily reified metaphor, *the self*, which he initially conceived of as a content of the psychic apparatus. He also continued to rely on the concept of a psychic structure which had such qualities as strength and flexibility.

In a few more years, the self had become his organizing principle of the mind, and it resembled the structural model in having its own anatomy. I believe this to be a great disadvantage—of which I will say much more, later. The advantages of the self as a theoretical construct include its being easier to convert to actual experience than the structural model, its variability from time to time within the same person and between people, and its integration into the world of relationships. His view of the self as imbedded in interpersonal life and the description he gave of clinical interactions undermined another philosophical pillar of psychoanalysis as it had been up to then: objective reality. I am not sure that he realized he had done so, but Robert Stolorow and his coworkers recognized it a few years later and elaborated the idea that reality is known subjectively, and that ideally analysis consists of the negotiation of a joint view of reality—intersubjectivity.

I believe that a revised, more sophisticated notion of reality can be of great benefit to psychoanalytic theory and practice. To begin with, it can explain the appeal of the concept *mind* and suggest a substitute. We have been in the habit of making models of the mind that we believe to be in each person. Instead we can recognize that each person constantly makes models of the world, and that those worlds are most of what we think of as *mind*.

Freud, though he was a great model maker, did not think of each person's reality as a creation. He worked with the concepts of reality and perception that were current at the time of his education, and we inherited them. In that view, reality is constant and knowable, with more or less distortion, and its perception is more or less a passive receptive experience. Freud thought of (and even drew) perception as a kind of eye through which stimuli passed and were focused. In this version, an image is formed and viewed by some part of us, something like a little person inside us watching a movie, but this is the start of an infinitely regressive series. Inside each homunculus viewing the images that perception generates, there would have to be a smaller homunculus viewing the image of the image, and so on.

Psychoanalysis itself, along with ethnography, gradually influenced the intellectual worldview so that the notion of a single reality, especially a single psychological or social reality, was increasingly in doubt. The crucial analytic concept was *psychic reality*. The idea that what is real to one differs from what is real to anyone else was subversive of the belief in a single objective reality. This was true even if the concept was originally intended as a way of explaining why things that weren't true acted within the mind as if they were.

Psychic reality and cultural relativism prepared the way for a purely relativistic view of the world. The relativistic idea arises inevitably from the notion that the world that each of us knows incorporates all of our personal distortions of the truth. The trouble is that there is no reality known to anyone except her or his psychic reality, unless the individual is so completely analyzed and has such good sensory organs as to have no distortions. Since no such person exists, we're stuck. The existence of reality is self-evident. The nature of reality is not, and reality can only be approximated by study, by comparison of various people's versions, and by negotiation among those people. Further doubts about the passive reception of perception were raised by the direct study of perception, which in all species seems to consist of interaction with the environment.

Freud himself has left us a way out of these difficulties. He defined thought as trial action, pointing out that as we develop we learn to react to frustration by undertaking imaginary actions in a fantasy world—experiments designed to see how the activity will work out. Thought, then, is interaction with an imagined environment. If the imaginary version is a useful one, the predictions will be accurate, and if it is not, it will ordinarily be revised. In this way we all create and correct our worlds. Much of our experience and all of our thinking is trial action: rehearsing or planning something we want to do, or have happen. I think that it is the ease with which we can create a model of the world by fantasy that explains the appeal of such concepts as *the mind*, *the inner world*, and *mental contents*. We all constantly have the experience of turning our attention away from our immediate surroundings to an infinite variety of other scenes and experiences. It is natural to think of a stage or place within us where these dramas are played out.

The question then arises, "Where are these dramas really occurring and what is the nature of the action?" Unless there is a disembodied soul the dramas have to be bodily activity, and I believe that quite a lot of that activity can be specified. The prominent portion of thought that is verbal is partially inhibited speech. Most children, when they first learn to read, read out loud. Usually they progress to whispering the words they are seeing, then they simply move their lips, and finally they are outwardly still while the words sound in their heads. I believe there must be a neural mechanism analogous to a clutch in a car. Just as the engine can run with or without connection to the drive wheels, I think that the engine of speech can be partially or perhaps wholly disconnected from the muscles of breathing, the larynx and the various organs of the mouth. It doesn't seem to have been as widely noted, but children have to learn to think without moving their lips, too. Their earliest thought in words is quite audible to anyone standing near them. Just as they teach each other—often by somewhat brutal means—to read (or count) silently, they also teach each other to quit whispering to themselves.

But is it really to themselves? I believe that they, or anyone who is thinking in words, are speaking to an audience. A rehearsal is in progress. As I write I hear the words, but I do not think I would be able to if I did not believe in you, my audience. In addition, there are a number of people, including a discussion group, who I think will read this to themselves within the next few weeks. Not only am I experiencing your presence, I am also being you, imagining your reaction and writing accordingly. For example, a minute ago I wrote the parenthetical phrase, "without moving their lips," after the words, "read this to themselves," but as I did so I felt several of you criticize my tone as too flip; I felt mild embarrassment, and backspaced it off the computer screen. Then I thought of using it as an example—possibly as a clarification and definitely as a way of sneaking the joke back in, and the number of you who were critical declined slightly; so I have left this in so far, though I am a little anxious about it.

When I read this aloud I will be alert to see if my models of you were accurate, and will increase my confidence in the veracity of some parts of the world that I am experiencing now, and eliminate or revise other parts. After I have finished reading, your reactions will have a similar effect on me as will the comments of the discussion group and other readers. My reality will be changed by our interaction, as almost all people's reality is changing constantly.

The exceptions to this kind of change are the psychotic. If I were paranoid, I would be sure what your reaction was going to be and I would know that any variation from my expectation was your attempt to fool me. No matter how hard you might try to convince me of your sincerity, I would easily explain away your efforts as a result of your seeing that I was on to you. But, except for psychotic people, we all spend much of our time jointly examining and negotiating reality. I think that a large portion of all human interaction is for this purpose.

Since right now I am writing, verbal thought is the example that comes to my mind first, but there are many other kinds of thinking. As I sit here writing I am being me reading aloud and I am being you listening. In addition, I am me scanning your faces and listening to your breathing. I am you looking at me and thinking my posture is poor and I am standing up straighter. As I do these things, the activity is not restricted to my central nervous system. My eyes move around as they will do in a short time when I have given up for tonight and gone to sleep and am dreaming. It is easy for any therapist to observe that many people when they are deep in thought trying to decide what to say next will have rapid eye movements as they scan some part of their world. I do not know what I do when I am imagining listening, but I suspect that my tensor tympani muscles as well as other parts of my ears are doing something at the same time that my apparatus of phonation is almost producing an imitation of the sounds you are making. Certainly I really do straighten my spine or at least increase the tension in it when thinking about my posture.

When we think of the world, I believe that our whole bodies are involved in simulating it. In urology there is a clue to urinary sphincter problems in women and girls known as the curtsy sign. It occurs when the affected person sees water flowing; she flexes her legs to clamp the urethra because thinking about flowing water involves increasing bladder pressure. I think that at least many of the gestures that are part of speaking are ways that we simulate the world through actions. For example, almost everyone while telling of a phone conversation will hold a hand up, partially closed, close to one cheek.

The space we imagine and call *the inner world* or *psychic reality* or *the mind* or whatever is a culturally determined, learned abstraction of the experience that we all have all the time of creating a world by our activity. But where do we think that world is? I think that we think it is the same world that we live in all the time. When I imagine reading this to you, I remember the room where I will be doing so. I am not imagining a different world. I am anticipating a different time. I think that usually when people do what we call withdrawing into thought, they are not primarily traveling in space but in time.

Time travel, and other magic we do all the time, is understandable in terms of the elusiveness of reality. As I write, the room, you and your reactions are very real to me; when I am reading this to you they will be just as real but probably different, and when I have finished reading and am talking with some of you they will be different still, and even this is a gross oversimplification. While I am writing, your reactions change. No doubt there will be similar changes from moment to moment while I am reading and afterward while we are conversing. So which is real reality? All or none? Perhaps it would be worthwhile to say that some are more reliable than others, but that would be hard to determine. For example, I am pretty calm right now—maybe not dispassionate but not excited. During the meeting in which I will read this I will be anxious, excited, eager to see what you think and prone to exaggerate what signs of approval or disapproval you give me.

As I write this I feel mild shame because another audience who is always with me, a sort of composite of my analysts, my father and my wife, point out to me that I am asking for praise, and I (and my mother) answer defensively that it's a good example anyhow. Who is right? Both or neither? And so it goes, at enormous speed that my typing fingers couldn't possibly keep up with. Coming back to your real reactions, will you tell them to me? Partially. Do you fully know them yourselves? No. If some of us devoted hours to discussing the subject in more detail, we would come to some consensus. That, I think, is the best we could do and is what people do all the time to determine what is real interpersonally.

If we were talking about less complex reality (I do not say physical reality, because all reality is physical), it would be easier but not really more certain. We could attempt to determine the temperature in the room. If one of us had a thermometer the answer would be easy to find. If two of us had thermometers it would be harder. If we went to great pains and calibrated a thermocouple, using melting ice and boiling water as standards (and allowed for our elevation above sea level and the current atmospheric pressure in determining what temperature to assign to the boiling water)—if we did all that and much more, all we could do would be to come up with a very sophisticated, precise consensus.

We construct reality all the time, and we change it all the time, as is most easily seen in conditions of reduced sensory input. Someone driving down a strange road on a foggy night may see a barn ahead, but on getting nearer the barn may transform itself into a billboard. Both perceptions may be quite convincing while they last, and the second may persist, but both are based on past experience with other persons that helped define barnness and billboardness. The crucial point is that thoughts are real until they are invalidated, and invalidation is never entirely convincing. We are all like the Golux in Thurber's *Thirteen Clocks* when Prince Zorn said to him, "I place my faith in you, and where you lead, I follow."

"Not so fast," the Golux said. "Half the places I have been to, never were. I make things up. Half the things I say are there cannot be found. When I was young I told a tale of buried gold, and men from leagues around dug in the woods. I dug myself."

"But why?"

"I thought the tale of treasure might be true."

A woman's father died when she was first in the school that would start her on the same career as his. Years later, she delayed finishing her lengthy training and became depressed. Unconsciously, she believed that somehow time could be turned back to the days when she and he had loved talking about their mutual interests and had looked forward to doing so for many years. Besides the world she lived in with so much pain, there was the one where everything was still all right. The better world, the world of the past, was present to her and she cherished it. What made that possible was the magical belief that somehow time could be reversed. To finish training closed the way back. She did not think of this consciously because to think consciously means to tell it (in thought) to someone, and all the people she could tell it to would not believe it; their skepticism might invade her and so that, too, might close the way back. When her therapist detected the time travel idea and told it to her, she reluctantly recognized it as her own, and in the following months mourned her loss—the loss of the chance to go back and do it right with her father alive.

This vignette is not novel, and it is no news to psychoanalysis that we all believe in magic, that we think the wish is equal to the deed, that a part is equal to the whole, that all time is now, and so on. The trouble is that we explain the fact that we believe in magic by saying that there is a powerful thing inside us, the id, the primary process, the system unconscious, and so forth, which has odd qualities of thought, instead of simply saying that we all think that way as well as in other ways.

I think one of our motives for adhering to that clumsy and tautological concept is that we want to deny the ubiquity of magic. People who have been less trained to think scientifically do not keep so much of the way they think secret from themselves. (They still keep most of their thought unconscious, but not on the grounds that it is magical.) If a moderately traditional Navajo man wants to speak of the possibility of someone being killed in a dangerous rodeo event, he will do so in a heavily veiled hint. To really say so might make it happen, or at the very least make his listeners think he wanted it to happen. If a moderately traditional Jewish insurance salesman wants to speak of policy benefits he will say, "If, God forbid, you should have an accident." These people, if asked why they spoke as they did, would be able to answer without difficulty. They, and we, acknowledge the magical belief, but in cases like the one of the graduate student we encumber ourselves with intervening abstractions instead of speaking simply of her beliefs. Mardi Horowitz, Joseph Weiss and Harold Sampson, and Theodore Dorpat and Michael Miller are among the psychoanalysts who are currently demonstrating the usefulness of speaking primarily in terms of what people think, believe, want, or fear, without recourse to the nature and state of the organs of the mind or the inhabitants of the object representational world.

In most of even this body of literature, and to a greater degree in current work in the object relations tradition, it seems to me there remains more than a necessary dependence on the tradition of a mental apparatus and its contents. Human experience is a constant flux of interweaving elements such as desires, hopes, fears, images and memories. One of the most difficult requirements of any general psychological theory is that it account for the vast variety of experience even within the same single moment as well as the inexorable persistence of certain patterns over a whole lifetime. The notion of structure is well-suited to the persistent patterns, but not so well designed for their complexity and variability, and it introduces endless possibilities for unnecessary confusion.

The object relations tradition offers more flexibility and more immediate resemblance to life than does the structural point of view, but its metaphor of beings interacting with one another in inner space has, among other disadvantages, a tendency to lead to a confusion of introjection with perception. If I see a tree and pay attention to it, I have created the tree. Someone else would create a different tree, but we could, if needed, reach a workable consensus version. In an inner world/outer world way of thinking, there is now a tree inside me (or at least a tree representation), but the tree is not introjected. If I did introject it (by identification, for example, if I were told that my father had planted the tree and tended it for years), what would be happening would not be moving something from the outside world into my interior, but my moving the tree representation into the representation of me.

This is complicated and confusing enough, but a simpler case, introjection without identification, is even worse. The tree—or more reasonably, a person—would be moved not from the outside of me to the inside, but from the realm of transient perceptions inside me to another part of my interior, a special zoo of internal objects such as the object representational world, where it would have long life and great significance. In this case, something—the perception that was already in the mental apparatus—is moved to another part of the mental apparatus, an idea that is logical and consistent, but so poorly named by the word *introjection* that it gets us all mixed up. It seems to me that we lose nothing by relatively simple statements such as, "That person from then on had great significance for me whether or not I was conscious of it."

The characters who are important in the stories of our lives are ones we have lived with or met, or long or fear to meet. We invent many of them from parts of others we already know; an infinite number of combinations and recombinations are possible, and therefore lots of characters. Each of us defines her or himself by the entire repertoire of relationships that are remembered or anticipated with love, hate and/or fear.

38

Almost all older and most newer object relations accounts of how life works have a distorting emphasis on the characters instead of the relationships among them. Even the newer accounts, which emphasize that it is a relationship that is internalized, suffer from being prone to reification—a certain inflexibility and needless abstraction and complication. Statements about fictitious beings in a fictitious personal interior can be replaced with ones like, "He always longed, without realizing it, for someone who would assure him that he was perfect, as his mother had."

What I am saying is in agreement with Roy Schafer's idea that the truest, most useful accounts of life are stated in terms of action—a preference for verbs over nouns. One of the concepts that has mostly remained tied to nouns instead of verbs is that of *affect*. We usually think of an emotion as a state of a person rather than as a person's action. Yet I think that affects are most essentially interpersonal behaviors that convey information about wishes—what they are and whether they are being fulfilled. If we speak of someone as sad or if we speak of sadness, it sounds as if we are talking about a quality or state, like a fever or arthritis, but what we mean is different. We mean that someone behaves or wants to behave in a certain way and wants a certain kind of response from others. People are described as sad if there is something about the way they look or talk or otherwise communicate that gives us the information that there is something they don't like about their situation, and they can't change it. (If their appearance conveys the information that they expect us to change it or else, we say they are angry.)

We talk as if the sadness is the basic variable, and the behavior expresses it. Actually, the sadness is an abstraction for behavior that expresses desire, such as crying in the presence of one or more others in the hope that they will be comforting, give certain benefits, or suffer. When we say that we are feeling an emotion, we mean that in our current fantasies we are behaving in a way that expresses our wishes. Commonly, the details of the fantasies and even the wishes are unconscious, and all that we are conscious of is some part of the nonverbal action. The term *emotion* is a convenient way of indicating the sensations of behaving affectively: crying, sulking, accusing, and so on, in the same way that verbal thought is subvocal speech, the sensation of talking.

Some years ago when I was a minor federal bureaucrat, another bureaucrat withdrew his agency's cooperation from a joint effort that I believed to be valuable. He did so because the plan had been made in collaboration with his predecessor, whom he hated. We met to discuss the situation. After all else had failed to change his mind, several of us yelled and pounded the table. No use. One of the last things I said was, "This has been a waste of time."

"No, it hasn't," he replied calmly. "It was good for you to express your feelings."

Anger is not pressure inside the mental boiler nor is it a substance which becomes toxic with age, as Freud once thought. Anger doesn't exist in the real world. Angry behavior does, and angry behavior is a tool we use to try to change things. When it doesn't, we are not better off except in such subsidiary ways as having the satisfaction of not having given up without a fight. Many people have tried going out into the wilderness and yelling, or into their bedrooms and weeping, and generally they aren't any better off for the effort. They try it because they believe in the steam boiler model of human nature, or more likely because they have a secret plan that someone will hear after all and do something.

One of the reasons that the notion of affects as states appeals to us is that it helps us to avoid responsibility for our behavior. Much of the time, we have a number of things we want to happen between us and various other people. To say to someone, "I would like it if you and I were to do such and such," is risky. If the other person says no or, worse yet, says that it is one of the last things he or she would ever do, we are hurt. We may be accused, by ourselves among others, of having been presumptuous, foolish, selfish or the like.

If instead of making a direct statement, we portray (to ourselves as much as to anyone else) being overcome by a feeling, some of which leaks out against our will in the form of a tear or a sigh of romantic longing, then at least we can claim that we couldn't help it. We were trying not to do it so we aren't really selfish, and so forth. Tears, sighs, angry or exuberant shouts, declarations of love and many other strong communications can be among the best things of life, but calling them passions, that is, things that affect us as opposed to things we do, is an anxiety-reducing illusion.

Many events have inevitable effects on us, such as pleasure or pain, and there are situations that we inevitably long for. These are strong motivations, but they are simply motivations, goals that we decide to reach by various means, including nonverbal communications which have at least partially neurologically predetermined meaning to other people. The affective behavior, or the wish or fantasy of performing it, is a means to a goal—not the goal itself or a determinant of the goal.

What is going on when we feel an emotion is that we want something or fear something. Even if we are completely satisfied, we have a want for things to stay the same. Being happy usually means that we have rising expectations of satisfaction. Being unhappy means that we have falling expectations. Being angry means that we want something that we think will require overcoming opposition and we think that there is at least a slight chance of winning some part. If a thing we fear has happened, or is about to, and we can't imagine anything to do about it, we feel panic or apathy. In panic we are still trying in a nonspecific, disorganized way to achieve something—by screaming, for example. In apathy we have given up and initially do nothing. Later we may try to correct the situation in which we feel dead by doing something desperate, such as cutting ourselves to restore feeling, or even by constructing a new world impervious to consensual invalidation—that is, by becoming psychotic.

Short of apathy, we experience various states of motivational tension. Something we want to happen isn't yet, or something we don't want is happening or seems likely to happen. The precise emotion we feel depends on the outcome of the fantasies we run through in order to solve our problem.

For example, if I imagine your being harshly critical of what I am saying, I try out an extreme case to see what I might do. I think that someone among you is going to interrupt me and say, "This is drivel—a combination of truisms everyone knows and illogical simplistic theorizing. I'm not going to listen to another minute of it." I take out a gun and shoot him. That doesn't work. I don't have a gun and wouldn't shoot anybody. I imagine the rest of you yelling at him to sit down. That works pretty well, but leaves me still worrying about the person's opinion. So I invite him to say more about what is wrong with my ideas and I answer him point by point until he admits that I am right after all. This doesn't seem likely.

I take a radically different tack. No one came to the meeting after all. Your loss. And so on, much faster than I have been able to write and much longer than either you or I would want me to describe. During the gun version, I felt angry. During the version in which the rest of you shouted him down, I felt a little sorry for myself and a little self-righteous. During the answering point-for-point version, I felt angry and anxious. These statements are oversimplifications because there is always a complex, rapidly changing mix.

The oversimplified general principals can be stated. Feelings of motivational tension are compounds of three elements: fantasies of advance; fantasies of retreat; and anxiety, which is the sum of all the bad outcomes of our trial actions and our assessment of their likelihood. The relationship among them will approximate the equation:

$$\text{motivational tension} = \text{advance} + \text{anxiety} + \text{retreat}$$

At any moment, the quantity of tension is given by the strength of the wish or the severity of the threat minus the amount of satisfaction that is present. The reciprocal balance among advance, anxiety and retreat is determined by the outcome of the trial action fantasies. If the person estimates the chances of winning a struggle for satisfaction as good, advance will predominate. If the estimate is less favorable but success seems possible there will be more of a balance between advance and anxiety—the person will be poised between fight and flight. If the estimate is bad, retreat will be the main component. On any real occasion the participants, as they interact, rapidly review their tactics and re-estimate their chances so that at one moment advance may predominate, and at the next a mixture of anxiety and retreat may take over.

The terms *advance* and *retreat* each stand for a range of behaviors. Advance includes everything from a loving request to murderous rage, and retreat everything from cheerful acquiescence to abject surrender. The exact nature of the affect, which is to say the imagined behavior, is determined by the situation as the person sees it. I will give a far from exhaustive series of examples. If the situation is one in which one's wishes seem likely to be easily achieved, the feeling is pleasurable excitement. If it is one in which a single important wish is impossible to realize, but other wishes appear possible, the feeling is sadness. If the wish is so important that no other matters, or if no wishes appear possible, the feeling is hopelessness and helplessness. If the outcome is surrender to an opponent or to the moral forces of the universe, the feeling is guilt. I believe that this kind of surrender is analogous to the surrender behavior, for example, exposing the jugular, seen in other species that live in packs. If the outcome is retreat and giving up on being able to achieve what had been hoped, the feeling is shame.

These schematic descriptions hardly do justice to the rapidity, variety and complexity of our thinking. One of the most important dimensions of experience that I have been neglecting is the one which in some ways is most essentially psychoanalytic—symbolism. Symbolism is not just part of one or another theoretical structure; it is a key phenomenon observed by all analysts (among other people). In symbolism, any element of thought stands for other elements in other thoughts. Psychotic people, if they are able to be self-observant, know this best. "A little means a lot," one of them said. Another, when she had largely recovered, told me that one of the reasons that she had starved herself at the height of her illness was that every kind of food was a kind of person. For instance, beans, which in Spanish are called almost the same thing as Jews, looked in the can like a picture she had seen of bodies stacked up at Auschwitz. "I thought I would be eating you and your relatives," she said.

In the schematic description of the meaning of affects, I did not specify the grounds on which we make judgments of the likely outcomes of conflict. Some of them are based on here-and-now assessments of a current situation as such. Most judgments are more complex, being based on lifelong accumulations of instances of particular kinds of interactions, especially some of the earliest ones in our lives; and the connection to earlier times is by way of symbolism. I recognize the severe critic who interrupts me as one of the versions of my father that is always with me. The rest of you who defend me are the complimentary version of my mother. I don't think I know the earliest edition of this story, but an early one I do know is that my mother seemed to me to hang on my every word and regard each one as a gem; but that criminal, my father, unfairly and cruelly questioned the value of some of what I said and did. Fortunately for my mental health, my mother generally did not seem to defend me against his more sensible assessments or even agree with me that his hurting my feelings was a crime. For that reason, my fantasy of the rest of you defending me against the crook who attacks me is unstable, and I have to resort to one in which I defend myself and I am anxious and guilty about the outcome.

Thomas French's concept of *the focal conflict* is useful in organizing a system in which to accommodate the way that conflict and the mechanisms of defense can be discussed nonmechanistically. French, following Hegel, saw life as a constant flux of synthesis, antithesis and synthesis. Starting at the thought of killing my heckler as the synthesis (French's *disturbing motive*), the antithesis (French's *reactive fear*) is that either I will be killed (or severely damaged) myself or I will lose a person I love dearly. The mechanisms of defense are not really mechanisms but common ways that the stories we tell ourselves are revised.

The formation of the next synthesis (new disturbing motive) is the kind of revision called *projection*. You, and not I, will attack my enemy. The antithesis is that I'm not sure you (my mother) won't side with him, and the new, more independent synthesis arises from that. I am leaving out ninety-nine percent or more of the dialectical steps that actually are going on in my thought, and about the same proportion of the detail of the antitheses. Nothing is new about this description except for its leaving out parts of the mind struggling against one part, and substituting conflicting parts of the world constructed by each person. Since this is a dialectical scheme and I am arguing for a description of life that does without metaphors of physical things inside a physical space, and since I grew up a Marxist, it appeals to me to call the system dialectical immaterialism.

One of the main hopes I have for this point of view, whatever I call it, is that it can be used to accommodate in one theory two views of the world that psychoanalysts of various persuasions have almost always kept apart. The schism has had endless versions but is basically the same from Freud v. Adler to Kohut v. Kernberg and beyond.

Alfred Adler was the first to state the non-Freudian side. Harry Stack Sullivan and Heinz Kohut were among his successors. Adler emphasized what people thought was wrong with them and the ways they tried to make themselves good enough. He spoke of people's doubts that they were who they thought or hoped they were. The issue is security versus insecurity.

Freud took as primary the question of what people want to do to and with each other, and he derived their personal doubts from their defenses against their impulses. The issue is security versus guilt.

If the difference had not become a schism, I think that a more balanced theory would have resulted, but as it turned out over and over, each side rejected the other's ideas instead of trying to see them as complementary. In some ways, it is a chicken-and-egg problem. Are we angry with other people because we are afraid they may disapprove of or otherwise hurt us, or are we afraid other people will hurt us because they know we are angry with them? All analysts have to balance the two versions, but this is hard to do clinically and seems to be next to impossible theoretically. For example, for Freud the prime mover is impulse, and anxiety arises from the vicissitudes and consequences of impulse, while for Sullivan the prime mover is anxiety, and all impulses arise from the need to avoid it.

It is overstating the case that it is next to impossible to balance the two versions theoretically, except that a balanced, inclusive theory is so rare. In 1971, Kohut published one in *The Analysis of the Self,* but in the next year or two he abandoned it.

The way I think that dialectical immaterialism can help is that it provides a way of thinking which collapses the two positions into one. If we focus on the stories we elaborate all the time, there are two critical questions about each story: how will it come out, and is it true? Kohut's main contributions have to do with the ways that people conceal from themselves who they think they are—especially their biggest and best version. In his system, their motive for this concealment is fear that their version of themselves will not stand up to exposure to others, and that they will be injured, or even shattered, by the damage to their grandiose self or to the idealized other people whom they experience as part of themselves.

In my opinion, a better way of talking about these issues is to speak in terms of consensual validation and invalidation of our world of relationships. Ordinarily only one part of our relationship world is at issue at a time and therefore only one aspect of ourselves. At the moment, my relationship with you is at risk and therefore so is the aspect of me that is a psychoanalytic writer. I think that even if you dislike or don't get what I am saying, I will still be basically all right, though shaken. If I were as fragile as some people are, the invalidation of my existence as a reasonably worthwhile writer would literally drive me crazy, since my whole sense of myself would be shattered, and therefore my whole world.

The result of invalidation ranges from mild embarrassment through shame to humiliation to fragmentation, all experiences we try hard to avoid. But they are not the only ones. If the opponent I imagined shooting were to show up I would fear being shamed by his attacks, but I would also fear hurting him too badly. If I did drive him from the room by logic, wit and sarcasm, I might feel triumphant, but I would also feel guilty. In other words, I would fear not only that the character I am in the story is unreal, but also that even if I am perfectly real I might do something that would lead to guilt or punishment.

The avoidance of guilt and the avoidance of shame are equally powerful motives, and both are present in all of us all the time. Guilt and shame often lead to each other. For example, guilt can motivate impotence, which results in shame, and a fear of shame may lead to lying, which leads to guilt.

I think it is worth speculating as to why one person has emphasized one side and another the other. Freud had his share of horrible conflicts, but he seems to have arrived in maturity with a particularly secure sense of who he was. Sullivan, on the other hand, not only had horrible conflicts but also an important period in his life when he wasn't at all sure who he was. In the Freudian account of life, emphasis goes on what people want to do to and with one another, not on whether they are secure in their identity. The Sullivanian account emphasizes whether people know who they are, and what they do to try to establish and prove some bearable version of themselves.

To some extent patients tend to group themselves similarly. A child of the Orthogenic School who had recovered from his earlier autism said that the thing he had hated the most when very young was riding in a car, because when another car passed going in the opposite direction, he couldn't tell which car he was in. On the other hand, an analysand who early on seemed unsure of who he was and eager for me to tell him proved to be kidding both of us. He knew for sure that he was smarter, more important and richer than me, and feared terribly what I would do when I found out.

Early in my career I thought of myself as a Sullivanian when working with severely disturbed people and a Freudian when working with neurotic ones. In 1971, I was delighted to find in Kohut's book a way of being both at once. The trouble is, though, that Kohut saw some of the difficulties in his account and abandoned half of it—the specifically Freudian half—while remaining tied to a particularly physical metaphor, the self.

The Analysis of the Self could be called *"I Discover Harry Stack Sullivan* by Heinz Kohut," and *The Restoration of the Self, "I Become Harry Stack Sullivan* by Heinz Kohut." I think that both works are of great importance because Kohut was in many ways a superior Sullivan whose clinical insights expanded psychoanalysis greatly, and whose theoretical constructs can be revised into something that works quite well.

I think that the necessary revisions have to start at the foundation. There is no such thing as *the self*, and as a consequence there is no such thing as narcissism. But the word *self* is highly useful. Attaching the word *the* to it is unfortunate. The difficulty goes back at least to Hartmann, who pointed out that prior to 1920, when Freud wrote about "the ego," most of the time he meant "the self." I think that part of the trouble arises from the definite article having different connotations in German and in English. "The I" doesn't mean the same thing as "Das Ich," and "the ego" is even further off. It would have sounded awkward to translate "Das Ich und Das Es" as "I and It," but no more awkward than "The Ego and the Id," and at the same time more lifelike and immediate.

If that had happened perhaps Edith Jacobson would have called her book *People and Their Significant Others*, and Kohut might have written about persons and people instead of the self. He could have solved the problem of what to call his 1971 book by making the grandiose fantasy rather than the grandiose self its focus. That would have been an improvement in many ways, because the grandiose fantasy is an interpersonal concept, a real thought and not a fictitious thing. In our grandiose (or any other) fantasy, we are defined by our relationships. To extend D. W. Winnicott, possibly in agreement with Robert Stolorow: there is no such thing as the person. In that case, there is no such thing as the self, and it follows that there is no such thing as narcissism.

There are many concepts of narcissism, and some of my main objections to all of them can be seen in a paradox in the idiom *self-centered person*. Few people are as interested in the activities of others as are the self-centered. At the end of World War II, there was a joke about what Hell would be like for two of the leading Nazis. For Goebels it was to be a thousand microphones and no loudspeaker, and for Goering, a thousand uniforms and no mirror. The joke, if taken literally, was wrong. The two war criminals would have been punished properly with endless loudspeakers and mirrors but no one to hear or see them. "I love me" is a plausible, meaningful statement, and so is "I love you," but the verb does not have quite the same meaning in the two sentences. When I am deeply involved in loving you, I will spend relatively little attention on anyone beyond the two of us, but when I am deeply involved in loving me, I will be just as deeply involved in attending to everyone else and getting them to see how wonderful I am. What is centered on the self-centered is the attention and care they want from everyone else.

In 1971, Kohut accommodated the distinction by emphasizing two kinds of libido, narcissistic and object instinctual. In ordinary language, the difference is that object libido is an attachment to others and narcissistic libido is an attachment to other people's attachment to us. Object impulses are desires to affect others. Narcissistic impulses are desires for others to affect us.

In considering the sentence, "I love me," people have tended to forget that the difference between the nouns is only grammar—subjective versus objective case. Most of the time, *self* is used reflexively. For instance, "I love myself," is more natural than, "I love me." *Herself* and *himself* are in the objective. There is no *heself* or *sheself*. *Itself* and *myself* are almost always used in the objective.

The exceptions are when *self* standing alone and the pronoun–self combinations are sometimes used for emphasis or to indicate that absolutely the whole person is indicated, as in, "I, myself, was responsible," but even in this usage there is a flavor of the objective case, a reminder to think of me (as the person responsible). Nowadays, it is common to read phrases like, "the self as originator of action," that is, the objective case person in the subjective case. This is not absurd, only confusing. It refers to the originator of action in his or her appearance to the world—how others relate to me when I act.

Freud in his early use of "Das Ich" was writing about who we feel we are, but *the ego* became a pseudo-organ. Had *Das Ich* been translated as *I* or *the person*, the disadvantage would have been to leave *it* and *over I*—id and superego—out of what sounds like the whole personality. But Freud, I think, meant it rather like that because it is how we feel: pressed by our desires and oppressed by our guilt—forces that feel like they come from outside the essential us—and if we had grown up accustomed to using those words, we would have been less likely to invent the self as a companion organ to the ego.

I think that a lot of confusion would be cleared up if we realized that in most cases *self*, *ego*, and *person* are synonymous. Most of the time sentences containing the word *ego* would be well translated into ordinary English by substituting *I*, *she*, *he* or *the person*. Many sentences containing "the self" would then be more ordinary and real because it would be clear that what was meant was the person as object: what is experienced, loved, hated and so forth. "The self" as a human being makes sense. "The self" as a part of a human being does not.

What then of the concept, *selfobject*? One of the greatest of Kohut's contributions was his pointing out that we experience ourselves as including other people or things, or as being included in them. "Selfness" is a characteristic as movable among the characters in our fantasies as the highlight on my computer screen. We all can put ourselves into the other car as easily as the autistic boy could, but we can take ourselves out more easily than he could. I can be me reading aloud or I can be you listening. If you praise what I did I will make you part of me, but if you then express reservations I may kick you out. Similarly, I am a part of the Chicago Bears, and if they win the Super Bowl, we will be number one, but if they don't make the playoffs they will just be a bunch of overpaid jocks I never even met.

But there are several difficulties with the term, *selfobject*. For one thing, after Kohut threw the rest of psychoanalytic theory overboard there was no other kind of object. I agree with Stolorow and others in saying that others are selfobjects to the extent that they are involved in the maintenance of our self-esteem and that they also function as objects of conflict. Another problem has to do with the generally favorable connotations that *self*, as in *selfobject*, has. In the writings of the self psychologists it usually sounds as though having selfobjects is good for one, and in many ways that is true, but I think they tend to neglect some of the disadvantages. They are clear on the vulnerability to loss that is entailed in having selfobjects, but less so on the possibilities of enslavement.

Kohut took that into account clearly in *The Analysis of the Self*, particularly in his conception that the part of the grandiose self that is vertically split-off is a product of a childhood in which people feel themselves to be a necessary adjunct to one or both parents, and under the control of the parents, in order to serve the parents' needs. This is a particularly critical idea, not only because it can serve as a warning of the possibility that the transference can become a similar enslavement, but also because it is a point of articulation with the work of a whole other group of analysts, those who study and think in terms of separation and individuation. For ten years I worked with a woman whose relationship with her mother consisted largely of the performance of rigid, compulsory rituals of mutual regard. Adherence to the family party line was strictly required. Two aspects of my relationship with this person were difficult and essential: her need for me to be available and in tune with her, and her need to be free to be somebody I hadn't thought she was or ought to be.

The other two aspects of relatedness that Kohut helps us to account for in one theory are just as important. This woman not only needed to know that she really existed and that we were connected even if she were an independent person, she also needed to be able to have sexual impulses toward me in spite of the fact that she had previously considered them bad, and she had to be able to hate me without fear or guilt as well. In working with her I was helped by having a theoretical framework within which I could see the danger that her sense of being real and coherent was vulnerable to destruction by my invalidating her world, and that instead I had to fairly gently negotiate the differences between our worlds. At the same time, the theory enabled me to see that what went on in her world felt dangerous to her not only because she might cease to exist, but also because she might be punished for her sins.

In conclusion, I hope that these ideas have some usefulness in reframing the psychoanalytic account of thought and its relation to other activities. I believe that they provide a means of discussing psychoanalytic data without resorting to mental anatomy and physiology, and that they lead to a clearer view of the problems of treating anyone, but particularly so-called narcissistic people.

I doubt that much that I have said is new except for the way of saying it. But that is something, and if I am right at all, it could be a way of relating our findings to those of scientists who investigate the real structure of humans and the actions and interrelationships of the components of that structure. It is, I think, a better solution to the problem of metapsychology than its abandonment in favor of the clinical theory, which is in danger of not being a theory at all but rather a highly valuable tradition of folk wisdom; good enough for psychoanalytic practice, but not so good for the psychoanalytic exploration of human nature and culture.

Shame as an Interactive Phenomenon

A neuroscientist, one of my friends in the study group, said in a meeting that he wasn't clear about the difference between shame and guilt. I bragged that I was. Confronted with a request that I explain it, I got nervous and said I would write a paper instead. As I worked on it, I kept thinking of more angles on what seems to me a topic which has grown more important over the last century.

FOR THE PAST TWO OR THREE DECADES, PSYCHOANALYSIS has been in the process of resolving one of its essential paradoxes. The joint work of an analyst and analysand (or of any two or more people involved in psychotherapy) is as interpersonal an enterprise as is possible. Both participants act on one another constantly and the behavior of each is always a reaction to the behavior of the other, but to a large degree analysts have conceived of and discussed their task as if the scene of action was inside the analysand. To the extent that analysis was seen as a joint effort, that effort was thought of as a cooperative exploration of the mind of one of the people, and the mind was represented by metaphors of a self-contained physical apparatus. The analysand opened a window into this apparatus by free associating and the analyst looked inside and described the structure and function of the machinery he saw or inferred.

Almost a century ago, Freud realized that what appeared in the window was influenced by the presence of the analyst. At first he thought this influence was an unfortunate distortion of the field of observation, but he always made advantages out of obstacles. In this case he saw that he was represented in the free associations as much more than a simple scientific observer, and he came to regard the more elaborate and passionate views of himself as a particularly valuable kind of data.

Transference came to be a *sine qua non* of analysis, but countertransference, when it too was recognized, tended to be considered for rather a long time as an unfortunate imperfection which ought to be minimized. The next step (one of the many oversimplifications in this account is to represent these developments as an orderly process) was the realization that the analyst's impulses toward the analysand were important data, too. But these data were regarded as being important as evidence of what was going on in the internal apparatus of the analysand. It was generally accepted that, with proper training and care, these data were valid and reliable. The belief that the analyst was a disinterested and expert observer whose observations and conclusions were correct, or at least approximately correct, descriptions of a reality that was independent of his or her presence was largely maintained for some time.

Analysands, from the very beginning, had not always believed the truth they were told by their analysts, and their disbelief was considered understandable since it is evident to anyone that people in general dislike hearing the truth about themselves. This dislike, which became known as resistance, was also seen as an important kind of data, but the possibility that the analysand was right in rejecting some of the interpretations he or she heard was ignored as much as possible for a long time. Thirty years ago, one of my favorite supervisors, Aaron Hilkevitch, said, "The most embarrassing moment for an analyst is to be at a case presentation and hear the analyst say, 'The transference distortion of me was to see me as such and such,' and for everybody else in the room to know that's what he's really like."

Among the many influences that gradually undermined the notion of analysis as the work of a subject on an object was the tension in analytic theory of the nature/nurture conflict. Freud's original position on the subject was that neurosis was always the result of trauma. When he realized that this was too simple a position and that he had overstated it, he substituted conflict for trauma in his theory and established inherent biologic tendency as at least the equal of traumatic experience. It didn't matter if the disturbing thoughts were memories or were fantasies created by libidinal force. What mattered was that people were coming to unsatisfactory, unconsciously arrived-at compromises between these thoughts and the demands of society. The heredity versus environment question was left open, which is a good way to leave it, except that it was also left strangely undiscussed.

Individual analysts have been and still are apt to believe that they know the right balance between inborn tendency and life history, and that everyone in analysis knows and agrees on this balance. But there are big differences in analytic theory and bigger ones in practice, based largely, I believe, on the personality of the analyst. I think that, in general, each analyst tends to be more interested in the environment than she or he is willing to admit. In any case, if one listens sympathetically to a person tell about suffering in an unsympathetic world, the experience is likely to lead to both people feeling good about their relationship and to thinking that it has been beneficial. Sixty years ago, the notion that analysis was a corrective emotional experience first became prominent and then notorious because it was used as a rationalization for naive, simple and sometimes unethical interventions. In reaction, there was a resurgence of purist thought: analysts must simply tell analysands how their minds work, how they deceive themselves and why, and let them heal themselves with that knowledge if they will. That puritanical reaction still lingers but is much attenuated by the passing of generations and the power of the analytic relationship — an influence internal to analysis has simply asserted itself, and its importance cannot easily be denied.

External influences have been even more powerful. Throughout much of the world, and especially in the United States, professional relationships in which the professional's authority was not to be questioned have become passé, and logical positivism has withered. A more egalitarian conception in which both parties observe one another, and the observations of both are regarded as potentially valid, comes naturally to many analysts nowadays. To a large degree it is now accepted, or at least acceptable, to think that models of reality are negotiated between and among people.

Prominent careers have been based on exploring how analyst and analysand together construct analytic reality. Aaron Hilkevitch's joke is now an analytic growth industry, as it ought to be. On the other hand, more impressive work has been done on the nature of analytic practice than on theory. We are less naive about what we are involved in doing in our offices, and more confused about basic questions about the nature of human life.

This ponderous introduction is intended to frame a discussion of shame, an experience of central clinical importance whose nature can be better understood in a constructivist context than in an intrapsychic one—that is, as a product of the interaction of people (perceived one way or another) as opposed to the interaction of organs of the mind of one person.

The theoretical difference can have big practical effects. An analyst hearing a tone of apology in an account of something is likely to say, "You think that what you have revealed about yourself isn't good enough." Starting from a constructivist point of view, one is more likely to say, "You fear that I will think that what you have revealed about yourself isn't good enough," in my opinion a statement that will seem more true and meaningful than the first, and one that does not hint at a negative judgment.

Analytic hours can be seen as consisting largely of efforts to negotiate the construction of a shared model of the reality of who the participants are and what their relation to each other is.

(I prefer to speak of models of reality because I am old-fashioned enough to think that reality exists, in the sense that there is a gradation of correctness and usefulness of various accounts of it. We do not construct reality, though we create or change it in the course of making models—especially interpersonally—and some models, such as racism, are never valid, no matter how many people accept them.)

Analytic hours are intended to be discussions of what is or isn't so, and therefore it isn't surprising that so many of them are taken up with reality modeling. On the other hand, much of the negotiating is covert, and the participants are well-acquainted with one another. By contrast, in the rest of life we frequently interact with people we don't know well, in circumstances that are at least as ambiguous as an analytic session and far less carefully circumscribed, and therefore requiring even more energy to be expended in negotiating a shared model. Therefore, what has been recognized and studied in analytic sessions applies generally. A thoroughgoing acceptance of the constructivist viewpoint implies that much of what people are doing all the time is defining personal shared reality.

Words fail me here, because we are so accustomed and our language so adapted to individual psychology that to write about reality as worked out interpersonally, and only interpersonally, strains the connotations of ordinary psychological language. What I mean is that who we are is the sum of our relationships—"relationships" defined quite broadly, including our connections to groups as well as individuals, to nonhuman things or abstractions, to anything that can be personified. In addition, I mean that who we feel we are includes alternate versions of each of our many relationships in various degrees of consciousness. Just as we try not to know about all our wishes and fantasies, we try not to know the extent of our great uncertainty that our preferred definition of ourselves will be validated by others. Every greeting, farewell, anecdote, observation about the weather, and so on, to an infinite number, serves at least in part as an experiment to determine if the other believes your relationship to one another to be what you think or wish it to be.

Since our uncertainty about who we are is so much greater than we like to think about, the experience of invalidation is particularly painful and damaging. If we communicate one way or another, directly or indirectly, a message such as, "You and I are friends," and the response or lack of response is that we aren't friends at all, we are shaken, and the pain we feel is somewhere on a spectrum on which embarrassment, shame, humiliation, mortification and panic are points. We will do a great deal to avoid that experience, and if it occurs we try to undo it, magically or otherwise. Long ago, I was delighted to see at a party a man who had been a valued supervisor two years earlier. I thought we now were of equal status and that it would be gratifying to renew the friendship on that footing. I called out his name enthusiastically as I approached him, and he ignored me completely. I never saw him again. I never fully appreciated how much I wanted to be able to discount that experience until, about twenty years later, I heard that he had done something disgraceful and it had ruined him. I am ashamed to admit, because I want to be thought of as a secure, forgiving person, that I was as glad to hear the news as I had been glad to see him at the party. Years of wishing that I could prove that he didn't matter had magically worked.

What he had done to me used to be called cutting someone dead, a phrase that I believe correctly expresses the meaning of the experience to the person whose greeting is ignored. The feeling of being killed or at least damaged psychically by invalidation is reflected in the past tradition of dueling's lethal consequences of a gentleman's believing his honor had been impugned, and in the dueling present by a gang member believing that he has been dissed. In either case, the social wound is intolerable and must be healed by a physical one. The presence on earth of someone who has an insulting opinion can't be lived with. The opinion has to be taken back by an apology, or either the offending person, the offended person, or both must die.

Consequences almost as serious occur when adolescents or young adults reach the conclusion that there is no way that they can try to satisfy urgent needs without at least risking complete rejection. Panic and psychosis may be the result. One such young man who had made significant progress—though not as much as I thought he had—told me of his despair of ever going out on a date. I said that perhaps, since his feelings about things were changing, it might someday be possible. He produced a .45 caliber automatic and put it to his head, saying, "I will now decorate your office with my brains." It took a long, frightening struggle to let him know that I did, after all, understand how impossible acceptance seemed to him, and how horrible rejection would be. When I finally made that clear, he put the gun down.

I do not mean to imply that psychosis is a product of experience alone. The perception that others are or will be rejecting arises from an interplay of disabilities, some of which are undoubtedly determined at conception.

Whatever brings it about, the perception of social failure causes trouble—often lasting trouble—for anyone. I think everyone has a collection of horrible memories of faux pas and other fiascos which come to mind unbidden and insistently, often to the accompaniment of self-denunciation: "Idiot!" "Fool!" "I wish I were dead." The memories are like intolerable foreign bodies we cannot extrude, no matter how we try. What is going on at these moments is that we are trying to undo the experience by wishing it away, and we are certainly making great efforts to avoid new ones. One of the things that everyone dreads the most is to be revealed as a fool: one who lets others know that he has mistaken self-confidence. Discrepant awareness is a tool of the playwright doing comedy. Malvolio, the steward in Shakespeare's *Twelfth Night*, believes that Olivia loves him. The audience is aware that she does not—very amusing for the audience, horrible for Malvolio. We all fear being in his position. For this reason, an enormous number of friendly remarks and other potentially desirable interactions are suppressed.

I believe that significant insecurity about these questions is much more prevalent in our present cosmopolitan society than in other, more homogeneous cultures now or in the past. My father-in-law has lived in the same small rural community for seventy-five years. Most of the people he encounters from day to day are ones he has known all their lives, and whose entire extended families he has known most of his life. Negotiations as to who is who and how they feel about one another are pretty complete. His ambitions as to his standing in the community have been largely achieved. When he comes to Seattle or otherwise meets strangers, he enjoys the experience as an interesting novelty. He is at ease and gracious on these occasions, and his friendly interest in learning who the new people are and what they think about things is almost always received with pleasure and eagerness. His security, I think, is based on his having a reliable home base. He is only slightly perturbed by the possibility that strangers will think him old-fashioned, out of it and rustic. Indeed, he sometimes cultivates that impression, which amuses him because he is pretty sure that his way of life is more sensible than more urban ones. I believe that, to the extent he takes a poor reception to heart, his knowledge of his standing with his family and neighbors more than compensates for the partial invalidation of his sense of himself as a decent, competent, attractive person. His standing has, of course, been earned by a lifetime of hard work, intelligence, friendship and generosity, but he can take it for granted now because it is known to the people that matter to him.

Most of us today are in constant contact with people with whom we have no history and only some shared agreement on what is a desirable self-presentation. The mobility of most of the population has made it relatively uncommon for people to live long among others they know well. Even when we are on intimate terms with our neighbors, we usually work with a completely different group. People who share our personal lives are often completely different from the ones who share our careers.

The mixing together of people from all over has destroyed our certainty that we know how to live, because neighbors, coworkers and often spouses come from different cultures or at least subcultures. We can never be sure that what we do will seem to make sense and be admirable to many of the people around us, and we care more than our ancestors did because society is less stratified. People used to be able to count on being seen as a member of their class, based on various symbolic ways of dressing, speaking and behaving in general. Being seen as a lady or a gentleman, a good ol' boy, or whatever, was often good enough. In addition, being thought weird by someone could often be dismissed because the other person was clearly the weird one—a member of a group that is beneath one, or is the oppressing enemy, or any other disqualification from full humanness. People in general used to be like my father-in-law, knowing pretty well where they stood and how they should act. Today most of us feel, at least sometimes, that everyone else is a member of the club and knows all the rules, and that only we are in ignorance, and we have to earn our standing continually.

Whether that task disconcerts us depends on our reserves of favorable history and on our optimism about the impressions we can make in the future. As these self-esteem issues have become more important, it has become ever more fashionable, especially in mental health circles—including psychoanalytic ones—to value independence of the judgment of others. I believe that this is a false value, one which, no matter how advantageous its achievement, is of no use because it is unachievable. No one can remain intact without a sense of security that comes from at least a modicum of positive relationships.

The issue is immensely complex, because an individual's stock of relationships is not congruent with what could be observed by another person. What counts is what each of us thinks—thinks consciously, in an automatic, unattended way, or thinks quite unconsciously. Most of us have illusions about how we appear and, as is well known, depressed people are more likely than those who aren't depressed to be accurate in their estimates of the opinions of others.

There seems to be a golden mean of optimism about these matters. Self-confidence is often rewarded by actual success, but excessive vanity leads to defeats the person does not anticipate, and feels keenly. It is not easy to distinguish the overconfidence of someone whose experience has been particularly easy from the arrogance of someone whose conscious or unconscious doubts lead to a frantic, relentless effort to disprove them. Independence of the opinions of others is a therapeutic goal that leads to a pseudocure along the lines of The Emperor's New Clothes. On the other hand, increased optimism about the opinions of others so that one can be less preoccupied with them is often achievable.

An even more difficult and subtle complication is the way that ghosts of the past constantly insinuate themselves into our perceptions of people now around us. This is one of the main contributions that psychoanalysis has made to our knowledge of human nature: the main characters of our early life, including ourselves, are constantly being perceived in the people now present. Therefore, we often misperceive each other. We pursue goals with each other that are more a part of an old relationship than a present one. For example, a spouse can be seen as likely to be accepting or rejecting as a parent was, and the repetition of old pleasures or, more dangerously, the repair of old damage, can be a cherished if unattainable goal.

The (oversimplified) principle is that we have learned too well from experience. The convictions from the past are shaken only with the greatest difficulty, and one of the least valuable parts of our nature leads us to stubbornly court the same defeats over and over in an attempt to undo them, hoping magically that they will come out right this time. That rationalization of the compulsion to repeat may be a false reassurance. Freud's opinion that there is a basically destructive side to our nature may be the only finally adequate explanation. Whatever the reason, people are continually offended by each other in ways that are inexplicable to one or both. They frustrate each other's ambitions and fail to live up to each other's idealizations without it being clear to anyone what the ambitions and idealizations are.

The occurrence of shame can be understood as being a consequence of any of these frustrations. If I tell a funny joke and happily expect laughter and approval, my audience's turning away in disgust or scorn will mortify me. As comedians say, "I'm dying up here!" The story of the little boy saying, "Say it isn't so, Joe," is touching because all of us can identify with him in his distress at learning that his hero had thrown the World Series. Security is derived from participation in a relationship (even if just as a fan in the grandstand) between people who are each regarded as admirable, or at least all right. The emphasis can be on one participant or on both. (One participant can be a group, a thing, and so forth.)

If the emphasis is on the subject in the desired relationship, the desire is an ambition. If it is on the object, it is an idealization. Mixtures such as relationships of mutual admiration occur. We are not usually in the habit of thinking of ambitions in these interpersonal terms, but I believe they are helpful. Someone who wants to be a movie star wants primarily to be in a certain relationship with the rest of us. Probably John F. Kennedy's ambition to send a man to the moon had to do primarily with being the president of the nation that was most powerful, accomplished, admired and envied.

Ambitions arise in the earliest relationship of infant and parents. Complex and partially instinctual interactions make a baby and the other participants happy. Among traditional Navajos, the person who first makes a child laugh gives it a present in return for the honor and pleasure. The experience of being loved, admired and understood is perhaps more critically necessary at the beginning of life than later, but never becomes optional. Being understood is as essential as the other two ingredients. An infant requires a well-timed and modulated response to its gestures, expressions and utterances, and throughout life we need to be with others who get what it is we are communicating. The ambition to be our own particular kind of person develops in the interaction of our particular qualities and the particular responsiveness of our caretakers.

The principle is that we need to be accepted, or more than accepted, for who we really feel we are. One of the many things that can go wrong is that children may find that their own spontaneous actions are not well responded to, and that they must follow a specific, rather rigid scenario their parents have in mind in order to be pleasing. The result, among other things, is a sense of not being really good enough and having to pretend: to be false or fraudulent. On the other hand, being praised for anything we do is only good for small babies.

This enviable situation, in my opinion, has given rise to another false value: unconditional positive regard. Like absolute independence, it is a response to the insecurity-generating qualities of the times. Parents inflict crippling damage on their small children if they ignore any defects and instead always tell them that they are just perfect. In a relatively common family situation, parents do not get along well and the mother tells the child that he (usually he) is better than the father. This seemingly spares the little boy from feeling quite so disappointed in his ambition to be the biggest and the best. The father is bigger, but according to the mother the child is best, and maybe small and incompetent is better in some special way that only special people can understand.

For many years, I have been treating a man whose mother did this. She told him that she and he were a better kind of person than was to be found around them, and that any criticism or blame he got from the father, and there was a lot, was just a sign of what a drunken brute the father was. If the boy depended on her, she was pleased by this token of her importance and her closeness to him. If he ventured away on expeditions of his own, she let him know that she was disappointed to learn that he was not the person she had thought he was.

He developed such severe school phobia that for several years he was tutored at home. He consulted me in his early twenties because the school phobia had become travel phobia. Over the nineteen years of our work he freed himself from the relationship with his mother and his symptoms, but not from me. Our relationship replaced the one with mother, and he experiences therapy as the special nurturance that keeps him going. My demands for loyalty are considerably less than his mother's were, but there remains this relatively small area of his life where he is still the trapped little boy. Considering how long it has been already, I doubt that he will ever free himself from the need for a special relationship with a special person, even though he is well aware of what is going on. Though he has done quite well in his career, and fairly well with his wife and children, he remains intensely shame-prone. Any failure to live up to his ambition to be the best in his field leads to pain and rage at whoever has not appreciated him or has competed successfully with him. He still feels, fairly strongly, the sense he learned from his mother that whoever competes successfully against him is a member of an awful lower order.

If the dawning realization that one is not the biggest and best in the household or world is not cushioned in a dangerous way, and if it's not too harsh and sudden, it can lead to a modification of ambition in the direction of what is reasonable, and to the other segment of self-esteem, idealization. It is as if children say to themselves such things as, "I may not be very big, but my mother can even reach things on top of the dresser and she is part of me, so I'm big too." This kind of security remains essential throughout life. Our sense of self includes others who enhance us. They may be really closely connected next of kin or strangers paid to play baseball, but the essential elements are that they be admirable and that there be some plausible connection that makes identification possible.

Two kinds of things can go wrong with idealization and lead to shame. The first is failure of the idealized other. The Seattle Mariners may play badly or the Chicago Black Sox consort with gamblers, and we are disappointed, or worse. If it is a fanship we usually extrude the offending party from our sense of self. "It's just a bunch of overpaid kids playing a stupid game." If the connection is marriage, there may be some kind of rupture.

The second way idealization may fail is by a disowning of the connection by the other person. Rejection by an idealized spouse causes unbearable feelings in both categories: the ambition to be loved and admired and the need to have a real connection to the admired person. Murdering such a person remains effectively legal in some states.

One of my heroes in childhood was a first baseman named Peanuts Lowery. I was hurt when he was traded away, but not so much so as a young woman who was the president, and maybe only member, of his fan club. She arranged to see him when he was in town once with his new team, and when he didn't take her seriously, she shot him.

Failure in the development of either category of self-esteem leaves a person excessively subject to shame and related difficulties. Ideally, babies are adored at first and sensitively weaned from adoration in accordance with the particular schedule of their development. People whose parents were neglectful, abusive or with whom for some inborn reason they just couldn't click, tend to go through life depressed, or aggressively exploiting others in an effort to avoid depression. Or they may fear

others and live in considerable isolation, while maintaining themselves
the best they can with a very active fantasy life. There are a number of
other variations of interpersonal distress, and precautions against it. The
avoidance of shame is the main motive of their lives. Unless they die of
marasmus their ambitions remain, not given up but largely unconscious,
and since they are the ambitions of an early period of development, they
are likely to be grandiose and imperative. If their parents had been more
welcoming they would have experienced a gradual wearing down into
reasonableness so that they would enter adulthood with ambitions that
were a little bit, but only a little bit, beyond their capacities. But what is
unconscious doesn't get worn down by experience, and so we see lots of
patients whom we diagnose as character disordered who feel awful about
themselves, are tormented by shame and who, if we give them only a
little encouragement, suddenly seem to expect endless admiration and
service.

In my opinion, the dynamics of what are often called splitting and
rapid cycling involve the expansion and constriction of the sense of self
as the social circumstances seem to the person to warrant greater or
lesser optimism about how they are going to be received, or as they feel
themselves to have been cruelly wounded by the failure of someone to
give them their due.

Psychoanalytic opinions differ considerably about how to understand
the anger that emerges on these occasions, and the theoretical persua-
sion on this point makes a big difference in clinical practice. The majority
opinion is that such people are enraged at the unsatisfactoriness of their
lives, and envy the power of those who frustrate them. The therapeutic
task, according to this view, is to facilitate and accept the expression
of their anger so that it can be amalgamated with other more positive
feelings, and so that they can achieve an ordinary, relatively peaceful
ambivalence. Interpretations along these lines often make the patient
mad. This anger is seen as confirmation of how mad the patient really
was already and as a salubrious lifting of repression. Such analysts then
attempt to convey an open-minded acceptance of the patient's feelings,
but usually not of the patient's reality. At this point in the action, the
patient is usually complaining about the character and behavior of the
analyst who, according to this point of view, will now interpret these

personal remarks as transference. The argument will then boil down to something like who is trying to control whom.

The argument sometimes goes on for years and is usually settled at least somewhat satisfactorily. Two other fairly frequent outcomes are that the patient leaves therapy, or (the worst outcome from my point of view) that the patient makes a big effort to comply and feels great shame at being such an angry, demanding person. This does not do him or her much good. I don't mean to argue that patients feeling shame is necessarily a bad thing, but that there is a level of shame, easily reached in the kind of person I am discussing, that is so disorganizing that little thought can accompany it. Harry Stack Sullivan, who called this kind of horrible sudden shame, "severe anxiety," said that it was like getting hit with a board, and that few people can learn something while they are being so hit. Patients who become compliant are likely to adopt a belief that the treatment has been very helpful—that it has revealed what wretches they basically are and that they now understand the origins of their troubles in their infantile demandingness, envy and rage. Some feel better. Others feel that they have benefited by the moral enlightenment but are otherwise still pretty miserable.

I believe that better results can be had by seeing the shame rather than the rage as the prime focus of interest, and seeing ambition as the prime mover of the symptoms. In the atmosphere that such a focus creates, patients are likely to allow themselves to express in any number of guarded, indirect ways, bits of the sense of the importance they really have or feel they have to have. These hints are accompanied by intense shame, or fear of intense shame; that is, a conviction that the analyst dislikes them, or will. My usual comments at these times concern the way patients are protecting themselves by being indirect, apologetic and tentative. Ultimately, I am likely to say something like, "I think you are hopeful that I will appreciate what you have to say, but if I don't, the things you are talking about are so important and so fragile that my not accepting them, or not even getting what it is you're talking about, would be a disaster that you don't want to take any chances on."

Unfortunately, pretty often, I don't catch onto something important, or I get caught up by some judgmental attitude of my own and make judgmental comments, or at least hints, and then people will be hurt and/or angry. Seeing these occurrences as unfortunate but inevitable, and trying as hard as I can to persuade people to help me to reconstruct and understand what went wrong between us, often works out well. The other person's pain is assuaged, she or he learns that it is possible to negotiate relational reality without being killed off, the rift in the relationship is healed, and we both learn something.

It is true that all people want more love, approval and importance than they can have, and that some people are particularly demanding of it, but an acceptance of the sadness of inevitable disappointment is quite different from a tacit condemnation of what are called immature traits. Particularly fragile people (who may look pretty formidable when aroused) teeter even more precariously than the rest of us between opposite opinions of themselves. Helping them to stabilize that teeter will decrease their fragility and, at the same time, increase their willingness to see that their ambitions are excessive, and to tone them down to ones that can be realized after all. Usually these changes can be accomplished without lecturing about the excessiveness of the ambitions. Before that, they are likely to have despaired of reaching their goals and blamed themselves, others, or both for the impossibility. As the therapy or analysis becomes safer for them, they reveal more of themselves, and what they reveal is often a marvelous invention. People who have felt locked into some awful corner survive through fantasies of possible relationship—sometimes to the nonhuman or to the ideal. They create secret cherished worlds, and the saving scrap of self-esteem may be that they are the special ones who know those special places, and others are excluded.

Analysts who are let in on these secrets had better be prepared to see that they are being given a special privilege, and react accordingly. In the midst of telling, patients are often so afraid that the importance of these secrets will be missed or scorned that they will themselves temporarily discount them. An analyst needs to react like an art critic—not a critic in the sense of judge, but in the more basic sense of one who is able to grasp the essential and beautiful in the work of another and make it explicable and appreciable by other potential audiences. In this case, the critic addresses the creators themselves and helps them to have the courage to be in touch with their conviction of their own particularity and worth in the presence of another person, when they would ordinarily feel shy or defensively angry. This kind of contact makes it easier to give up some of the demands for proof of love and admiration that they have been accustomed to making.

This kind of work is often what goes into a second analysis when the first has been more or less a failure. One first analysis I know about lasted six years and was largely a compliant false-self performance. The analysand planned his "free" associations in advance in order that he could fill the time to the analyst's satisfaction. Another one, which lasted a little longer before the analyst called it off on the grounds that the person was unanalyzable, got stuck on the analyst's insistence on talking about how angry the analysand was. She is a person who almost never gets angry overtly and directly, and who continually sacrifices herself.

It was true that she was angry, and grew more so over the years, and she felt terribly ashamed of being so. In childhood it had seemed impossible to please her mother. She had tried very hard, and continues to try very hard, to please both the elderly mother and the many substitutes for her, and continues to feel that it is impossible. The mother had been a strict disciplinarian and was especially intolerant of any defiance. Being angry was a serious failing, and being angry at her was absolutely out. The analysand experienced the analyst as confirming what she believed to be her mother's strongest accusations against her.

In many cases, I believe, people—far more often women than men—grow up feeling that being different from their mothers or what their mothers seem to want them to be is a particular crime, and anger one of its worst forms. Interpretations of their words or behavior in analysis as showing that they are angry usually induce shame and/or rage. Interpretations of the shame or fear of shame help.

Most such people, and in addition some who are more capable of being openly angry themselves, are excessively frightened by the anger of others. Usually the basis is not a fear of losing an argument or fight and being really or symbolically injured, but of being written off. They have had the experience of parents who would quickly recategorize them as not themselves or not a member of their family: "I used to think you were a... but now I see...." One of my analysands spoke of being annihilated whenever someone disapproved of her. From the point of view of the other person, including me, it is she who makes herself disappear. In either case, a feature of everyone's life, and a particularly obtrusive feature of the lives of people who are easily hurt, is the appearance and disappearance of parts of one's self.

To put it a slightly different way, we expand and constrict more or less automatically depending on our assessment of our circumstances. When it feels as if the people around us, or particularly a special individual, is likely to get what it is we are all about and to appreciate us, more of what we are all about suddenly becomes conscious and available to be lived. Conversely, if we are disappointed in others' response, or feel that we probably will be, things that we cherish about ourselves are suddenly gone. An everyday example is the person who can't remember jokes. They disappear, because she or he can't believe they will really be well-received.

I vividly remember "The Little Lame Prince," a fairy tale I knew in childhood, in which the imprisoned prince was safeguarded by a fairy godmother who gave him a magic carpet on which he could escape his tower prison to any wonderful place he wanted. When no one was around the carpet was itself, but if some dangerous captor appeared it rolled itself up small and went off into a corner in the guise of a tattered, worthless old rag.

These fluctuations in our size and shape are determined by our estimates of our condition as well as our estimates of the receptivity of the others. When we are well-rested and healthy, have recently been successful in what we have been doing, or otherwise feel at the height of our powers, a person whom we might otherwise be afraid to approach seems more approachable, and in our increased daring, we expand. The converse is also true, and both expansion and constriction have a life of their own as vicious or benign circles since, within limits, self-confidence is often rewarded and self-doubt punished.

The sense of ourselves in this way is greatly influenced by drugs. Alcohol, it seems to me, is more likely than any other—at a medium blood level—to increase one's sense of being interesting and admirable to the people around. That phenomenon seems to correlate well with observations that alcoholics are frequently shy people who would isolate themselves without the alcohol, and who are helped by AA or other groups that facilitate their being able to express themselves. I think that antidepressants, especially SSRIs, also help in this way.

This phenomenon suggests that at least some depression or some portion of depression is the interplay of whatever biochemical system (serotonergic?) mediates a sense of personal power/weakness with experiences that generate changes in self-confidence. It is my clinical experience that many extremely insecure patients—particularly as they improve—go through rapid and large fluctuations in this dimension. They are apt to be diagnosed as rapid cyclers or as bipolar type II. Whether this is all the same thing, or if there are people whose cycling is more close to being purely a matter of experience and behavior, I don't know. I am also not sure to what degree this type of psychodynamics influences the appearance and disappearance of full-blown mania. In a number of cases, nothing apparent to me as therapist influenced it very much except medication, but I'm not sure.

In this connection I have puzzled for a long time over what seems to me a set of potentially valuable coincidences: Full-blood Native Americans don't suffer from bipolar disorder. They do have an enormous prevalence of alcoholism, and they are more than usually susceptible to serious conflicts and panic precipitated by unusually strong positive reactions. On one occasion, I observed a brief, manic-like psychosis in a young man unexpectedly singled out for personal praise by people he experienced as being of great national importance.

Whether there is anything to these speculations or not, Native American people tend to differ from most of us these days in having more self-esteem resources of the other-idealization type. These configurations have their origins a bit later than ambitions, and have a milder, less driven kind of emotional component. Where ambitions drive and torment, idealizations, and especially ideals, lead and console. In their beginning they are based on the very young peoples' ability to recognize differences between themselves and their caretakers—especially ways in which the adult has qualities (size, strength, power and the like) that the child can only wish for personally.

This is an area of child development theory that comes from reconstructions based on the analysis and other introspections of adults or older children, and on observation of actual infants and toddlers. It can never be more than a useful construct. Freud called it a myth. Strongly competing versions differ at exactly this point: how does the young person react to seeing this difference? Much of the analytic world says, "with envy." The answer that is more convincing to me is that it is first with admiration, and I believe that this is in agreement with what is observable. One can see the very young looking at their parents with love and something like awe, but not with rage unless they are frustrated, and it does not seem necessary or lifelike to assume that their rage at not being fed, for example, is envious. In my opinion, envy arises when someone else arrives on the scene and diverts the admiring attention of the parent. At any rate, admiration of caretakers and identification with them is the start of the capacity to sustain oneself, partly by this more reliable means when the failure of ambition would otherwise lead to shame.

The reliability of either means to self-esteem increases gradually as the child adapts to non-traumatic frustrations. If frustration is so sudden and severe that the child cannot adapt, it interrupts the line of development and leaves maladaptive motives: wishes to undo the unbearable experience. If the frustration of ambitions is too severe for the particular child at the particular time, he or she will remain ambitious at a relatively immature, unrealistic level. The presence of infantile, grandiose ambition may be conscious and lead to a constant, desperate struggle against a shameful feeling of inadequacy by attempts to be the center of adoration by one means or another, or it may become unconscious and leave the person feeling empty and lifeless, deprived of the energy of his or her important goals.

A worse outcome occurs when there is so little attention or understanding available from any meaningful audience that the person begins to exist in almost constant severe shame and panic, and other means of self-soothing become necessary: rocking, head-banging, frantic behavior that results in painful (but therefore convincingly real) engagements, and a whole spectrum of addictive behaviors, including addiction to various drugs. Worse yet is a giving up on a real audience altogether and a reconstitution of the world along purely private lines: psychosis.

If the frustration is not too great, the child will invent new ways of thinking and behaving to overcome it. If a child's wish for admiration is denied because the parents (or other audience) are inattentive or lack attunement, the child is likely to withdraw temporarily into a state in which satisfaction is looked for from fantasied audiences, which means audiences in the future, whether they are possible in the real world or not. The maneuver amounts to something like the idea that *someone, sometime will appreciate me even if these people don't.*

The accompanying state of mind usually includes some bittersweet feeling that the future appreciation will include admiration for how much they suffered and how little understood they were. A lot of art gets created in this emotional mode. Gradually, successive, manageable failures of the right audience to materialize reduce the ambition to reasonable levels. It is a series of mourned losses. Similarly, when the failure to win the hoped-for regard is based on an actual inability to perform as hoped, the reactions include adaptive measures to improve performance and gradual mourning of the more elevated and unrealistic levels of ambition so that the goals become closer to what is possible.

The evolution of idealization is similar, but somewhat more complex. Traumatic frustrations take the form of a failure of the idealized parent to have the qualities the child is counting on, a rejection of the idealizing child, or both; for example, a parent hitting a child. In the film *The Bicycle Thief*, the despairing father, tortured by the expectations of his adoring son, hits him, and the boy walks off crushed. The father is overwhelmed with guilt and fears the boy has drowned, because he knows he may already have killed something vital in him. Such experiences leave a person with a desperate need for idealizable others, and prone to terrible shame when an idealized person lets them down. This desperation in the case of neglected and abused children is often expressed in its denial. Tough delinquents, terrified of their longing for a hero, are often out to prove that there is no one that they have any reason to admire. They are particularly susceptible to becoming the blind followers of someone they turn out not to be able to beat, and who then presents him or herself as a savior, or at least a leader that will bring some degree of fulfillment. The development of the Nazi and other fascist parties is a good example.

Non-traumatic frustrations lead to greater flexibility and versatility in selection among possible ideal others, as well as a wearing down of the extremes of what the idealized other needs to personify. A further step also occurs and is even more desirable. When the idealized parent fails to have a desired quality, the quality itself can be adopted in place of the person. An ideal is formed. Even if parents don't know everything, one can be devoted to knowledge and its pursuit. Almost anything can become an ideal: frugality or generosity, caution or bravery, universal love or the purity and superiority of one's tribe or race, etc., but the quality of ideals is more or less invariable. They are cherished and pursued with devotion. The great advantage of this relatively late step in maturation is that an ideal rarely fails and is much more reliable than any idealized actual person. The same qualities may be objects of ambition as well, but the reaction of the failure to live up to an ambition is shame, while the reaction to failing to reach an ideal is more like longing. We are still able to take solace in the fact that we have the ideal even when we don't quite live up to it—a devoted scientist can take pride in being a scientist and trying hard to extend knowledge even when she or he doesn't extend it very much.

Two of the ways in which this description of development is over-schematized is that it leaves out the effects of rivals and the effects of anger at poor audiences and disappointing idealized people. We react as if it is built into us to equate good with best until considerable maturation takes place. Before a best can be conceived of, there seems to be a demand to be the only. It is bad if our adoring parents are busy with their own concerns and don't pay proper attention. It can be worse when they give that attention to another. Jealous rage is the result if someone else is having the relationship we have lost. Envious rage arises when someone possesses the qualities or things we believe we need in order to be properly admired. In the rough and tumble complexity of real family life, all possible combinations occur frequently. We simultaneously cherish people who appreciate us, cherish them because of the qualities we admire in them, hate them for failing to appreciate us or to live up to our idealizations, hate them for rejecting us, and hate them as rivals for the love and admiration of someone else.

As we develop the capacity to see that we can lose or damage another person, our hateful fantasies and actions give rise to sadness and guilt. If someone simply doesn't attend very well, or if we mess up our performance, we are ashamed, but if we feel that we have lost them because we have destroyed or hurt them we are guilty. A somewhat too simple but largely valid distinction between guilt and shame is that shame refers to damage to the self and guilt to damage to the other. Guilt has a moral quality and usually shame does not. Shame motivates rage, retaliation, efforts to improve performance, efforts to hide, and so forth. Guilt motivates confession, punishment seeking, acts of repentance and reparation. A probably infinite number of confusing interrelationships occur. Shame often occurs without guilt, but guilt rarely without shame. If we have harmed someone we are almost certainly failing to live up to one of our ambitions. Guilt can lead to shame through our feeling that we are awful and that no one could like us. Guilt can cause behavior that causes shame, and vice versa. A man may be impotent because of guilt and ashamed because of impotence. He might hurt or kill his lover out of rage at the shame, and feel guilty for the harm he has done.

Envious rage itself has a line of development that is intertwined with the maturation of ambition and idealization. Primitive envy leads to the wish to destroy rivals or to rob them of what is envied. As children become more capable, and as they develop a feeling for others, they become competitive. Competition arises when there is hope of besting the opponent. For some time, and in some people forever, defeat in competition leads to recurrence of envious rage and the wish to destroy, but if the parents are secure enough and playful enough to happily compete with their children, victory and defeat lead to mutual admiration and enjoyment.

This development is particularly crucial in adolescence. To establish oneself as separate from one's parents and equal to them or better is invariably opposed by irrational guilt based on fantasies (sometimes reality) that the parent is hurt by our achievement. Rites of passage and the giving of parental blessing help to ease the situation, but particularly nowadays, when most such rites are defunct or empty, pleasurable competition can replace them. The impulse to outdo the parent is clearly expressed and the parent isn't hurt. The parent ideally enjoys the child's growing ability even when it surpasses his or her own. Ambitions can then be strongly pursued without guilt or guilt-induced failure, which leads to shame. At the same time, a parent's graceful acceptance of defeat eases the substitution of ideals for idealizations. The increased availability and popularity of competitive sports for girls is a great help in undoing an inequality in which boys were given an aid in maturation that girls were denied.

Since these complex developments can never go entirely smoothly and particularly not at the present time, there is plenty of need for all the understanding of shame that we can muster. Psychoanalysis in its first century has had a considerable effect in increased understanding, tolerance and alleviation of guilt. The idea that guilt is often irrational and can be overcome is common knowledge now, and wasn't in the nineteenth century.

Understanding of shame has lagged behind. It is a hard subject to discuss, not only because of its subtleties and complexities but also because of its unpleasantness. Being ashamed is one of the most painful and destructive of experiences and leads to other kinds of destruction. To make matters worse, we are often a little proud of feeling guilty, but we are ashamed of feeling ashamed. Enlightened therapy and enlightened attitudes are developing and will help. The acceptance that a need for each other is unavoidable and desirable can replace puritanical insistence on self-reliance and independence of the opinions of others. Frank acceptance of our horror of shame can ease the horror itself.

Tough Customers

I had the good fortune to be taught early on by Otto Will and Bruno Bettelheim, from whom I learned so many things that are now so much part of me that I don't know what is them and what is me. Both of them specialized in the psychotherapy of seriously disturbed people, and I have always tried to do that work myself. As I wrote my mindless papers, and thought more and more about the work as a negotiation between two people about what is really happening and who we really are, it seemed to me I did better work with loosely put together people, and that I could say better what that work was about. So I wrote this.

TOUGH CUSTOMERS, UNPLEASANT PEOPLE WHO ARE impossible to please, make angry scenes and are dangerous sometimes, turn up almost everywhere. Any business that offers products or services has its share, and people who have to wait on them understandably resent them. A few years ago, most garages and service stations seemed to have posted a copy of a cartoon showing a service manager asking if having all the mechanics shot would be an adequate solution to a client's problem.

Most of us in the psychoanalysis/psychotherapy business have even more reason to resent tough customers than do people in other lines of work. For one thing, we ourselves have generally been easy customers. Those of us who have had training analyses, especially those of us who had them a long time ago when training analysts used to report on our suitability to continue our candidacy, had powerful reasons to be agreeable. So it hardly seems fair when we have to work for ingrates and complainers. Most of us have war stories about people who were particularly hard to get along with, who yelled at us, wouldn't leave the office, called all the time or defamed us publicly. A friend had a patient who, more than once, made harmless but spectacular leaps into the Chicago River after announcing his name and her dissatisfaction with him to the crowds that were present.

Opinions differ about how best to work with such people. A popular answer to the question is, "don't." That solution becomes possible only with time and success. Most of us at the beginning of our careers can't be that choosy. The result is a bit like the old joke about the dude and the sadistic cowboy: "Never rode before? This horse will be just right; he's never been rid before."

But in my opinion tough customers can be good ones. Not only do they spend lots of time and money in our business establishments, but in the long run they are often rewarding to work with because they are interesting, teach us a lot, and make big favorable changes in the way they live. It seems to me that emotional expressiveness is a favorable prognostic sign. People who seem to be exploding all over the place are much more accessible, even if they seem more angry and forbidding, than those who are invariably quiet and agreeable. Even determinedly mute people can be quite dramatic and communicative in their silence and, in the long run, much easier to be with than one of my early analysands was. He was so agreeable that on several occasions he apologized for being compliant again.

It's easy for me to look on the bright side in the abstract, but not so easy to put up with the real thing. About twenty years ago, when I was psychiatry residency director at the University of New Mexico, I did a therapy demonstration seminar in which I saw a patient weekly in the presence of the residents. Before beginning, I asked the chief resident to find me a nice, verbal, mildly neurotic person. For his own reasons he provided an exceedingly angry, impulsive young woman who was living a chaotic and self-destructive life. Many of the hours were devoted to her addressing the residents on the subject of my horrible failures as her therapist. Often she demanded to know how they could just sit there and allow me to be so terrible to her, and several times at the ends of hours she pulled the fire alarm on her way out of the building.

Putting up with all the bitter complaints is one of the biggest problems for those of us involved in such a relationship. I think that some of the most natural, and therefore usual, means of coping with the other person's dissatisfaction are mistakes that do immediate harm and generate vicious circles which perpetuate and intensify the trouble. The simplest method is labeling. People who are making us anxious, ashamed and guilty can be explained away by diagnosis. They are doing objectionable things because they are the kind of people that do those things. They are borderline, narcissistic, entitled and so on. That would seem to explain it, and it also can rally the support—real or imagined—of our colleagues. Too bad we have to put up with this bad behavior, but it isn't our fault because all people of this category act like this.

A somewhat more sophisticated and individualized method is to employ the concept of negative transference. Almost all difficult people had difficult childhoods. If, in a first hour, we hear a history that includes mistreatment by one or both parents, most of us will predict that sooner or later the person will be angry with us, and usually the prediction will come true. The success of the prediction may encourage us to explain the anger as originating in the past and not, as the other person believes, in our present behavior. If the other person is provided with that explanation, he or she is likely to become even angrier, which may lead to further explanation based on transference. The person will probably get even madder, leading to more interpretation that blames the figures of the past and exonerates the therapist, which leads to further increases in anger, and so on.

I am oversimplifying. Skillful therapists may seldom trigger the vicious circle or may escape from it by acknowledging their contribution to the situation even as they are thinking that the real cause is in the past. It seems to me that the critical variable is the therapist's defensiveness. To whatever extent an interpretation is made defensively, or for that matter to whatever extent we do anything defensively, we are asking for trouble. When I was a counselor at the Orthogenic School, Bruno Bettelheim often said, "I only know three things, and one of them is that the customer is always right. If I saw things the way he does, I'd act exactly the same way. I forget the other two things." He claimed that this was the central lesson of the work of Sigmund Freud.

When put upon by unreasonable people we are all too likely to think that psychoanalysis teaches that the customer is always wrong. Unconscious frustration, anger and fantasies from early life are causing her or him to distort our helpfulness and the necessary rules of our method so as to see them as sadistic. I believe that it is common for therapists to dismiss complaints by saying that they are a result of the negative transference, and to put the dismissal as crudely and as simply as that. Even if we recognize that we may indeed have done something hurtful, there are still a number of ways that we can prove that the customer is wrong; for example, projective identification: you made me do it.

Unfortunately, I am an unusually sleepy person and have considerable experience with hurting people by drifting off while they are speaking to me (I rarely fall asleep while I am speaking). Early in my career I tried to claim that I wasn't really asleep. That claim got me into more trouble than ever. I don't think I ever blamed the other person, but more than a handful of times I have heard accounts of colleagues who did, and it never seems to have gone over very well.

Another common form of defensiveness depends on talking about the other person's view of things as though it weren't true. I think therapists often say something like, "you feel that I wasn't understanding you," when they know perfectly well that they weren't. Frank acknowledgement always works best, but what makes it so hard is that some people are unreasonable and their reactions extreme. Since I am claiming that explaining their unreasonableness as negative transference is a mistake, I need to suggest a less defensive, more helpful explanation.

I think that the basic shift needed is from thinking of them as recreating the past to thinking of them as unusually vulnerable to re-experiencing the past; that is, some action of ours is damaging them in the same way that they have been damaged often before. A good-enough inherited temperament and a good-enough childhood equip one with some resilience in responding to shame, but many people not only are undone by shame but are made ashamed by almost any interpersonal event. I think that this proneness to disastrous shame can be understood better in intersubjective and constructivist terms than from older points of view. In addition, the mindless point of view I prefer is somewhat protective against making the mistakes that cause one's customers horrible shame.

According to my mindless version of life, each time people encounter each other they negotiate a version of reality that they can more or less agree on. People start with their own ideas of what their relationship is to particular others, and, if people are well-acquainted and attached to each other, the negotiations will be easy and pleasing. For example, this evening (from my standpoint as I am writing this) I intend to visit my daughter's family. It is a part of my reality I don't usually think about, that she, her husband and her little daughter are people I like to be with, and vice versa. When I get there, a profusion of small signs will—I expect—be exchanged as confirmation of our pleasure in seeing each other. The negotiation of shared reality will be easy with the adults but may be a little trickier with my 19-month-old grandchild. If something should go wrong; for example if it's the wrong night, and they're not expecting us to come to supper and are surprised and dismayed by our showing up hungry, I will be embarrassed. It won't be a big problem for me or any of us, I think. We will reassure each other verbally, and especially nonverbally, that we do like to be together and that we'll figure out something to get us all fed. It would be a much bigger problem if I were planning to visit people I didn't know so well and mistakenly believed liked me enough that they would be glad to see me appear on their doorstep. The pain of that situation leads to the custom of telephoning first.

Even though I am embarrassed quite often, painfully ashamed occasionally, and once in a while humiliated, I usually am not shattered by the experience. From the beginning of my life, and most importantly then, I have felt welcome most places I've been. It's like having money in the bank. If I'm proved wrong in my belief about my connection to one person or another, I have resources to fall back on. Memories, whether summoned up consciously or not, reassure me that on such occasions I can sometimes win someone over, and that, failing that, there are other people I can think of who are glad to be connected to me.

Since I am someone who fears loss of relationship more than loss of stature (or anatomical parts) I am likely to become a little downcast—tending more to blame my deficiencies for the failure than the other person's malice or other faults. Accordingly, I will try to stay connected and fix things. On the other hand if I am anxious and disoriented; for example, if I am in a foreign country where I don't speak the language,

I am likely to become suspicious, ready to believe that people are envious and eager to reduce me in some way. People who fear loss of stature (or organs) more than they do loss of connections to others regularly blame interpersonal failures on others and withdraw. They would rather be alone than reduced.

Many tough customers don't have the kind of resources in their past that I do. In fact, many have been unwelcome in their own families, schools, potential play groups, the army, work and on and on. People who were able to find a foothold somewhere, especially among other children, are often worse than tough customers—they become delinquents. Banding together, and proving to themselves that the adults whose relationship they secretly long for are actually corrupt, weak and contemptible, they can form gangs, fascist political parties and other menaces that may cause us trouble but rarely do in our professional capacities, though I did once have the interesting experience of treating a Nazi. (He actually wasn't too tough since he surprisingly formed an idealizing transference, which was helpful to his symptoms and was based on his discovery that it wasn't the actual Jews like me who were responsible for all the world's problems, but rather the fake Jews like George Bush, Senior.)

Most of the people I am trying to describe have had little social success, and though they can be terrible pains to have around are not criminal or dangerous—except to themselves. Some people have been pretty much unwelcome no matter what. I have known someone whose psychotic mother considered the daughter to be a real menace to the mother's well-being or even continued existence, and whose selfish father didn't care to incur the pain and inconvenience of opposing the harridan he was married to. (A friend glancing at a magazine cover read it as being a copy of *Worst Parents*, a publication she points out that most of us therapists could contribute to.)

As miserable as are the lives of people who were purely unwanted, they are usually not terribly hard on us therapists. Tougher customers are often people who were unwelcome as independent beings but were more or less intensively used by parents or other so-called caregivers.

The uses of children vary but include sexual abuse and less obviously wrongful treatment. Probably all persons have served to some degree as a part of their parents' positive identities. (Millions of Christmas letters with glowing accounts of children's achievements are annual evidence of the sort of thing I mean.) Two dimensions make this parental failure more or less serious: its pervasiveness and its rigidity. If parents respond favorably only to what their idea of their children should be in order to be a prop to their sense of themselves, and especially if they write and direct the dramas in which the children appear, one of the likely outcomes is a false self, a personality, no matter how successful and polished, that nevertheless is desperate and hollow.

I think this type is what Edwin Arlington Robinson had in mind in writing "Richard Cory." Cory as an analysand would have been challenging, but he probably wouldn't have raised hell with his analyst. That kind of thing is more likely to arise if the false self the parents sponsor is not good enough to succeed out in the world. Often parents who feel the need to dominate their children in this way are pretty hollow and unsuccessful themselves, and not with it enough to provide a script that works outside of the family.

The trouble with much false self functioning is its woodenness. It is not centered in the performers' basic impulses or sense of themselves, but in their ideas of what others want or will respond to. Its motive is the wish to belong, to be accepted, to be socially effective. Within the family where this kind of behavior originates it is often simple and ritualized. Cue and response—"I love you." "I love you too, Mommy"—are unvarying, unvariable and therefore coercive.

As I've said previously, it gives rise to what I like to jokingly call *falseselfobjects*: concretely used symbols that are intended to coerce proper reactions. One stands up and salutes the flag. We are abashed if told that our clinical conduct was not analytic. The most satisfying and genuine interactions are the opposite of these stylized ones. We express what spontaneously occurs to us in reaction to each other's real characteristics out of a confidence that we will be understood and accepted.

When life is going that way, social space expands to accommodate multiple meanings and emotions that are both strongly felt and playful. Skilled falsity can mimic this kind of interaction, as with conmen and seducers, but many people feel so empty and without real resources that they are stuck in their social behavior with relatively crude models of each participant. "You, a psychotherapist are here to relieve my suffering. Here it is. Relieve it."

That example is not a real one but a translation into simple and direct words of what is conveyed by a display of crudely manipulated symbols. Lots of people who come to see us have had enough previous clinical experience that they have learned a vocabulary of mental health clichés, and not uncommonly they include some previous experience with a therapist who was highly satisfactory, somehow no longer available and far superior to us. Sometimes we are faced with the choice to respond as we are prompted to, or be regarded as a failure. But I am getting ahead of myself.

The use of false relating is intended to protect people against terrible shame and its shattering effects. They are susceptible to such experiences because of a lack of a reserve of past good experience and an excess of bad. Their lives not only have left them pessimistic about what is likely to happen anytime they meet someone, but often with no coherent version of themselves, real or false.

This incoherence seems to be particularly prevalent among those who were used most abusively as children. Sexual abuse, and especially incestuous sexual abuse, cannot be incorporated into a general scheme of family relations that can be felt or represented as real membership in a good family. To some extent the abuse can be represented between the participants as conferring a special connection, but it is not one that can be made a part of life as a whole.

The results, covering a big range, include those who use a sexually provocative or merely available persona as a partial false self. Men and women in the sex industry, many of whom have this history, may know how to use sexual contact as a way of producing a semblance of relationship and a livelihood, but I believe they are often quite clear that their performances are feigned and empty except for contempt for the others and/or themselves. Other people with this experience may have no way to incorporate sexuality into any version of themselves, even a false version. That lack of integration leads to their getting into spots in their lives that are baffling. The situation calls for something that is not in any way part of themselves, and they are thrown into despair and panic.

Severe anxiety is the principal moving force in the lives of many angry people. The anxiety itself is generated as a result of the expectation of shame or humiliation, events that are likely because of limited resources. Central or true ambitions and ideals are repressed much of the time for protection. Since toddlerhood, if not infancy, those precious senses of self have had to be protected against the unresponsiveness or attacks of parents or others. Not even the persons themselves are allowed to know of these grandiose fantasies, because they are threatened with destruction merely by the thoughts being thought. Because they have been repressed and therefore not modified by the ordinary wearing down that infantile grandiosity is subjected to in the course of a good-enough growing up, they are unreasonably and unrealizably wonderful. Since thought is trial action, letting them into consciousness exposes them to failing the trial unless the person is psychotic enough to create a pretty much idiosyncratic world.

Completely psychotic people have mostly given up on the process of negotiating shared reality with anyone else. They are therefore protected against further shattering by having someone invalidate their version of who they are and how people relate to them. In actuality the cost of that situation is so horrible that no one would choose it unless it was the only possible way to stave off complete disintegration, but the idea of being immune from invalidation is appealing enough that the fantasy of carefree psychosis is popular except with those of us who happen to have some experience, vicarious or personal, of being psychotic. In our practices we rarely meet completely psychotic people nowadays, but we see plenty of people who are psychotic enough that they spend an inordinate amount of time and energy on their own versions of themselves and others, and too little time and energy on seeing if they are right. One of the results of this way of life is that they have ideas that are so idiosyncratic as to be not only unlikely to be shared by others, but even unlikely to be understood by others.

People come to us with these brittle expectations, and we fail them. They often have in mind a quite precise idea of what we will do in response to their doing or saying a certain thing. It may be obvious to them that the response they want is what we should do, but it may be quite mysterious to us. If we don't figure it out and do the right thing there will be trouble. At first meeting it may not be too bad, because we may not have become essential players in their dramas. The customers may give us the benefit of the doubt because we don't know each other yet. Often, of course, the result is the customers' taking their business elsewhere. Failures that come later are worse. If the people are still enacting the various parts that make up a false self there is a slight protective effect. Failure is almost invariably experienced as real or threatened abandonment, but what is being rejected is not a truly precious sense of self. Often they have a conviction that they have a right to a correct response, and so they can protect themselves from the full force of shame by being irate.

Under the circumstances, we are likely to think or say the words *narcissistic* or *entitled*. What we may not realize is that the grandiosity being enacted is not connected to an experience of being grand or at all worthwhile.

Many years ago, and in another state, I had a very tough customer who had many angry complaints about me. She had come to see me in the small town where, one day a week, I was the psychiatrist, but soon she moved to the psychiatric ward at my home base. Occasionally I took her with me on my weekly trips so that she could visit her family. Returning unexpectedly late one evening, she had missed any chance for supper at the hospital. She complained angrily, but when I answered by inviting her to join me and my family for a meal she was speechless for several seconds and then said, "But I'm the bitch of all time."

Before my invitation she had been thoroughly in character as an afflicted patient whose suffering should automatically command at least the other person's anxiety and guilt, but the idea of being an ordinary guest of my family startled her out of her usual frame of reference and led to her frank statement of how devoid of real social standing she felt. She believed that as her doctor I owed her a lot, but as a person I owed her nothing and could be expected to be repelled by her.

The most disastrous failures are when something that is part of a genuinely felt part of a person is invalidated. This kind of thing is most likely fairly late in therapy when the false self is occasionally or frequently abandoned.

I once worked with a woman whose mother had provided little sustenance to any of her spontaneous activities or interests, but had imparted a well-developed picture of the family as being unjustly treated by the world and a repertoire of angry and often effective responses to mistreatment. The daughter grew up feeling empty and inadequate much of the time, but she was wonderful at complaining. Hearing her accounts of her effectiveness in dealing with desk clerks or airline agents, I often imagined hiring her to accompany me any time I was having trouble getting good service.

Her big successes in this department, however, gave her little satisfaction and no sense of personal worth. After we'd spent a number of years together, she had allowed herself to feel that I understood and appreciated what felt to her like her real qualities, though quite frequently I would fail in one way or another, and the result was almost always her breaking off treatment for a time, during which she wrote me long vituperative letters. As she felt we were more involved in a real way, and her life in general improved remarkably, she was even more deeply wounded by my errors.

She got a job that she was good at and proud of. Once, in the course of her work, she produced a brochure about her employers. I heard about her various adventures in getting it done, and then she brought me a copy. I looked at it carefully. I thought and said that it was beautiful. Then, after looking at it some more, I handed it back to her. To my surprise she abruptly left in a rage. My mistake was in not recognizing that the copy had been a gift and she had been sure that I would gratefully keep it. It took careful thought and careful reading of the thousands of words she wrote me over the two weeks that she stopped coming before I figured out what I had done. It was a double failure, because my not keeping the brochure was a less appreciative response than she had counted on, and also it was based on a disowning of my importance to her. In giving back the copy I was feeling as though I was not important enough to merit a copy.

I think that we must keep a precarious balance in our attitude about our inevitable failures. In order to make progress we have to recognize and understand what we did or didn't do and its effects, and explaining them away defensively will make things worse instead of better. If we are guilty and ashamed of ourselves we won't feel very good and won't do good work. I try to keep in mind that the customer needs certain things desperately and will be harmed without them, but that unfortunately they are often beyond my capabilities.

If I felt that many other therapists could do much better I would have a hard time accepting the situation, but in general I feel I do as well as can be expected, even though that frequently isn't good enough. I am sorry when I do the wrong thing, worried about the bad effects and how to help repair them, but still fairly confident in myself as a person and an analyst in spite of the failure. There are cases, however, where I do feel guilty and ashamed, and sometimes I hear of cases that lead me to feel considerable disapproval of other therapist's faults. The fact that some victims are outrageously over the top in their ire can often distract others from seeing that they are right.

Many years ago I undertook seeing a woman I had already heard about casually. She was said to be so crazily angry and out of control that, to whatever extent possible, everyone avoided her and pitied her husband. It appeared that he was self-sacrificing, long suffering. People thought that, since she was obviously so nuts, he must have had to take complete responsibility for the family; they had three children. Though her complaints were about him, their friends' opinion wasn't altered by them because they were so loud, continuous and hyperbolic that they were discounted.

I did work with her for several years, and also, for a time, I saw both of them. Winning her trust was difficult but turned out to be possible, and I was surprised by what I learned. Her complaints were justified. He was selfish, punitive, and dependent. The seemingly disabled wife took complete care of the seemingly capable husband. For example, he claimed not to know how to shop for clothes, and so she purchased every item that he wore. He had strict religious principles and demanded that the family observe his rules. Since he believed that the true meaning of Christmas had been lost in commercialization no presents were to be exchanged in the family, but each December he bought himself (he could shop when he wanted to) some expensive gadget or toy.

I learned that she was so sure that she was worthless and likely to be abandoned that she never did anything effective about her situation out of fear that it was the best that she could do. Her earliest memory was of being driven by a large building that her parents said was the orphanage. They told her that because she was bad they were going to leave her there permanently. She begged them not to and they relented, but the exercise was repeated. After a couple of years of our work she learned to be less noisy and childish in asking for change. That helped make her demands harder to discredit. She was right again. Her husband wouldn't tolerate her more effective self and they divorced.

I have encountered a number of people even more enraged with their therapists than she was with her husband. I once was asked to see a person with the unappealing history of having recently burned down her previous psychiatrist's office. After a time she and I overcame enough of our suspicion of each other that I heard the story. During a period of several years she had become quite attached to her psychiatrist, even though she was frequently disappointed by feeling misunderstood and put down. When that had happened she had become angry enough to frighten the doctor, who ultimately decided that she had had enough. She wanted to get away from her patient but was too frightened to tell her so in person, or even while they were in the same part of the world. She went to Europe, leaving behind a letter to the patient saying that she would no longer see her.

When the therapist returned, the patient called to ask to see her and was refused. She repeated the call many times, and after a while called many times in the middle of each night. The doctor called the police, and the patient was jailed for harassment. When she got out, she vandalized the doctor's car and went back to jail. Then she burned the office down.

Somehow, she escaped jail in spite of the greater seriousness of her last crime, and she came to see me. She felt that she would never be all right as long as she felt that she was to blame for what had happened. In one way she felt sure that some of the blame should go to the psychiatrist, but in another, as long as the other person maintained her innocence and was supported by the community, she could not feel all right about herself.

I told her simply that it was wrong of her doctor to have abandoned her as she did. My saying so was of some help but not enough. In my opinion, it is helpful to think of the connections among false self, vertically split-off grandiosity, and separation-individuation. The disavowed self-importance is a feature of the false self, which is often the continuation of the parent-invented mythology of a symbiotic relationship. People functioning in this way have particularly great trouble believing any opinion that is not shared with the actual parent, or someone who has come to be in that role. Without the psychiatrist's agreement the office burner couldn't believe that it wasn't all her fault, and she was psychologically destroyed by that belief.

The revenges she had attempted were partly motivated by the wish to get even in the sense that if the psychiatrist had destroyed her, she would destroy the psychiatrist—at least in effigy. Beyond that, there was perhaps even more urgency to the wish to stay engaged with the doctor in some way that might provoke her to do something good that would re-establish the old affirming connection, or cause her to do something so bad that she would be exposed and have to admit her wrongdoing. Only by re-establishing the relationship, or by the other person's acknowledging responsibility, could she restore any sense that she was a decent human.

I called my predecessor and asked her to meet with me and her former patient. She was appalled by the idea, and even more aghast when I suggested that it would be helpful if she would acknowledge that it was not a good idea for her to have ended their connection in the way she did. She was afraid even to be in the same room, and the idea of admitting error added the fear of a lawsuit. I said that she had already suffered substantial damage and there was no guarantee that it would not continue, but that I was almost certain it would end if she agreed to my plan. After some days' thought, she agreed, and we met. The conversation was calm and almost friendly, especially after the doctor somewhat graciously apologized. The patient accepted the apology somewhat graciously and thanked her former therapist for good times and real help given. Everyone was greatly relieved, and for the next four years, as long as I continued to live there, there was no more contact between the two.

Toward the end of that time I began to receive phone calls in the middle of the night. At first the caller didn't speak, but later a furious woman would shout obscenities. I couldn't engage her in conversation, but one morning she screamed, "If you're a friend of Dr. X, you're a fucker." Resisting the impulse to call Dr. X at 4 a.m. I made the call somewhat later, and learned that the situation of the person who was calling me was almost identical with the one who had burned the office. I was then running a psychotherapy referral service, and Dr. X, in his letter firing his patient on the occasion of his having already left on vacation, had suggested that the person call me for a referral. I called her. She was a little embarrassed and quite suspicious, but my expressing a bad opinion of the method of Dr. X resigning from her case helped. She came to see me. I made a referral, which worked well enough that she later wrote me to express gratitude for it. I don't think a meeting with Dr. X was necessary. I have encountered one more case of a psychiatrist firing a patient in that manner with almost equally bad results.

What scares therapists that much? I think there are several notable forces. The anger is often implacable, and its aim is not to win a particular point, but to destroy. When we fail to live up to what the other has in mind that person is destroyed and wants to destroy in return. In some cases the attacks are shrewd, directed at real weaknesses of which we are ashamed, or at cherished parts of ourselves: our families or our religions or especially our professional competence.

As I said earlier, people sometimes come to us with some previous wonderful experience of therapy to which they contrast us. Some frequently mention our failure to live up to this standard. When this happens to me, I usually think of the story about the shopper who demanded to know why the hamburger was so expensive. "My usual store sells hamburger for eighty cents a pound." The butcher asks, "Why don't you go to your usual store then?" "They're out of hamburger." "Oh, we sell hamburger for twenty cents a pound when we're out." The ideal therapist is unavailable, but occasionally there is one whom the customer calls on the phone, or visits in another city, and usually the ideal therapist is reported to have agreed with the customer's complaints about me.

Attacks on my clinical competence can be even more painful when I start as the favorite. All previous therapists were terrible, but I have come highly recommended and the person can see right away that the recommendations were justified. I have often heard it said that this sort of talk is simply a buildup for the reverse and is part of a sadistic plan of exaltation and contempt, or that it is a manifestation of splitting. I don't think of it that way. It seems to me that people whose sense of self is primitive have ambitions and idealizations that are both impossible to realize and inflexibly essential to their staying in one piece psychologically. When idealization, the need to be a good person by being connected to a wonderful one, is the predominant theme, the initial idealization is desirable but precarious. When I fail, the results are often disastrous to the other person and painful to both of us.

No matter how well I have seemed to prepare myself for this event I still always feel terrible—worse than when I was no good from the start, but I try to regain my balance by reflecting that we are on a roller coaster whose hills will gradually get lower and tamer. With luck, and with acknowledgement and exploration of my error and its results, the disasters can be overcome. By small increments, the requirements I have to meet are lowered a bit, ultimately to the level of the possible. At the same time, the person will have realized enough of his or her ambitions independently to be less in need of me as proof of personal worth. It would seem as if having been through the process successfully would help me to feel less bad when it starts with someone new, but that is true only to a limited extent. My clinical self-esteem is like a greedy voter who asks the incumbent, "What have you done for me lately?"

Being denigrated effectively is not only painful, it is also provocative, and that stimulates another force that scares us—our own rage. With the exception of a few sadistic people in our business, most of us don't like to find ourselves attacking the people we went into this work to help. Many of the people we are trying to help will twist that particular knife by pointing out how angry we are with them, saying in effect, "You promised me you'd be different, but here you are attacking me, just like my parents and everyone else."

I hate to think how often I have found myself denying the charge before I could think and catch myself. That defensiveness makes things worse in every way, among other things giving the other person a chance to point out, often derisively, how I am trying to fool myself.

The same situation often arises from provocations that are not in the form of direct attacks, the most frequent being demands that cannot be met. The best example I can think of is the refusal to leave at the end of an hour. Usually the worst that happens is that firm insistence will get the person out, but once in a while someone comes along who will not leave without threats of ending treatment, the police, the MHPs or something. Then there may be a noisy scene that is a problem for the person or persons in the waiting room and the people in adjacent offices. My experience has lead me to believe that if I can remain relatively calm, and can use the least coercion that is still effective, the next time will be less bad. I try to be like a rock by the ocean, unchanged by the waves breaking over it.

If I can manage that at all, I believe the other customers will be able to shake the belief that they are so horrible that knowing them will destroy me or at least destroy my willingness to be with them.

Because many people feel so little confidence in their welcome they try to compel it. Some do that by living in a permanent state of emergency—another force that scares us. In many ways the emergency can be real enough. People who live constantly on the verge of disintegration that can be triggered by seemingly small failures which produce great shame are constantly at risk, since their disintegration is not only horrible in and of itself, but it may lead to self-destructive emergency measures such as cutting or burning. These attacks on oneself are sometimes angry and sometimes not, but they serve the purpose of restoring some sense of coherence, agency, or simply of being alive.

A person I worked with for a long time subjected herself to terrible injuries, which she said were punishments for trying to involve me with her. She traced them historically to a time when she asked her sister to form a club with her. The purpose of the club was to beat each other so that they would be inured to beating and therefore less afraid of their mother. The sister declined to join, and so the girl carried on the abuse of herself unaided. The physical punishment was later carried out not to prepare for punishment but to punish preemptively. It was to teach her not to try to connect with anyone because the other would only be hurtful.

The tactic worked in several directions. When I "dropped her," as she called my frequent failures, her cutting herself punished us both and restored a bit of feeling of effectiveness. It alarmed me and kept me on my toes, proving that she needed help, and tested my ability to stick with her really as well as in form. To the extent that I could keep from withdrawing out of fear and anger, I was helpful.

Of course some self-destructiveness can be lethal. Over the years that we worked together the woman who had said that she was the bitch of all times attempted suicide repeatedly, and each time would have died if not quickly discovered and rushed to the hospital. On one occasion she called me and seemed calm, but in the background, I could hear a toilet flushing. Since I knew her by that time, I asked what she had flushed down the toilet. "Some lithium," she said. "What did you do with the rest?" "I took it." She was in the ICU in less than an hour, but still had to remain there several days.

Sometimes the emergency is a little less real. In the middle of the night once, I was called by someone from the crisis clinic at the mental health center. "C's husband called. C just set her dress on fire!" "Was she wearing it at the time?" "Just a minute, I'll check. No."

Phone calls can occasionally be life-saving and occasionally amusing, but mostly are important as a way of maintaining attachment when it is threatened. Some people cannot maintain a belief that they are in mind when out of sight, and more cannot believe that they are thought at all well of when they can't see and hear their therapist looking and sounding friendly. Some therapists hate to receive phone calls, and I think that they shouldn't try to pretend to feel different about them and shouldn't suggest them, but many of us don't mind them, and a willingness to talk on the phone can be a big help to some people.

I often suggest to people who are having a hard time between appointments that they call me, I give them my home phone number, and sometimes tell them before a weekend when I will be home and when out. I fairly often give people the number where I can be reached out of town when I travel. I think it is particularly important to say that they should call any time they feel like calling. If they say that they would only call if they have to, I urge them not to limit themselves to those times. I usually say, "The indication for calling me is that you want to." This statement not only stirs up useful discussions of what they think I feel about them, but is also, and even more crucially, a step toward reducing the number of desperate situations that occur.

I have been following this course for many years and it has only once resulted in my receiving excessive numbers of calls. Many people call me a few times to find out if it is true that they will be welcome, and once they have found that out they may call rarely, if at all. I almost never talk more than I want to, which is usually for about five minutes. As soon as I feel resentful of the call, or as soon as I feel the need to attend to something else I say that I have to go, will talk again later or see the person at our next appointment. Once in a great while someone will call when I don't want to talk at all, and if for some reason I have answered the phone I will say that I can't talk then, but will suggest a time that they call again or arrange a time I can call back.

One excessively guilty and self-effacing person never calls, though it is clear that at times it would be useful for her to do so. I regard her never calling as symptomatic, and discuss it as such. Straightforward treatment of this sort of ordinary issue of life increases the directness and genuineness of the relationship and decreases the occurrence of strange and unconvincing performances.

The unreality of some of the ways some people present themselves in treatment is one of the problems I have the most trouble with. In general I favor the approach for which Lou Shapiro was for many years famous in Chicago. He said that when the character came in he dealt with the character, and then someday the patient would be able to come in without the character, and that would be wonderful. But, since genuineness is one of the qualities I most value, I can find working with the cruder sorts of false selfhood trying.

I especially dislike getting involved in "as if" performances of two people doing analysis or therapy. It is one of the contemporary forms of hysteria, which I think of as a strategy for expressing requests indirectly. In its old-fashioned form hysteria consisted of symptoms that were alarming but with a denial in words that they were any cause for concern. Many an elderly person has been brought to the doctor by relatives and has apologetically said, "I'm so sorry to bother you. My children insisted I come, but I know there's nothing wrong with me." After working the person up for the winces, twitches or gasps that frightened the family, the doctor agrees with the patient. The person wanted to see the doctor and to be worried over by the family, but would have been ashamed to say so.

The form of the syndrome is often, as we say in cross-cultural psychiatry, culture-bound. At any particular time and place some set of symptoms, sometimes with a theory of their etiology, is well-known and widely performed. The grand hysteria known in Vienna, Paris and other capitals over a century ago was stylized and detailed. Old textbooks included drawings of the customary postures that were characteristic of the various stages of an hysterical attack. Now such things are as rare as top hats and spats. Thirty-seven years ago I saw a case of hysterical blindness, but I have never seen another. I think that such cases may still occur in parts of the world where people are more naive psychologically than they are around here, but with being wised up about psychology, people have learned psychological syndromes and catch phrases of psychotherapy. "I need so desperately to get in touch with my inner child, but I just don't think I'll ever be able to have enough trust to do it."

Talk like that is not exactly intellectualization, partly because of its lack of intellectual soundness, but more so because of its being used expressively but indirectly, as an hysterical seizure was used. The fact that words are being used instead of gestures, postures or physical complaints is distracting because the words have an overt meaning, but may not be what the person means any more than people mean to seriously inquire about each other's health and announce that it is good when they say "How are you?" "Fine, thanks. How are you?"

I was arguing a while ago for the customer's always being right, but in this sort of communication the customer's correctness comes in two particularly different forms. In the first, it would be as rude and incorrect to say, "You're just talking the way you think a psychotherapy patient is supposed to talk," as to say "You don't really want me to tell you how I am." In the second form it is essential to know that the customer is right in talking like a patient. My first assumption is that he or she wants me to be interested, concerned, and favorably impressed.

That's all fine with me, but problems arise if the performance is prolonged. The difficulty that I find myself being drawn into is what I think of as following too close, getting caught up in the surface of the discussion to the exclusion of the more real message that is being conveyed by the form of the surface. It's easy if the other simply goes on at length, because then I can be quiet and wait for a moment when I think I can see some real issue that I can comment on tactfully enough not to cause shame: something like, "I think maybe you're worried that I may try to impose my ideas on you."

At times of trouble, some people are straightforward and direct in their complaints: "You told me I could say anything to you but then you got mad at what I was saying and attacked me." But others are sometimes crudely histrionic. One person that I have been hearing about lately leaves tens of voice mails consisting mainly of wailing. Complaints may be more coherent than that but still come across as phony and affected. The trick is not to get caught up in their details, but instead try to figure out and state what really went wrong. Not to say, "It's terrible that you need to trust me but you can't anymore," but instead, "When I said I thought you were ashamed of what you had done, I was implying that you ought to feel ashamed."

By consistently talking about what is really happening, it is possible to gradually edge the interaction toward greater and greater genuineness and reality, but what seems to me to be the most important is the promotion of an atmosphere of playfulness. False self interactions are generally concrete, formal and coercive. They are hard to pull off if you're laughing.

Gentleness and tact are necessary in promoting ease, freedom and lightness, though occasionally one can be tactless, if deft. A woman once came into my office saying, "Oh! This has been the most awful time of my life." She went on to spend forty-five minutes telling in great detail about the death of a neighbor she didn't know very well and her ensuing involvement with the bereaved family. When she finally paused for breath I said, "Makes a hell of a good story, doesn't it?" She said, "You God damn son of a bitch!" but she was laughing.

As I'm saying, it's hard to know the proper distance at which to follow, but I try to follow the maxim of C, the woman who set her dress on fire. My vacations were hard and dangerous times for her, and I always found someone to look after her whenever I went away. The last time I was to see her before one trip she asked, "Did you tell Dr. Summers about me?" "Yes I did." "Did you tell him all about me?" "That would be impossible." "Good. He shouldn't believe all of my bullshit, but he should believe some of it."

The Trouble with Psychic Reality

This concept has always seemed more like a stumbling block than a help to me, and as I became clearer on how I think reality is constructed in dialogue, I could be more precise about what faults I find in it.

THE COMEDIAN SEVERN DARDEN USED TO DELIVER a philosophy lecture entitled, "A Short Talk on the Universe." It began,

"Why," you will ask me, "have you decided to speak on the universe instead of on some other topic?" The answer is very simple. There is nothing else.

The trouble with psychic reality is the same: there is nothing else. The universe, or at least the tiny portion of it that is near us, is palpably, convincingly real, but our awareness of it is our own idiosyncratic creation. My awareness is, in many ways, different from anyone else's, but I rely on it, and my natural inclination is to call it reality.

It often mystifies me that yours is so different from mine, but I want to be big about it. I don't want to dismiss your universe as an illusion. You believe in it, and so I will generously acknowledge that it is real to you. I will call it your psychic reality. Calling it "psychic reality" instead of just plain "reality" may not seem fair to you, but I have various traditional answers to your objections. Your perceptions are dictated by powerful unconscious forces whereas I am an objective outsider to your life.

Even if I suffer from distortions caused by my unconscious, I am well analyzed. I know what my distortions are, and correct for them. Furthermore, I can ally myself with other experts who agree with me about your distortions and where they come from. If you keep on arguing that your reality is real, especially if you are strenuous about it, I will be able to tell (and tell you) that I must be right, because look how defensive you're getting. The truth hurts, and therefore what hurts must be true. Aggression is making you distort reality, and it is also making you try to destroy my mind, which is okay because I don't believe I have one. For the past twelve years I have been trying to express the main concepts of psychoanalysis without recourse to the idea of the mind.

I have been indulging in this caricature mainly to support the idea that the seemingly sharp distinction between intra- and extra- psychic is pretty blurry, except that your intrapsychic is my extrapsychic, and vice versa. The intrapsychic is supposedly psychic reality and the machinery that generates it. The apparatus and the energy that fuels it—no matter how conceived—is seen as primary, generating motives which in turn affect perception. Recognition of how difficult and varied perception is can turn this primacy around. If each person's perceptions are different from every other person's, then motivation can be seen as flowing from perception, and not the other way around.

In a non-mental conception of analysis, thought is an activity primarily of the brain that generates ideas, and is in turn determined by ideas. We speak of models of the mind, but I have come to think that what we call *mind* is a set of models of the world. For example, what is called *superego* I believe can be better represented as a set of ideas or fantasies that guide our actions. The fantasies concern ourselves and others who are expected to approve, disapprove, punish and so on. The people whose actions are hoped for or feared usually include living people, the dead, the unborn, the supernatural, and so on. The fantasies may or may not be conscious, and they are complex, ever-changing, and yet essentially the same throughout life. They are much too multifarious to be represented by a set of internal objects, and the use of the word "internal" is itself misleading because the distinction between external and internal is illusory.

But what we mean by *internal objects* as well as what we mean by *ego*, *id* and *self* can all be accounted for in terms of fantasies. For example, the mechanisms of defense are ways in which fantasies are revised, promoted toward action or temporarily abandoned. These events can simply be seen as bodily—mostly brain—activities. Leave out the mind.

One of the reasons that I think analysis should lose its mind is that the mind is supposed to be a real thing, rather than a collection of ideas about real things. Speaking of the mind as if it is a real thing, rather than an activity, leads to tautology and confusion. Some of that confusion was built into analysis because it was born in the heyday of Cartesian dualism, and analysis, as well as other psychological disciplines, increased the confusion by introducing another split. Earlier, the mind had been a person's experience and its locus. Then psychoanalysis and other psychological disciplines gave it more metaphorical substance. The topographic model of the mind includes, as its largest part, the unconscious, which cannot be experienced. In the structural model it has anatomy and physiology like a second body. Object relations theory similarly includes a collection of inner objects like a menagerie of homunculi.

The result of these approaches, as I have claimed before, is an unacknowledged triad. Where there had been two realms, experience and the body, there were now three: experience; the mind, whose structure and function gave rise to experience; and the body, which was related to the mind in only partially specified ways.

The project of trying to reformulate my ideas without a concept of mind has affected my clinical point of view and the way I speak when doing analysis, therapy and supervision. What I am attempting to do now is to give an account of those changes and what I believe are their benefits. The most basic change is that I focus my attention on the negotiation of reality, the development of shared versions of what is. That negotiation comprises much of human interaction, sometimes obviously, as in:

"You're late."
"No I'm not."

—and sometimes less obviously, as in:

"How about those Mariners?"
"I don't really pay attention to sports."

—a partial translation of which might be:

"You and I are similar and friendly. We share an activity, an enthusiasm and an identification."

"No. We are strangers and different and I am more unusual than you, and probably better."

Though most of the reality that is negotiated is social reality, because we are such social creatures, it is worth noting that physical reality is also the product of negotiation; for example, the international agreements as to what a kilogram weighs and what time it is.

The negotiations between psychotherapists and the people who come to see us are often in bad faith, in that one or both parties may only pretend to negotiate because they are unwilling to change some beliefs. Insanity does not consist of having incorrect perceptions, since we all have plenty of those, but of unwillingness to adjust our perceptions by interacting with others.

The extreme case is paranoia, the construction of a set of perceptions which are impossible to disprove, such as, "You are patiently waiting to kill me, and the fact that you have shown no sign of even trying to do so merely shows how fiendishly patient you are."

Some psychoanalytic perceptions take that form, such as, "Your anger at my interpreting as greed your wish to borrow a magazine from the waiting room shows just how greedy you are."

I believe one of the most important parts of my job is to remember to doubt my version of things and to promote the other person's having similar doubts. Whenever analysands tell me something about my character or about what I am doing at the moment, the first possibility I consider is that they are right. Experience has demonstrated the validity of this principle, which seems to me to be generalizable. It has been my observation in working with couples in therapy, or simply listening to any group of people, that what they say about each other is much more likely to be accurate than what they say about themselves.

Of course, my analysands can't always be right, but even if they aren't (and how can I be sure?) is there harm in acting as if they are right? I think there may be, if that means acting guilty and apologetic. I think that once in a while an apology is called for if it is clear that I have made a serious error such as being significantly late. On the other hand, almost all people in therapy recognize that it is a complex interaction in which strong impulses naturally arise and affect both people. Even if the other people are furious with me, I hope that they will ultimately be able to take an interest in examining what happened without insisting on more than a recognition of the legitimacy of their position. It usually works out that way, even if it may take a while.

Thinking intrapsychically makes it hard to take the attitude I am recommending, because it leads to theorizing about what is making the other people distort their perceptions of me. I think it is more helpful to think socially, but the social thinking I try to do is shaped by the premise that there is no single social reality but many realities—more than there are persons involved.

To begin with, there are at least two versions for each person: what he or she thinks, and what he or she thinks the other person thinks. Really all I mean by this is that there are pairs of realities, because each person has many primary versions of what is going on and each has its reciprocal version of what the other thinks. Usually there is a preferred version, a most feared version, and a number of intermediates. Many of these are unconscious, but usually can readily come into consciousness if mentioned by the other person.

Disavowed or unconscious versions may also become conscious if the other treats the avowed version as legitimate. It may sometimes work even if I am doing what we used to call in my Chicago childhood, "using psychology on them," saying the reverse of what I think so that the other will argue for my side. Artificial, tactical agreements usually (at least when I do them) come across as phony and condescending, but if I really am seeing a possibility of truth, or a lot of truth, in the other person's version, the lack of need to defend themselves, and surprise and satisfaction in being respected, often leads to their temporarily identifying with my former point of view and seeing that a feared version may be correct, but in this interpersonal atmosphere it is not so bad.

Talking about these matters in general comes across a little blood-less, I'm afraid. There have been many people with whom I have worked who were dissatisfied and angry with me for long periods and, to a large extent, I with them. Sometimes it seems to me that those people were simply less tactful than the rest of my clientele, because when I managed to listen nondefensively enough I could see justice in their complaints and was chagrined to think I had been the same way many times with others without being called on it. But even so, some people seem to me to be pretty unreasonable and hard to get along with; touchy and likely to take almost anything extremely personally. I am fond of quoting the late Richard J. Daley, mayor of Chicago, who said, "I have been vilified. I have been crucified. I've even been criticized!" Often something I say or don't say will lead to an explosion or a sulk that surprises me, and sometimes thinking it over doesn't lead quickly to my catching on to what my offense was. Asking what it was sometimes doesn't work either, and at those times I try to resist the strong temptation to look for and make an intrapsychic interpretation, e.g., one involving projective identification.

I try to take the attitude that the customer is always right, but that doesn't mean that I think the customer is reasonable. No one can possibly be intuitive enough to know in advance how all things will appear to another person, especially if the other person is exceptionally vulnerable. What I mean about their being right is that if I can think my way into their dominant ways of seeing reality, I can find what went wrong and speak of it.

I should admit that in this kind of effort I am sometimes guided by an intrapsychic crib sheet: I resort temporarily to the structural model, object relations theory or self psychology, whichever seems to be the most fruitful at the moment, but the way I do that is to use those principles as guides to how other people are likely to structure their worlds. I use special or mechanical models to help me to think what the crucial issues are. I do not think that my use of these old-fashioned study guides is necessary, but it is a product of my personal history and professional development. I think that in the future—maybe already—many analysts will simply use general principles of how we organize the world, principles learned over the century of analytic practice which have been represented as the mind and its contents, but they will dispense with the old forms and go directly to conceptions of how people build models of the world without first going back a step to how Freud and others built models of the mind.

In practice, what all this means is that I try to come up with statements about conflict between me and the other rather than statements about conflicts or forces within the other. Those statements may not be my own first view of what happened or is happening. I try to state my best guess as to what the other person's most important view of the situation is, whether I think that view is conscious or not.

For example, if someone tells me of a new accomplishment and then falls silent, I say, "I didn't respond to something important to you." This remark seems to me preferable to, "You are angry that I didn't say anything about it," or "You need me to confirm your sense of accomplishment." Those interpretations usually will be heard as putdowns, and often enough, if the other person wasn't overtly angry before they were made, he or she will be afterward.

So what's the problem? If I say that a person is angry, and sure enough he or she then gets mad, hasn't the truth of my interpretation been established and a harmfully repressed emotion been beneficially released? I don't think so. That view promotes something from the status of a reaction to the status of a cause, which view begins to leave me out as a contributor to the whole situation. My lack of response to the person's account of the accomplishment was the primary cause. The character of the analysand also determined the nature of the reaction, but focusing on the anger implies various judgments about that character, such as that the person is demanding and controlling, having to have it all his or her own way. Such value judgments are often made as though they were not culturally determined and self-serving, as I believe them to be, but rather as though they are scientific and detached, made from a point of view of superior understanding. Regarding these value judgments as scientific observations leads to the belief in dangerous, unconscious instinctual forces that need to be dragged out into the open and curbed. This belief will often pour fuel on the fire or, worse yet, induce a resigned, self-abasing acquiescence.

The analysand's anger and resignation are attempts to deal with the shame that the interpretation caused. I do not think that it is always destructive to say something that causes shame, but it often is, especially if the person is relatively fragile and intensely involved with the analyst. My idea of those situations is that the other people have few beliefs about themselves that lead to optimism about their acceptance by others who matter to them. The belief that the analyst finds them worthwhile is often the cornerstone of a shaky structure of fantasies by which they define themselves at all favorably, and is opposed by threatening sets of fantasies defining them as worthless, hateful, dangerous, or otherwise likely to inspire hatred or worse in the those they care about. Their fantasies of good relationship tend to be quite pure—purely good or purely bad—and an instance in which the analyst is critical of them may convince them that the analyst is only critical. Their whole sense of security may come tumbling down, producing a dangerous situation: panic, in which they can only pull together some coherent experience of themselves by desperate measures such as rage, compulsive alcohol or drug use, cutting themselves, getting themselves in trouble with the law, or any number of horrible things like that. One often hears, as a general statement or as a particular instance, though almost always third- or fourth-hand, of some poor person being driven crazy by therapy gone wrong—too much insight for their ego strength, or something like that. I don't think it actually happens very often, but I think it does occasionally, and my view of how such things work is that after suffering some sort of severe shaming, people find themselves unable to conceive of any way that they feel capable of behaving that would be acceptable to anyone who matters.

Cases in which trouble is all too apparent, though awful for everyone concerned, are relatively easy to discuss theoretically. What are much harder, and more common, are situations in which the other person makes no objection to the analyst's behavior as such but implies them by a shift in mood, a slowing or other change in speech or subject, the appearance of self-accusations, or an infinite number of other signs of some reaction that isn't being spoken about. I mean, roughly, unawareness of transference, but I mean it only roughly because I think we grossly overestimate what is unconscious, and underestimate what is conscious but not said.

I will use as an example a small incident in an analysis I am quite familiar with, which has gone well and is nearing a successful completion. One Monday the analysand began with an account of a problem at work over the weekend. She was being expected to do something that she thought was poor professional practice. The analyst said that he agreed that it was indeed poor practice. The woman went on to say that her supervisor ordered her to proceed against her better judgment. She said that she felt like quitting the job and reporting her workplace to public authorities, but she said that this would be a problem because she needed the extra job to pay for the analysis. The analyst made an uncharacteristically unhelpful remark: "You feel burdened." The woman, who had been animated and engaged, became quiet and a bit withdrawn. She said, "I don't know why I was thinking about that." I believe that earlier in the analysis she would have remained in a position of criticizing herself for bringing up something that she thought was not so important after all, but because of the good work that has gone on over a number of years she rallied enough to say, "Your response was generic." She went on putting herself down until she again rallied enough to ask the analyst what he thought was going on, and he spoke of her disappointment in his lack of skill. That helped.

I have a large assortment of ideas of what the analyst might better have said than, "You feel burdened." The woman's communication was rich with implications about herself and the analyst that I'm sure all of you are aware of, but I want to focus on one particular feature of the generic response. One of the generic things about it was that it began, "You feel…," a common first couple of words for analytic interpretations. I think they are almost always a mistake. I think that as a first shot at beginning a discussion of the story of the weekend, the words, "What a terrible problem," would be much better. I do not believe that the analyst thought that his analysand was making too much fuss about what happened, but I feel pretty sure that she thought he did.

One of the troubles with telling people what they feel is that they almost always hear us as implying that they shouldn't feel like that. "You are burdened," would have been a bit awkward but at least it would have sounded as thought the analyst thought the problem was real and important, as he had in fact implied by his first remark in which he agreed that she was being asked to do something wrong. The contrast between the first remark and the second might have caught the woman by surprise and led to her feeling a bit betrayed.

"What a terrible weekend!" would have encouraged her to go on with the account and her thoughts about it. I imagine that then there would have been lots of good spots to say things like, "The analysis costs you a lot." The reaction to that might have led to an opportunity to say, "I'm influencing you to do things that are wrong," a big issue for this person. With luck, she might have stopped and thought about that and said that actually she isn't so helpless. There are ways that she could refuse the order and still keep the job, and she is capable of getting better jobs. Then there might have been an opportunity to say, "As a general rule, you feel less confident and capable over the weekend."

I feel odd advising against speaking about feelings, since we analysts think emotions are more important than most people think they are. It is my experience, however, that analysands speak more freely about their emotions when I talk about the circumstances that give rise to their feelings instead of trying to name the feelings myself. This is particularly true of anger. I believe there was a time when ordinary people being analyzed thought being angry was perfectly respectable, and would react to their analysts' saying they were angry with a straightforward and self-respecting yes or no. Sex was a different matter in those days, and interpretations of sexual impulses were often hotly denied. It may be particularly true of analysands in the Pacific Northwest, but people I work with tend to be matter-of-fact about sexuality and embarrassed or ashamed about anger. Whatever the explanation, I find it much more useful to say things like, "This is a terrible time for me to be going away," or "My remark changed the subject from what you were most interested in," than "My going on vacation makes you mad."

Besides being shame-inducers, interpretations which use emotions as one of their main terms are imprecise because our concept of emotion is confused. We lump together affects as communications to others, affects as impulses and affects as self-assessments. In my opinion, the correct starting point for a discussion of affect is a situation with which a person is dissatisfied. For the sake of fitting it into this relatively short talk, I will combine all the causes of a situation being different from what we want under the general heading of "The Pleasure Principle." We want something changed when our best predictions of what will happen next include pain and/or do not include a pleasure we think we might be able to have.

If I see you yawning as I read this, I will want a change in the situation: perhaps I should ad lib a bit. If I smell coffee and it appeals to me, I may want to hurry things up here so as to get to eat sooner. In either case I will experience some kind of tension. What kind depends on my assessment of my chances. If you really look hopelessly bored or disapproving, and I don't think there's much chance of changing your minds, I will feel depressed, or angry, or both. I probably will also feel anxious. It will be depression if I judge that not only can't I change your minds but also I won't be able to convince anyone, for example, my wife, that you were dumb not to like this talk. If I think there is a fighting chance that I can convince her, I will feel angry and anxious. If I'm sure I can convince her and other people that you were dumb not to like me I'll be even madder, and maybe hardly anxious at all.

The point I am trying to make is that emotions are secondary to the motivating situation, not prime movers in and of themselves. I prefer to think of fantasies as the next step into higher abstractions and as the immediate explanation of emotion. We are constantly comparing fantasy to reality, or what we think from moment to moment is the most likely fantasy to be real. Since the two blend and are hard to distinguish, it may be better to say that we compare wishful with realistic fantasy, and the degree of our tension is proportional to the difference between them.

The wishful fantasies are in constant flux as our circumstances change. The changes may be physiological, such as the emptying of the stomach or the filling of the seminal vesicles, or they may be external, such as the arrival of a friendly or an unfriendly person. My way of thinking of the notion of derivatives is that each immediately operative fantasy is only the latest in an almost infinite series of fantasies from which it is derived. Most of what we want is instrumental toward getting something that is instrumental toward getting something else that is instrumental toward getting something else, and so on and on.

The pursuit of money is an ordinary example of this. We experience our satisfaction in getting some cash fairly purely because it is a relief of the tension that we have felt in trying to get it, but also because of the good feelings that are produced as all the things we want to do with money seem more possible.

The other main way that fantasies are related to others from which they are derived is through editorial revision. This is my mindless way of describing the mechanisms of defense. For example, my example of the fantasy of telling my wife that you are dumb if I see you looking bored or disapproving is a revision of an earlier one of telling you yourselves. My whole mindless system is largely based on Freud's description of thought as trial action, and when I tried out that last fantasy it had several bad outcomes and no good ones, and so I changed it.

Similarly, as I have already said, my fantasy of telling my wife was based on thinking I might convince her; it would have to be revised if it seemed as if she wouldn't believe me, while if I thought the fantasy was actually workable, I would feel angry and anxious. Saying that I would feel angry means that I would be imagining telling her, with indignation, about your failures. If that felt like a sure success I would just feel angry, but since I can't be sure how she would receive such a story I would worry about the outcome. Worrying about it means that I would feel tense and have a large number of bad fantasies of what she might think, say and do, and contingency plan fantasies about how to convince her, retreat from my position, go off alone to lick my wounds, or even how I would live to fight another day and think about who I would fight and how.

The defense mechanisms with which we are all familiar are, in my version, the rules of how our stories can be restructured. One of the rules is that we can change the characters almost limitlessly. The subject and the object of the story can simply trade places, or each can be changed into someone else. The commonest way to change who is the subject is through *identification*. We call changing the object *displacement*. If I don't succeed with you here today I can think of various heroes of mine who succeeded with other audiences, or I can think of other audiences with whom I may succeed in the future. The hopeful fantasy that I will persuade you here today is itself a product of an unthinkably large number of such revisions. Most simply, it is derived from my determination to do better than I did on occasions dating back to the 1940s, if not the '30s, when I failed to impress some audience I cared about. Perhaps, even more, it is derived from my determination to repeat pleasurable experiences in similar situations. Our analysands' feelings about us, as we all know, are a product both of series of instrumental wishes and of revisions made necessary by the failures and successes of their past.

We tend to talk about feelings as signals to ourselves, and as pleasant or noxious experiences. Doing so leaves out what seems to me to be an essential element of feeling anything—nonverbal communication. If, while I read this, I do feel sad, what that means is that I will be changing the tone and rate of my speech, lowering the corners of my mouth, exhibiting even worse posture than usual, and so on. I think that these elements of my behavior will be designed to affect you instinctively, so that you feel sympathetic and not threatened, and you will be less likely to shame me in some way because I am already giving off signs of submission. You don't have to shame me because I've done it to myself already. Except for years of thinking about this stuff, I would probably not be aware of anything except a generalization which, if put into words—which it ordinarily wouldn't be—would come out something like, "I feel bad."

The point I am trying to make by these oversimplifications is that if, when I am working, I can accurately describe the basic situation that is giving rise to some complex reaction, I am likely to be rewarded with a nondefensive, relatively comfortable description of what the other person wants, what he or she thinks are the chances of getting it, what he or she would like me to do next, and what I should think about it.

To get that all at once doesn't happen very often, but things usually move in that direction. "This is a terrible time for me to go away," might be met with, "You're entitled to a vacation just like anyone else," to which I might reply, "My being entitled to it doesn't make it any easier for you," to which the answer might be, "I have no right to complain," followed by my, "What gives people the right to complain, and when don't they have it?" and so on.

With luck, we might be able to get to the point where the other person thinks I will dislike them if they complain about things. If so, we would be getting at a subject that in some ways is the quintessential intrapsychic one: guilt. I never had much success with saying, "You feel guilty about X." What usually happened was that the other people thought I meant they should feel guilty. The more interpersonal, "You think I will disapprove of you if you do X," works a lot better, but still may sound like an implication of actual disapproval. Sometimes an extra-transference interpretation works better; for example, "Your mother always told you never to do X." With luck, the reply will be something like, "Of course she did, because it's wrong," to which, on occasion, I will reply with, "What's wrong with it?" This may ultimately lead to my being able to say, "I'm causing you trouble by trying to corrupt you." If things are going at all well between us, that underlines a dilemma that can lead to a real rethinking of the issues involved, and their history.

The issues involved in guilt are complex and shifting, and I believe can be better described without the metaphor of the superego or the relatively stiff and limited concepts of an inner world or a bipolar self. Feeling guilty consists of a perception of the world in which, in any of a variety of ways, one is going to be punished, or should be.

Such narratives are characterized by a shift of identification away from oneself. The simplest form is identification with the aggressor. If I am driving (a somewhat unusual situation), and red and blue lights suddenly flash behind me, I feel chagrined, frightened and self-reproachful. I try to think—if I don't already know—what I might have done wrong. Since I am more of a depressive than a paranoid person, my first assumption is that the police are right in stopping me. Though I may defensively struggle against it, I shift into the officers' point of view and sympathize with their decision to give me a ticket. People who are more toward the paranoid end of the continuum will first be angry and frightened, and try to think why the police might be committing this injustice. If they clearly perceive that they have been speeding or something like that they will shift more into identification with the police. I, on the other hand, if I really convince myself that I have broken no traffic laws, may shift back into identification with myself.

A somewhat more complicated case is identification with one's victim. If my son wakes me in the morning by playing the piano and I angrily tell him to stop, I may then see him look hurt and disappointed in me. Then, if he reminds me that it is rather late and that he has a music lesson in an hour, I will cease to be the abused and irate hero of the story. He will become the abused hero and I the villain whose action I want to undo or rationalize.

These simple examples involve ordinary people in the here and now, and real actions. Most guilt is derived from perceptions that are supernatural. Mere wishes are believed to have real effects on others. Thoughts are known by others, including those not present, the dead or the divine, and magical punishments may be more feared than ordinary ones. Many people readily avow such beliefs because they are widely accepted as correct by those they live with. Probably all of us avow some such ideas, but for the most part I would think that present company tends to disavow them and even keep them out of consciousness. But they still play a large part in forming our personal reality.

The appearance of one or another personal reality is determined by the interaction of the immediately perceived situation and an array of wishes and fears derived from one's whole history and inborn temperament. Character descriptions are generalizations about these arrays of wishes and fears. My calling myself "depressive" means that I am more likely to be decided in any conflict by the fear of loss of connection to other people than by the fear that others will hurt me. More paranoid people would rather be left than hurt.

The injuries I have in mind are physical or social. Classical notions about castration anxiety seem to me to be perfectly useful if we make sure that it is understood that castration can be symbolic, that is, the loss of standing, authority, reputation and so on. These preferences are not always obvious. Paradoxically, in my willingness to be hurt rather than left, I may be quite fearful of the injuries I expect to receive, and a paranoid person may appear quite fearless about injury as he or she prepares for battle. The motivating point is that I would rather be humble than hated, while the paranoid person is willing, though often reluctantly, to be hated, but will try hard to avoid being humbled.

I am elaborating these specimens of motivational description to show how I think, and also to try to illustrate how they point toward the examination of the interpersonal negotiation of reality. If I see that an analysand is guilty or angry, my not allowing myself to think first of a superego or a ferocious introject leaves me little choice but to think of myself. Figuring out what I have done or not done that led to that result is likely to lead to a relatively nondefensive discussion of what is really going on, which can lead to exploring the array of wishful and fearful stories that determined the analysand's guilt. A thoroughgoing acceptance of the interpersonal view as a starting point can therefore do more to lead to understanding of the particularities of how someone characteristically thinks than discussion that starts with the other person's character.

I hope these stylized, broad-brush examples make my thinking clear, but they seem a bit pale next to real life. So I want to come back to the analysis I was describing earlier for another example of what seem to me to be the advantages of speaking of the situation rather than of the person's reaction to the situation. The analysand had often been in conflict with women who had authority over her, and characteristically she described them as evil and wrong-headed, and quit jobs which it might have been better for her to keep. The analyst had often spoken of her tendency "to discredit" such people. Now it was all happening again in connection with the order at work to do something against her principles.

A few days after the hour I described before, she reported that her objection to doing things the way the institution and her supervisor wanted them done had resulted in her being told that she was to have a conference with the woman in overall charge of the place. In the meantime, she had scored a major professional success somewhere else and was pleased and excited, but at the beginning of this hour she said, "The wind's been taken out of my sails, and I don't know why." She went on to talk about the proposed meeting with the boss and to say that the boss was just a figurehead who knew nothing.

She expanded on these statements at some length, and the analyst said, "You feel you have to discredit her as you have other women with whom you have been in conflict." She became rather angry and said that physicians all stick together and form a solid front against anyone who points out their malpractice. The analyst is a physician and the analysand is not. The analyst defensively denied that physicians are as powerful as she was representing them to be, and when things continued to go wrong between them, caught himself and spoke of her disappointment in him for not supporting her.

This interpretation was largely successful, but I think several issues were lost from the conversation. It's ever so easy to second-guess when I have all the time in the world to do it and am not caught up in the heat of action, so I don't know what I really would have done, but saying what I wish I would have done can serve as an illustration. If I had been the analyst, I wish I would have said, "You're caught in a tough spot. Not only do you believe in your point of view, but I also told you I agree with you. Easy for me to say, but you're the one that has to face the big boss."

I imagine that she might have said that it wasn't going to do any good, to which I might have answered, "I don't know what will happen, but I seem to have a higher opinion of your standing and your ability to argue than you do. Again, that's easy for me to say because I'm not the one on the line, but maybe you took the wind out of your sails so you wouldn't be dangerously brave going in to see her." I think that if these and related issues were explicated, the discrediting would take care of itself, and if it didn't it could have been dealt with in the form of something like, "Maybe I seem like I will side with her if you don't let me know about her faults."

Now I have another worry. My examples seem to me much too full of my talking and especially too full of my interpreting. That too seems like an odd thing for an analyst to say, because interpretation is supposed to be the main and the best thing we do, and I sort of agree with that. I do think that, most of the time, interpreting is much better than educating or advising, but, though some of my analysands have accused me of just being lazy and of being afraid of trouble, I continue to believe that one of the best mottoes for an analyst is, "Don't just do something. Sit there."

From having had the privilege of being an analyst for other therapists and analysts, I have learned that lots of people besides me worry about earning their fees and keeping their reputations by being productive, and that being productive often seems to them to consist of constantly figuring out fairly arcane stuff and talking about it. Any analytic hour is amenable to thousands of interesting interpretations. What seems to me one of the essences of our art is to pick which one is the most helpful, taking one's time in finding the best way to say it, and then waiting for the best time. I liked all of my analysts. The second one (of three) was particularly patient. He once waited six months to say something. My immediate reaction was, "You son of a bitch. Why didn't you say that last July?" But actually I could see that I was more ready to hear it in February, and I not only learned something about myself and about analytic technique, but maybe most importantly I felt well listened to.

And for my money, that's what counts the most. According to my mindless view of human psychology, thought is trial action (scarcely an original idea), and when we think in words we are rehearsing what we might say, trying to undo the past when we said the wrong thing, speaking to supernatural beings or rehearsing a speech to them, or any of an infinite number of other possibilities. Thinking in words, or in general ideas about words, is one of the main things that gives us whatever rational mastery of our lives we muster. There are many people to whom we can't say much, and a few people to whom we can say a lot. Analysands often complain that when they are with me they can't remember many important thoughts they had elsewhere. In imagination there is less risk that I will say the wrong thing, but there are things they never think because they can't imagine that I will say the right thing.

If things go well, that realm diminishes. What I miss most about being in analysis myself is having someone to whom I could say anything—well, almost anything. My goal when I am the analyst is to promote a feeling that the other person can say anything to me. If they can come anywhere close to feeling that, they can think anything, or at least a lot more than they used to be able to think, and that is one of the main things it's all about. Relentlessly interpreting can make it hard for the other person to say things to you. Often a chuckle of appreciation of something funny or even a returned funny remark can be more important than a heavy-handed defense interpretation of why the analysand made the joke. Getting what the other people are saying, and letting them know that you do, can go a lot further than making something conscious that was unconscious if what you're talking about seems like it was beside the point, even if interesting, and the other person is left in doubt as to whether you get what they're saying.

Now I'm afraid this all sounds like sweetness and light. My actual experience is rather different. In spite of my efforts to avoid shaming people and misunderstanding them and so forth, I still seem to have plenty of dissatisfied customers, or really customers who are often dissatisfied, and maybe that's all to the good. It seems to me that an analysis without contention would miss essential elements like envy and jealousy, and one that was all contention would miss the need for affiliation and the progression from idealizing a person to disappointment and the consequent ability to form cherished ideals. That balance is my cherished ideal, anyway.

Criticism and Defensiveness

People who pay to talk with me are mostly responsible for these ideas. Almost all of them have been intelligent and eloquent, and many of them are sophisticated about the profession we share. They have been adept at pointing out to me how I often am defensive when I don't know it myself, and how my being that way messes things up. As I tried to cut it out, and saw that when I succeeded things improved, I generalized my conclusions to the rest of life.

"I have been crucified. I have been vilified. I have even been criticized."
— *The Honorable Richard J. Daley*

AS A MINDLESS PSYCHOANALYST I HAVE BEEN TRYING to express psychoanalytic theory and practice without resorting to a conception of the mind and its alleged structures. Early in this attempt, under the influence of constructivist ideas, I realized that much of what we call the mind consists of a person's array of conceptions of the world. I have attempted to move from models of the mind to considering people's models of reality.

In my daily work, I have learned to think about the competing theories of what exists that each of us is constantly weighing and testing. One of the results of this discipline is to see what goes on between me and the people I work with as a series of negotiations leading to a shared version of reality; especially social reality and, most importantly, the reality of who each of us is, and how we are related to each other. Thinking this way has led me to have greater respect for other people's realities, and less certainty of my own. I am much less likely than I was at the beginning of my career to tell people that they are wrong.

This change seems to be most important when I am tempted to tell people that they are wrong about me. I have seen more and more clearly how much of what analysts and other therapists say is defensive, and how harmful our defensiveness is. In previous papers I have elaborated this idea in some detail as it applies to our behavior at work. Thinking about the bad effects of defensiveness in therapy has made me more aware of its bad effects in the rest of life, and I now want to extend my preaching to a kind of psychoanalytic Miss Manners of everyday life.

I believe that much of what goes wrong in life is a result of our being criticized, and reactively defending ourselves in ways that criticize the other, who then defends him or herself in what often becomes a vicious circle. These vicious circles can occur in the real interpersonal world, or simply in our imagination. The wish to be defensive when criticized is almost irresistible, but I believe that any time we can resist it we are much better off. Defensiveness consists of attempting to prove more or less artificially what best arises naturally: that others think well of us. It is uncomfortable while we're doing it, it doesn't work, and it usually makes everything worse.

Our sense of who we are is primarily made up of our relationships. We need to feel pretty sure that people we care about also care about and think well of us, and we need to be at least somewhat optimistic that people we are going to meet will be glad to meet us. Many psychoanalysts and others, especially in this country, have suggested that a well-developed person doesn't need the opinions of others to feel secure. Everyone admits that children need the good opinion of their parents, but what is supposed to happen is something like the internalization of the approving and disapproving parents to the degree that we are not only able to decide what is good or bad for us to do, but also to give ourselves all the approval we need.

Aspiring to this kind of independence is a false value. I don't simply mean that being that independent would be a bad thing, though I do think that it would; if we were all that oblivious to what others thought, society would fall apart because we would be unable to influence each other. But even if I am wrong and super-independence is a wonderful goal, it doesn't matter because it is impossible. I also do think that it would be wonderful to be able to fly by levitation, but to adopt that as a goal would be meaningless because it is unattainable. I cannot prove that there is no completely independent person, but I am sure I have never met one or heard of one and I can't imagine one. It is our dependence on others' opinions that makes us so vulnerable to criticism. This vulnerability varies from person to person. Some people go crazy and/or commit suicide after a criticism, bad grade, performance review, or other blow, and others take such things more or less in stride.

The areas in which the various forms of shame arise can be divided into four: two kinds of ambition and two forms of idealizing. The most overt ambitiousness, which we tend to call conceit, entitlement, grandiosity or narcissism—descriptions I dislike—is what I like to call *secondary ambition*. It is that collection of notions of what one must be that are derived from the parents' ambitions for children, who then feel that they must be something the parents had in mind in order not to let them down, to be loved, or even in extreme cases to continue to exist. Criticism that attacks this area is particularly shaming and frightening, especially if the critic is felt to be a symbolic successor to the parents. If the parents needed one to be brilliant or beautiful or something like that, it may feel as if a spouse will need the same thing, and if the spouse points out some flaw, it means that one isn't good enough to be loved anymore.

What I like to call *primary ambition* is a little sturdier. These are goals that arise more spontaneously from children themselves: things they naturally like doing from earliest times, fantasies they elaborate themselves and so on. Parents do influence these, too, by responding to them or not, but the parents function more as audience or participants, not as scriptwriters. As I noted earlier, people who have fortunate childhoods are quite grandiose in the second year of life and into the third but gradually, manageable frustration wears their ambitions down to more realistic levels. It also causes them to learn how to pursue goals effectively instead of wanting them to have been achieved already. These goals are more dear to us than the secondary ones, and so a threat to one of them can be terribly painful, but we can learn that we can right ourselves after a defeat and make new plans and efforts that have a good chance of succeeding.

The more fragile situation arises in less fortunate childhoods, in which the children's activities or fantasies are not noticed and admired or, worse yet, are derided or punished. When that happens, the primary ambitions have to go underground for their own protection, and since they are largely unconscious and not pursued they are not modified by experience. They remain grandiose and imperative. Under favorable circumstances such as a loving relationship, they may surface. Particularly at first they are unlikely to be realized and their frustration is awful because their coming to light produces a precious hope which is then dashed.

The two kinds of idealizing are idealizations of actual people and the establishment of abstract ideals. Idealization of real people tends to be the more troublesome of the two. It comes earlier, beginning with the admiration of the parents whose impressive qualities are cherished by children as they recognize that they themselves aren't as big, powerful and wonderful as they had hoped. Children who feel small, weak and uninformed comfort themselves by seeing that their parents are big, strong and knowledgeable. The toddlers are still great, because they own and belong to others who are great.

Just as with ambitions, favorable development depends on optimal frustration. If the parents remain reliably in the children's lives, and if their failings are not too obtrusive and severe, children's idealizations get gradually worn down to realistic size and at the same time the second form of idealizing arises. Where the parents fail, the child adopts the lost perfection as an abstract ideal. If the parent turns out not to know everything, the child may adopt knowledge as an ideal. When frustration is too severe to be manageable—a painful disillusionment—the idealization is withdrawn from the parent and the child may go through life searching for others to idealize. No one completely switches from idealization to ideals, but if that switch has been made to a limited extent, the person's idealized people are an especially vulnerable part of themselves. To see how bad it can be to criticize a primitively idealized person, think what happened sixty or seventy years ago to people who told some Nazi that Hitler wasn't perfect. It is generally not as likely to cause an emotional outburst to criticize someone's ideal of science or art, but criticizing falseselfobject religious or political symbols like the swastika, cross, Bible or flag can be explosive.

We sometimes speak disapprovingly of people as narcissistically vulnerable, but I think that more often than we notice, equanimity is as much a matter of our status as it is a matter of how well we think. People who are well-situated socially are seemingly less narcissistically vulnerable than those without much standing, but I think they are hurt less often because there are fewer people who have the nerve to oppose them, and fewer people whom they cannot dismiss as unimportant. Some board certified analysts I know speak, apparently quite seriously, of their certification examination as being a useful educational experience, but they tend to be the ones that passed the first time. Over the years, I have known many people who initially failed the analytic or psychiatric boards. I have never known one of them to describe the process as a useful educational experience and I have never known one that explained the failure as deserved.

Which reminds me of the story of Peter the Great and the prisoners. The Czar was inspecting a prison and interviewed the inmates. All but one told him that they had been wrongfully convicted, and asked to be released. The one exception said that he was guilty of terrible crimes, and richly deserved his punishment. Peter angrily told the warden, "Get this crook out of here before he has a bad influence on all the wonderful innocent people that he's in here with." Not being defensive doesn't usually have that good an effect, but it almost always beats the reverse.

The wish to defend is so strong because even the narcissistically not-so-vulnerable are thrown into disarray when someone whom they at least hope has a good opinion of them says there is something wrong with them. The effect is particularly strong if the complaint is from a person who is very important to the one being criticized, and it comes as a complete surprise. In extreme cases it can be like having the ground drop out from under them.

Some years ago, I knew a couple whose serious troubles began one day in the second decade of their marriage. They were out for a long walk, and the wife who had thought things were at least all right was devastated by the husband's suddenly confiding in her that he had never been happy. The idea that her marriage was good enough, that her husband was reasonably content was an important part of the woman's sense of who she was. In the same way, her idea of who her husband was and what he thought and was likely to do was also a part of her self-definition.

When he made his sudden announcement, her personal reality fell apart. His saying that didn't make sense. The question that presented itself to her with great force was one that people in that spot usually think and often ask: "How could he?" When a person who isn't crucial to our experience of our world does something we don't like, we say, "I don't like that," "It isn't fair," or something like that; but when the person is crucial to us, the event strikes us as impossible. Incredulity easily becomes denial, which usually fades quickly and is followed by anger and/or depression. The situation is intolerable and something has to be done.

The wife did ask, "How can you say that after all these years? Do you really mean to tell me that you've always been unhappy with me?"

"Yes," he said.

"I can't believe this. This is like a sneak attack. I even thought you were enjoying the walk."

He was getting panicky, too. "I didn't mean to make you so mad. It was being a good time and that's what gave me the nerve to finally tell you how I feel."

"What do you mean, gave you the nerve, are you usually too scared of me to tell me things?"

"Yes. You get so mad." That remark started the fourth turn of the vicious circle. At the time of his revelation they were in different realities. His was that the marriage was not very good because she was so bossy, but today she seemed calm and accepting. He imagined that if he took a chance and revealed his suffering, she would be sympathetic and sorry, and might comfort him and ask what she could do to make him happier. When her reaction destroyed that picture, he in turn was in an intolerable situation.

At the end of the first turn, each of them felt that something was said that had to be taken back or somehow corrected. She couldn't stand his being unhappy with her, and he couldn't stand her implying that he was a bad person to have finally revealed his feelings. If things could have been interrupted there, a solution might have been negotiated. He might have said truthfully that he was overstating and over-generalizing; that there had been lots of good times and, just as truthfully but not as easily, that he knew he was a gloomy sort of person whose unhappiness was not primarily due to her. She might have said she was glad that he was telling her so they could figure out how to make things better.

Nothing of the kind happened until after they had spiraled into an abyss and then had quite a lot of arduous therapy. The second turn gave each another intolerable statement to deal with. He had to do something about the idea that there was something wrong with him that he hadn't spoken sooner, and she had to do something about the idea that she was such a frightening person that her husband couldn't talk with her. By the time they got home from the park, each had heard many more criticisms that had to be destroyed or counteracted.

As I said before, defensiveness aims at proving something, usually that one is a good person after all. If you flunk your board exam, it becomes natural to re-establish your worth by showing that the examiners were stupid and prejudiced and the exam meaningless after all. An infinite number of other strategies are available: you were sick that day, your husband was unsupportive and didn't help you have time to study, and so forth. The strategies can be divided into the categories of excuse or counterattack. The strategies of counterattack can be further divided into those that prove that the criticism is invalid, or that the criticizer is just as bad. The second can be extended to all of humanity: everyone is just as bad.

Looked at from some distance the whole struggle appears a little odd. To whom is the argument aimed? Who is supposed to be convinced by the proof? If it is the person who did the criticizing, the chances of success are close to zero. If the audience is someone other than the critic, the chances are probably better than zero but not much.

In my earlier paper, "Audience," I suggested that the audience who is supposed to be convinced is only present in imagination: a reasonable person (as opposed to the one you're talking with), God, other members of your gender (as opposed to the person you're talking with), your parents, your analyst, and so on. How can we be so foolish? What could possibly make us think that telling someone we need that they are stupid, too angry, just as bad as we are, and so forth, will do us any good? The other person won't agree, and everything will get worse. When we therapists try to understand such situations we are likely to look at the structures and the forces that are involved; for example, with the couple on the walk, his passivity and her wish to avoid separation anxiety by keeping control of the people around her. That approach will help, but only so far. It is like the proper approach to understanding an earthquake—here is the fault and this is the shearing force—but most human conflicts are more like fires than earthquakes. They aren't a single disaster, but a disastrous process. Once the thing gets going, it will consume every flammable thing available.

Another foolish thing about defensiveness is that though the conflagration and its damage are real enough, the whole affair may get far from reality. If someone says to me, "Change your clothes before we go to the party," I may say, "What I'm wearing looks fine," even if I don't believe it. The person who is most likely to say that to me is too smart to think I believe what I said, and won't argue the point, but she will stick to her guns. Most of us aren't that smart and will take such words much too seriously. As a result, lots of tumult consists of people angrily arguing over positions that neither believes, but unfortunately the less sure of ourselves we are, the more angrily defensive we are likely to become. For that reason, the more accurate the criticism, the stronger the defensive reaction is likely to be unless the characteristic criticized is one that is not part of either our ambitions or our ideals. The criticism that will bother us the least is one that isn't true and isn't important, and the one that will bother the most is one that is true and is important.

Once or twice in my life someone has been obtuse enough or I have been sneaky enough that I have been said to be too silent and modest. I am perfectly comfortable with that criticism. Much more often I have been said to be unfashionably dressed. (Once before an event at a Seattle Psychoanalytic Society and Institute Open House, my colleague Fritz Hoedemaker asked me what the dress code was. I said, "I don't know. I intend to dress even worse than usual." "Is that possible?" he asked.) That doesn't bother me because the criticism is true but not a contradiction of my goals; but if someone says I have written something awkwardly, I get upset because I am all too aware of how far short of my ambitions I fall, and it does matter to me.

Criticism that hurts is such a hazard that we are constantly trying to anticipate it. We defend in advance: "I don't care about being politically correct and so I'm going to say...." "Not to be a know-it-all, but...."

Many years ago when I was first in analysis, I was obsessed by the fear that while I was lying on the couch I would think of my contact lenses, and because I was a great believer in the basic rule, I would have to mention them. Soon enough it happened. "My left eye is hurting. There must be something wrong with my contact lens. I've had them for several years now. I got them because I am involved in a lot of sports and my glasses kept getting broken and besides I see better with contact lenses than with glasses and they don't fog up when I come in from the cold. It's not because I care about my appearance." My analyst, Paul Kramer said, "Oh?"

Even trivial actions when no one is around—except in imagination—may be defensive. While working on this paper at my office I took time out to go to the men's room. People often turn off the lights in the one located in the front of the building. During the day, the window provides a dim light and I usually don't switch the lights on when I come in. Being in an even more self-involved mood than usual because I was writing this, I stopped to wonder why I left it dark. The first thing that registered was a mildly defiant feeling, which I was able to track back about ten years to a day when I hadn't turned the lights on, someone else came in and did throw the switch. I had felt criticized. Then a much older memory came to me. At eighteen I was attempting to teach a fourth-grade class. One day the children became obstreperous, and I lost control of them. A more experienced teacher came in from his room across the hall and restored order. The first thing he did on entering was turn on the lights. From there I got to a memory of my father seeing me at ten or eleven behave badly in school and being disappointed in me. From there I got to what is as close to bedrock for this subject as I can reach: pissing, as I was while doing this self-analysis, but pissing at age four next to my father who was also pissing and whose penis and urinary stream dwarfed mine. So I concluded that I don't generally turn on the lights because I want to prove I don't care that my father could beat me in a pissing contest.

Series of usually unconscious thoughts like this give rise to many needless criticisms. The vicious circle starts even before a word is said. I think that one of the most common forms this process takes involves our defensiveness against the charge of selfishness. It is risky to say to another person, "I would really like it if you and I were to do something or other." The something or other can be anything, but a typically troublesome example is make love, or at the opposite end of the spectrum: "I would really like it if we don't see each other this afternoon while I go do something with someone else." Since we don't want the other to say that we are selfish to suggest something that he or she wouldn't like, we avoid framing the wish as a request. It feels safer, though it isn't, to frame it as a criticism, a necessity or a right. Instead of taking the risk of saying something like, "I really like oral sex and would love it if we did that," people often say things like, "you have rather a limited range sexually."

The simplest and maybe most common defensive move is to use the word *need* in place of the word *want*. It isn't that we merely want sex or an afternoon out because we would enjoy it. We have to mention it, perhaps even reluctantly, because the need has built up to the point where we are forced to say something. In the service of that version of things, people often wait for the other person to do what they want without it being requested. If it doesn't happen, they cannot only defensively claim that they are forced to mention it, but also argue that the other is a bad person for not knowing that it was the right thing to do. The other person is thoughtless, lacks empathy, and is insensitive. Asking for the thing makes the thing no good.

Thinking about the words *I need* has led me to try to drop them from my vocabulary. On the other hand, I have tried to increase my use of the words *you need* because they are less potentially critical than *you want*; for example, in questions like, "What do you need me to do?" Most of the time when I want to say, "I need," I am kidding myself. When I say, "you need," I'm being tactful.

What's worse than talking about needs is talking about rights. Two of the worst things about marriage are the idea that one is entitled to rather a lot of different things from the spouse, and the idea that since one is married, it is not necessary to do much to keep the relationship intact. Over the years, one of the phenomena that I have found most depressing, particularly when doing couples therapy, is the way many people who are passive and compliant with everyone else give each other no end of grief. It is as if the marriage becomes the sewer into which they dump all the shit that they are afraid to put anywhere else. In the world at large, such people are afraid that if they do the slightest thing to offend someone that person will reject them, but they act as if being married means that their spouse can't, or at least shouldn't, reject them. It's a paradox, that the person whom they most need and whose contentment and affection are most important to them is treated with less consideration than strangers whose alienation would have few consequences.

One couple I knew a long time ago was as embattled as any I have met. Both people were severely insecure in all their other relationships, and each blamed the other for undermining them by not giving them what they needed and had a right to. Often when she was feeling down because her satisfaction in life was limited by her fears of trying to do what she wanted professionally or socially, she would think that her bad feelings resulted from being married to someone who didn't pay attention to her. She would often complain bitterly that he forgot the hamburger she had asked him to buy one day more than fifteen years earlier. He was shyer in public than she, and after the two of them had been in some group where he had been afraid to speak up and she had been lively, he would say that she was a terrible wife because she talked so much that he didn't have a chance, and because she didn't act as a cheerleader for him. These were intelligent, psychologically minded people who could see what they were doing, but they refused to change because each was sure the other wouldn't. She once said, "Why should I stop being childish if he isn't going to?"

Fairness is another term that usually arises in marital arguments about the partners not getting what they claim a right to. Fairness is a real and important value, especially in one's family, but it is useless as a term introduced defensively into a dispute over rights. It seems to me that it would be to the point in such dealings to consider whether the people involved really have the rights they claim, but it usually doesn't work that way. Angrily defensive accusations often are answered with denials, even if the accusation in and of itself doesn't make sense. I think that nine times out of ten if someone says, "You're angry at me," the person so accused will say, "No, I'm not," instead of simply, "Yes." It doesn't seem to occur to people that what they are being accused of isn't necessarily a bad thing and doesn't merit an accusation. By the same principle, a spouse accused of not being attentive enough will resort to fairness arguments such as, "You never pay attention to me," instead of taking up the question of whether a spouse is automatically entitled to the kind of attention he or she wants.

I suppose what it comes down to is whether spouses owe each other affection, and how its presence or absence can be proven. Forty years ago, when I was relatively newly acquainted with the interpretation of slips and other mistakes, and anxious about the love of the person I was then married to, I would point out signs of her unconscious wish to be rid of me. If I had had my wits about me, I would have thought about what I was doing or not doing to inspire such wishes, and I certainly would not have set myself up as an authority on her unconscious, but I learn slowly. Naturally, my interpretations made her mad, but she too was an inexperienced kid and she didn't say, "In the first place, save that stuff for work, and in the second place, if you're making yourself hard to be around, that's your problem." Instead she was hurt, and counterattacked by pointing out how I didn't appreciate all the things she did that showed she cared about me.

This point gets a little tricky. Most of us promised to love when we got married, which is a reason not to get married. If you are with someone who didn't promise that to you, you might be more likely to think that you had to be attractive and good to them in order that they would continue to love you. So one question is whether people have a right to their spouse's love, but usually people get stuck on another: What actions necessarily follow from loving?

"If you loved me you would..." is an old-fashioned cliché of the sexual skirmishes of adolescence, but in many forms it infests marriage, especially in relation to attentiveness and sex. A lot of people talk as if they know more or less the number of times a year a loving person brings flowers, or the number of times a month a loving couple has sex. Someone accused of not loving would do well to doubt both the claim that not doing what was wished proves a lack of love, and the implied claim that love is a right. If people get bogged down in defending against the charge of not loving, no good will come of it. Saying, "Maybe I don't love you as much as you want me to," might be productive. G. B. Shaw once succumbed to the importunate requests of a friend that he come to see the friend's play. He slept through it. The friend said, "How could you do that? I was so eager to get your criticism," to which Shaw answered, "Sleep is a criticism." Similarly, in my opinion sex or attention in marriage are things to be courted as they are outside of marriage.

The other relationship in which criticism and defensiveness are a major problem is parenthood. People are usually more critical of their children than of their spouses, and often more defensive.

Among traditional Navajo people, children are regarded as equal members of the family who are not to be treated any more highhandedly than are adults. Once I was discussing child rearing with a group of elderly medicine people (there are no non-elderly medicine people). One of the men told about what happened because his father was too mean to him. One day when he was five or six, he was out herding the sheep, and as often happened he was daydreaming and the flock scattered. He heard a horse approaching, saw it was his father's and knew he was in for an unpleasant time.

He was sitting on the edge of a deep arroyo and knew that the sand below him was particularly soft. So he threw himself over the edge and when his father came and looked down at him, he held completely still. The wall of the arroyo was too steep for his father to climb down and he rode a long way to get down to the boy's level. The son, however, knew a short cut out and ran away. At that critical moment a flash flood roared through. The boy went to his aunt's hogan and told her what had happened. She kept him hidden with her. Soon, everyone in the extended family except the father knew the story and for several days the father fretted and mourned. Finally the family produced the son and told the father that this should be a lesson to him not to be so mean.

Not only do people feel that they have even more of a right to be unpleasant to their children than to their spouses, they even think it is good for them. Oddly, even though they think they should be unpleasant they are defensive about it. Again, wishes are presented as necessities and rights, and since directions given to children are necessary and for their own good, their anger about them isn't accepted. Lots of energy goes into arguments over the justification of parental edicts. The parents say, "thou shalt" or "thou shalt not"; the children ask why and the parents more or less angrily try to tell them, not entirely recognizing that "why" isn't a question; it's an argument. In my opinion, the old-fashioned answer, "Because I said so," is less foolish than to explain one's good motives. I prefer, "Because I want you to." If the children say, "You're not being fair," I think parents do well to say, "You're right." Not only is that less likely to produce a prolonged argument, but it has the more important advantage of telling the children that it is reasonable for them to be mad. If they can be angry without guilt or shame, they are likely to mourn their loss and ultimately be able to think about the good reason—if there was one—for the demand or the prohibition.

Some parents to whom I have suggested this policy have said that they needed to explain themselves so that their children wouldn't be made insecure by the idea that their parents were bad. I think that idea is backwards. The children's frustration naturally makes them mad. If they have to think that their parents are right and if, as is likely, they also see that their parents are distressed, they end up thinking that they are bad to want what they want.

For that and many other reasons parents avoid saying, "I want you to," and instead say, "You need to," or "You have to." And when their children behave in ways they don't like, many people are defensive about it's being a question of what's wanted or liked or not. Instead of saying, "I don't like your doing that," or "It makes me mad," they say some version of, "That's bad," or, worse yet, "You're bad." It makes me just about as mad to hear someone tell a kid the supposedly milder, "That's not okay." I have heard lots of rationalizations for attacking the behavior or the character of children. Some people say that it is necessary to act as the mouthpiece of reality, as if telling a child, "I don't want you to play in the street," will obscure the fact of the danger. Others say that expressing directions in the form of wishes is less effective than issuing commands, and under certain conditions, I can see sense in that as long as the command is phrased as such and not as a criticism: "Hurry up," and not, "Why do we always have to wait for you?"

Whatever the rationalization, I think the real reason is usually that parents want to escape personal responsibility for things they say that the kids don't like. They would rather that the children think that the parents are good than that they, the children, are good.

Another situation in which parental defensiveness leads children to feel shame and guilt comes about when a child asks the impractical or impossible. Fortunately, my parents were good about not making that mistake. When I was nine or ten, I was in Marshall Fields and was astonished to find an airplane not only on display but offered for sale. It was small but perfectly real. I had never been so near one before. My mother let me hang around it, and ask the airplane man questions. That evening, I told my father that we ought to buy one. He said that it cost so much that we couldn't afford it. He listened to my arguments seriously, but told me the facts. He also let me know that he thought it would be wonderful to have an airplane and he was sorry that he didn't earn enough money to be able to afford it. I think this response was unusual. Most parents in that situation say that the child is being stupid, crazy and selfish in wanting something that is out of reach. I am not sure what would have happened if my father had taken that approach, but I think it would have been different from what did happen: My aspiration to fly remained proud, magical and unconflicted, and when it was realized, it was as good as I had thought it would be when, as a child, I mooned over the Ercoupe in the department store.

Most children are not as lucky as I was. Requests for things they can't afford make many parents anxious and ashamed, emotions they quickly escape by blaming the children for asking. I think that girls in particular are told not to be so greedy. I think mothers often tell their daughters, but seldom their sons, "You don't need that," and say it in such a way as to convey, "It's bad of you to want that." Not only are they promoting a moralistic self-denial, but they are also promoting the defensive use of the word need because they are telling girls that a wish for something is not a good-enough reason to get it.

I may be wrong, but I think that many women have been brought up not to be assertive or competitive and so are prone to be critical and to be particularly wounded by criticism. If a person can't comfortably say, "I want such and such," she is likely to wait to see if it is forthcoming without its being requested. Indeed it's my impression that women are generally better than men at figuring out what someone would appreciate their doing and going ahead and doing it without being asked, but if that fails there may be trouble.

These days I am happy to see girls much more involved in sports than they were when I was in school. Women who grew up before they were encouraged to compete at something other than being good or popular, value their popularity more than men do. Not just loyalty, but solidarity with the group is a necessity. As a result, being criticized is a serious matter. Someone who criticizes you is not your friend, and for many women a large circle of friends is proof of worthiness and a source of power. I know this is a generalization to which there are many exceptions, but I believe there is truth in it.

I think that the young women who are growing up competitive with one another will share the advantage that men have had of more often being able to take a contradiction or a suggestion as a competitive challenge that can be met than as a threat to their social survival. Those who are comfortable with competition are less threatened by its being said of them that they try to be better than others, and they are able to more or less happily take part in struggles with others that are experienced as fair competitions. A lot depends on the ability of parents to compete with their children playfully. Parents who have to win or who think that they should never win both cause trouble. I think that children whose parents play games with them but don't try are often experienced as patronizing. I think children benefit from manageable losses. If the children are given enough of a handicap to win about half of the time and the adults try to win, the children will master losing as well as learning that their own efforts can be realistically successful. Adolescence, when the kids no longer need handicaps, is a particularly important time in this line of development. Ideally, parents still try hard to win but also take pleasure in the growth and development of their children and so are happy to find them tough competition.

Seemingly harsh criticism in a setting of happy competition can be fun and attractive. I think one of the reasons for the popularity of Klick and Klack, the Tappet Brothers, is that they call each other stupid and crazy with such good humor and understood affection. Debaters, politicians (Mayor Daley to the contrary), lawyers, and scholars can usually go after each other vigorously without personal injury and without becoming defensive. One of the ways that attack ads and political dirty tricks can be effective is that they give rise to an unseemly defensiveness on the part of the target. I think one of the reasons Bill Clinton survived so many attacks is that in the main he didn't become defensive. The one time he did, it led to his impeachment.

There is not a clear and easy distinction between competition that doesn't wound and criticism that does. Mainly it depends on the result. Some people can't stand to lose, and so for them there is no distinction, but most of us can stand to lose if we don't feel that in the process we have been disqualified from membership in the groups we value. If, as often happens, someone rows past me when I am rowing my fastest, I am disappointed, but still feel I'm a rower. Though I may be inclined to make a defensive excuse, such as, "I didn't get enough sleep last night," it isn't a strong inclination. But one time when I did something so clumsy that I tipped the boat over, I was sure the rowers who fished me out of the water must have considered me not a rower at all and I had a hard time not trying to find some exonerating explanation.

Unfortunately, much criticism within families takes forms that do tend to disqualify people from something important, such as the class of all people who are good spouses. The standard psychoanalytic advice to express feelings about behavior rather than facts about character is very helpful, though frequently not followed, even by those who often give others that advice.

Not all of the advice we give or imply is that good. Since psychoanalysts have often claimed that their theory and practice are not judgmental or even that they are value-free, the value implications of analytic technique are infrequently considered as such. Freud told his analysands that the basic rule they had to follow was to say everything they thought without any omissions or any editing, and I believe that principle is one of the most valuable parts of our technique. I no longer tell people they must say out loud every thought that comes into their awareness, but I do one way or another try to convey to them that it is my goal to make it safe for them to say absolutely anything to me. When that safety is achieved it is a wonderful thing, but it shouldn't be inferred that it would be a wonderful thing everywhere. Yet that seems to have happened a lot. As far as I know, the analytic or therapeutic situation is the only one where it is a good idea to say anything, which is one of the reasons I miss being in analysis.

The application of the basic rule to other situations is appealing, especially in love and marriage. In intensely romantic moments it can seem that the two people are so united in who they are and what they want, and so accepting of one another, that knowing each other through and through would be wonderful. One of the less than wonderful things that often happens first is telling each other about prior relationships—almost always a mistake in my opinion. It can be a good thing for people to discuss the broad outlines of what went wrong with an earlier marriage or something of the sort. In fact, I think people deciding on a new partner should have some idea of why the same thing isn't going to happen to them as happened to their predecessor, or of how to keep it from happening.

But details, especially sexual ones, probably should be omitted since they so regularly give rise to needless jealousy. Most of us are insecure enough about our attractiveness and sexual skill that we do better if reminded as little as possible of our being in a sexually competitive world. We don't necessarily have the illusion that we are the only one that our partner has known in that way, but it is good for most of us to ignore history and to know as little of it as we can. A related subject that should generally be suppressed in conversation with our romantic partners is our feeling attracted to anyone who is not our partner. I think that suppression is a good one to impose in any conversation with someone of the same gender as the person we feel attracted to, but it depends on the situation.

Another stated or implied analytic value is assertiveness. Unquestionably an ability to stand up for ourselves is vital, but so is judgment as to when and how to do it. I have known analysts and therapists who were passionately angry at spouses without much thought because they thought that passion was a good idea. One person I once worked with believed that it was necessary for him to tell his wife every dissatisfaction he had with her and on that principle informed her that she was too short. I asked what she could do about that, and he said he had thought that it was just important that she should know his feeling. Angry defensiveness is also often believed to be a good thing because it consists of feelings that will cause trouble if they aren't communicated. They almost always cause trouble if they are communicated. When people say mean things to one another, it will sometimes seem to both of them that repression is being undone, that they are finally learning the awful truth that was always there and silently causing trouble. No doubt we all are ambivalent about everyone we are attached to at all, but the nasty opinions that are used defensively in fights are mostly a new product of the fight itself or at least that have become newly significant now that they seem to be needed tactically.

So if I think saying anything that comes into one's mind and being assertive on most occasions can be bad lessons of psychoanalysis, I should say what I think the good lessons are. This is the Miss Manners part. The main ones I have in mind are: Never be defensive and be critical as little and as judiciously as possible. These are hard lessons to live by. So a corollary lesson is to get analyzed until you are secure enough to do it. Analysis, when it goes well, does help by increasing one's flexibility and strength, both of which are severely challenged when one is criticized. On the other hand, I have found that besides my many years on the couch I have benefited from the discipline I imposed on myself some years ago of trying never to be defensive when at the end of the couch. As with learning anything, you have to think about it rather deliberately at first before it will at all come naturally. The first and hardest thing to think about is that the criticism may well be correct, and is a chance to improve oneself. Almost all criticisms have at least a grain of truth to them, and recognizing them not only will teach you something worth knowing, but acknowledging them to the other person will decrease the interpersonal tension.

A person I know who is particularly skilled at working harmoniously in groups says that three of the most powerful words are, "I was wrong." Acknowledging the truth in a criticism need not imply accepting the whole criticism or the way that it was delivered, but those issues can often be ignored since angry people usually exaggerate and know it. So saying that you can see they are right in a particular way may satisfy them even if you don't acknowledge that you are always that way or that you are worse about that than anyone else.

I doubt that many people can always avoid being defensive. So it's important to recognize, as dieters and alcoholics need to, that a slip doesn't ruin everything forever. Any time you can catch yourself during or after the argument, say, "I was wrong," and start over again, things may start to improve.

Recently I did two of the worst things I do. Some people have trouble going to sleep. I am the opposite. I have trouble staying awake. The other afternoon, I nodded off as someone I work with was telling me something important. Reasonably enough, he said, "You're falling asleep!" I was so chagrinned and so sure that I had been hearing everything that even though I decidedly knew better, I said, "I think I heard everything you said," and I even started to read it back to him. That claim was a worse injury than the first one. It took some time to restore at all the person's trust in me, but that process began with my saying that he was right to complain of both the offense and the defense. If I had blamed the other person for my sleepiness, it would have been much worse and that kind of criticism is always a mistake. But when is being assertive productive, and how can it be done without being critical?

The most important principle is to take the risk and the blame. The wise saying that I associate with the one about the three most important words is one I heard almost twenty years earlier from a homeless person I worked with in a downtown clinic. He said that the most powerful action is just to ask. If you want something, take the risk of being rejected and criticized. Ask for it. Don't wait around to see if the other person does what you want without your asking, unless you are sure you can bear not getting what you want and that you won't feel compelled to complain about the other's thoughtlessness, or something like that. If the other person says that you are selfish to ask, agree to that, but don't necessarily withdraw the request. It seems like a good idea to me to say you are disappointed if you are strongly so, but otherwise drop it. If the other person explains why your request is a poor idea or explains why he or she doesn't want to do it, listen as open-mindedly as you can; and if you think they have a good point, say so with or without dropping the request.

Similarly, if asked to do something that you don't want to do, refuse without defending the refusal. If you are certain that you are unable to comply for practical reasons—psychological reasons don't qualify for this—say you are sorry but you can't, and explain why briefly unless that seems likely to be inflammatory. I believe this rule is good for intimate relationships. In the case of ordinary social connections I think the usual white lie, "I'm sorry, but I can't come that day," is preferable to the true but rude "don't want to." Be extremely sparing with the word *need* when making requests, and use it generously when asking someone else's wishes. Unless you are convinced that a refusal would cause damage you can't live with, don't say you need something, because doing so already hangs a potential criticism over the other person's head. But if you ask people what they need from you, you are taking the risk of being the bad person and are making it clear that you really want to know their wishes.

If you wish your spouse or your child to change something they do, say so. Do not tell them that they are doing the wrong thing or, worse yet, that they are bad people, and above all don't make a psychoanalytic interpretation of their behavior. Always psychoanalyze yourself. Sometimes psychoanalyze your family but keep the results to yourself except to do something to resolve the problem. Don't say, "You won't do what I want because you want to get even with me for not doing what you wanted," but see if you can offer something that will make up for your earlier refusal before you ask for anything else. If you feel very strongly about something you want changed, say that as calmly as possible. Saying quietly, "I am very angry or very disappointed because I wanted X," is less provocative and also stronger than shouting those or more blaming words. Statements about anger that are expressed temperately are usually more effective than outbursts, because you can't as easily be dismissed as childish or nutty.

I think one can do without criticizing others in almost all situations, except for situations of debate or ones like supervision where criticism is asked for. In those situations it is obviously advisable to phrase criticisms as opinion that may be in error, criticize actions or ideas and not character, and never say directly or by implication that the other person is not a member of the group they aspire to because they aren't doing things the way we do.

Saying these things puts me in a position to be strongly and immediately tested. I am sure that you have disagreed with things I have said, and I will try to listen to contrary opinions as openly and flexibly as possible.

Violence and the Wish to Belong

When the Forum Committee planned the meeting for 2002, they suggested that papers submitted that year deal with violence. My bias is to look at the need for security as a first cause of behavior, and I thought the events of 9/11/01 presented a good chance to see what could be done from that angle in an extreme case.

SOME YEARS AGO, A YOUNG MAN INVADED THE HOME of a Seattle family and, under the mistaken impression that they were Jews and Communists, killed all but one of them. One of my patients at that time knew the young man and had been with him shortly before the crime.

Both were members of a crazy right-wing group with basic ideas that ranged from the wrong-headed to the delusional. My patient had at first frightened me, because he talked of how he and his associates were thinking about assassinating public officials. I never took any protective action, since from the first time I heard these ideas they sounded to me more like group fantasies than actual plans. As things turned out, that impression proved to be correct.

The group imagined ways of acting together to do something they thought would be noble. The actual murderer did something horribly real, all by himself. He had talked vaguely about killing Communists, but no one took him seriously. My patient, though scarcely a happy person, was at his most nearly content as a member of this group where he had achieved some prominence and respect. The murderer was only barely accepted by the others because they thought he was strange and a bit embarrassing. He murdered the family because he thought he was doing something great, since the victims were dangerous enemies of America, but mostly he seemed to have been moved by the wish to prove to the club that he was worthy of full membership.

We usually think of the wish to belong as a natural and good feature of human nature. Alienation is considered a misfortune. Sociologists and political scientists have warned about the decreasing lack of community in the United States. At the moment, at least in January, 2002, as I am writing this, most people—including some with actual data—believe that the situation has improved. One of the important improvements is the increased regard and decreased suspicion across racial and ethnic lines.

When I was in New York in December, I noticed this change on the subway. Subway riding is one of my favorite pastimes. So I have a time-lapse image of social change based on my annual exposure to my fellow passengers on New York subways for a week about once a year, for many years. The picture has shown gradual improvement, from dangerous hostility ten or more years ago to safe and comfortable neutrality more recently. This year, the improvement jolted forward. Much of the time, I observed and participated in actual friendliness: cordial conversations across all kinds of identity lines between strangers or among groups. People were getting off the train saying, "Merry Christmas. Nice talking with you." I was moved, but not so much so as by the memorials around what used to be the World Trade Center and around neighborhood firehouses. Aside from the letters to people who died from their families, what brought tears to my eyes was the profusion of tributes from everywhere. It seemed as if not only all regions of this country, but also all parts of the world, were uniting in sympathy with the victims and admiration for the heroes.

What bothers me is the thought that these wonderful reactions would have been less if the buildings had simply caught fire and collapsed, and quite different if the people responsible had been members of a larger and more American group. Like Adolf Hitler and Hideki Tojo, Osama bin Laden is reassuringly different from any of us. We hate him and try to find and kill him not only because he hurt us so badly, but also because the effort unites us and makes us feel as if we belong to something grand.

I am just old enough to remember Pearl Harbor and, with increasing clarity, the four years that followed. One of my most cherished possessions was an American flag. Marching around the house with it felt like being a part of the most important thing in the world. It seems to me that everyone, not just impressionable small boys, felt the same way. People grumbled about rationing but submitted to it willingly and even with a certain enthusiasm. We sang stirring songs like,

> Hi ho, hi ho
> We're off to Tokyo.
> We'll wipe those Japs right off the maps,
> Hi ho, hi ho, hi ho.

Unfortunately, that kind of high-spirited unification depends on dehumanizing the opposing group. In the case of Japanese-Americans, pre-existing racist pseudospeciations—regarding others as non-human—made it easy for most Americans to accept their persecution. German-Americans were spared because they were members of the more favored Caucasian race, and so the dehumanization of the enemy in Europe was focused on Nazis, who, Lord knows, cooperated by committing large-scale inhuman atrocities. It was the good war because the other side was so bad. As many people have written, no subsequent war until this one has felt nearly so good, with the possible exception of the war against the war in Vietnam. That one, like the civil rights movement that preceded and informed it, seems to me to be pretty close to ideal; not only did immense numbers of diverse people unite effectively, but also, and most importantly, the enemy—Lyndon Johnson, Richard Nixon, and the rest—though dehumanized were attacked nonviolently.

The same principles seem to apply to the other side as well. The motives of the highjackers, their colleagues and bosses must be complex, but I believe that their joining Al Qaeda must have resulted in part from a wish to escape being nonentities by becoming a part of something not only significant but even holy, and more important than their individual lives.

There has been a good deal said and written about the fact of their suicide showing that they were crazy, but we should be cautious about this conclusion. Friends of mine in New York, who visited their neighborhood firehouse after the disaster, spoke with firefighters who had been there. These men said that as they were in their truck on the way downtown with new alarms coming in every few seconds, knowing the extreme danger of fires in towers, they thought that they were probably going to their deaths, but they went willingly. It could be argued that the ideal that united the firefighters, selfless courage devoted to saving others, is quite different from an ideal that leads to killing others, but this too would be misleading, since the armed forces of the United States and most of the rest of us have been quite enthusiastic about killing enemies in Afghanistan, and even if need be people who aren't enemies but have the bad luck to be living near them.

Though I know nothing first-hand about the men who have joined Al Qaeda, and my study of them has not gone much further than reading the *New York Times* and listening to NPR, it seems reasonable to believe that many of them were either odd ducks like Zacariah Moussaoui, Richard Reid and John Walker Lindh, or people who were more socially skilled but were connected to seriously disadvantaged groups.

For it to be worth killing and dying, the group one joins must be able to convey a conviction of significance to its members. The prospective convert must see the group as possessed of either power or a great ideal or, preferably, both. Osama bin Laden in his videotapes has emphasized both power and ideals by saying that men are attracted to the more powerful horse and that the success of the September attacks has produced great numbers of converts, and by portraying his struggle as pitting the just and faithful against the enemies of God.

His version of what God wants is remarkably similar to the versions of the many other fundamentalist leaders who have gained prominence in most religions over the last several decades. The bin Laden explanation of September 11 is pretty close to the Falwell explanation. These men (that is almost always the gender) don't like cultural diversity, and they want a return to strict and brutal enforcement of God's laws, which they know. Usually their claim is not that others don't know God's law, but that they are evilly defying it. The defiance that most outrages them has to do with the place of women in society. In their outrage, some of them have murdered women for having jobs, and others have murdered people for providing women with abortions.

About thirty years ago, I attended a World Congress of Social Psychiatry in Athens. The host agency was an institute for the study of families, and as hosts they made one of the main presentations. They reviewed their studies of men whose patriarchal status had been diminished by moving from the country to the city. That kind of move was increasingly common, because it was hard to earn a decent living in the rural areas, and there was at least the hope of jobs in Athens. When the men got to the city, three main things went wrong for them. They lost the support of their cronies in the village. Their women were exposed to new styles of family life. And it was easier for unskilled women than unskilled men to get work. Our hosts told us that many of these men were terribly angry, that it was difficult to resolve their grievances in working with the families, and the men were often violent. They said they believed that these conditions were worldwide and would lead to popular movements to restore men to their previous levels of power through fundamentalist religion.

It was one of the best predictions I have ever heard, one that I could easily relate to my old neighbors in Chicago, the Nation of Islam. The Black Muslim beliefs were appealing to black people because they promised redemption from humiliation by the white devils, and they were particularly appealing to black men who, after moving to Chicago, found themselves in the situation the Athenian psychologists described. Elijah Muhammad decreed that women be neither seen nor heard.

All over the world, men who haven't been particularly interested in religion before have joined newfangled, often fanatical religious groups in an effort to rejoin the patriarchy. Patriarchy, whether newfangled or old, implies violence against women. Why do men see women as the enemy? For one thing, most people want the lion's share and if they are bigger, stronger and more independent—not being as tied to childbirth and children—they can take over. Those who take over always cite something like the divine right of kings that proves that God wants them to be in charge.

But I believe there are more mysterious sources of misogyny. When I was four and five, I had nightmares about witches. These evil creatures had the power to make me helplessly paralyzed. One morning, as

I thought about the terror of the night, I suddenly recognized the witch in my dream was my beloved grandmother. I was amazed and horrified. I was aware of lots of reasons to hate and fear as well as love my mother, but it seemed to me there was nothing bad about my grandmother. It took me many years to figure it out. The two women were about equally present and important in the first eight years of my life. Of the two, my grandmother was by far the more indulgent and the one who was most likely—though both were pretty good at this—to overestimate me or to tell me that my various deficiencies didn't matter.

My grandmother, who read to me constantly, often from the *Saturday Evening Post*, once read me something about photographic memory. She said that she thought there should be phonographic memory as well. I asked if I had one of those talents, and she assured me that I had both. I thought that it would be wonderful to spend a night with her in bed, and pestered her to do so. She always said that it would be lovely but tonight was just not quite the right time, but sometime we would do it.

Outside of the house I had to deal with a pretty aggressive bunch of neighbor kids; I was the youngest kid on the block. The contrast between their opinion of me and my grandmother's was striking. When I lost in some competition, I generally felt that something not only undesirable but also downright unfair and wrong had happened. I had enough sense to keep that idea to myself. Usually I didn't run home but I wanted to, and my friends could see it in my demeanor and laughed at me. There are African societies in which little boys are kept very close to their mothers and given wonderful service until they are abruptly driven out at five or six and made to live in a communal boys' house. When I first heard accounts of how they were kept from running home to mother by the derision of the other boys, I knew just how they felt. I want to be a tough guy about as much as most, and so it is a terrible menace to have an enormous longing for sweet merger with someone who likes me tender and little.

What a diabolical power you women have over us poor men! We have only to look at or even just think of you, and you cast your spell. The horrifying thing is the way you can cause immense longing to well up from the center of our being; longing that makes no sense and that seems independent of our will or judgment. Mere sex appeal can be bad enough, but usually it is more than welcome because it poses little or no threat to our machismo; but lurking within the supposedly adult sexual fantasy is the remembered, fantastic, magically powerful giant, the mother of our earliest days with whom we are dying to merge. We can all identify with Superman, omnipotent and invulnerable unless exposed to kryptonite, those fragments of his mother planet, which were always said on the radio and in the comic books to make him powerless as a baby.

There are even worse things. My grandmother was a widow so I didn't have to contend with a grandfather, but she did have the temerity to pay attention to my sister and even to my mother and father. All three were a lot older and more capable than I was. For those of us fortunate enough to ever have lived there, paradise is lost through our learning we can't and don't even want to be merged with our caretaker, and worse yet it is lost through the realization that even though we need to be the one and only in the adult's life, we aren't.

It seems to me that Genesis can be read as a parable of separation-individuation; humans have a separate and independent will from God's will. That story is followed immediately by a parable of sibling rivalry. With great good luck we are fortunate enough to reach the point where we can more or less see our struggle against a parent for the love of the other parent as a scary but productive and even ultimately exciting competition. However, even then, there remains in us the old insatiable craving for the woman we are paired with to think we are her one and only, or at least the best she knows. If other men see her, they will be charmed as we are, and then terrible things might happen. We don't want occasions for comparisons to be made—especially intimate occasions. It's therefore best to keep them barefoot and pregnant or concealed in burqas, or something like that.

The *New York Times* printed an account of the early life of Zacariah Moussaoui, the twentieth highjacker, the one who couldn't get on the plane because he had been arrested in Minnesota after he tried to book airliner simulator time just to learn to make turns, not to take off or land. His mother was forced in her mid-adolescence to marry a stranger who took her to France, fathered several children with her and then deserted the family. She managed to keep a poor but independent and respectable life together by doing hard, menial work. One thing that made this possible was that she brought her sons up to do housework. According to the mother, who was interviewed, things were all right until the arrival of a cousin from the old country who was scandalized that Zacariah and his brothers made their own beds. He told them that it was sacrilegious for their mother to make them do that, and that they should be sure to have at least two wives each when they grew up so that they would be properly cared for. Though his mother doubts the charges against him, she said that Zacariah began to change then and became interested in fanatical Islamist groups into which he ultimately disappeared.

Though I believe that the wish to belong to misogynist groups is one of the sources of the violence of Al Qaeda and other groups, I also believe that colonialism and its aftereffects are an equally strong source. Even in this country, converts to fundamentalism seem to come predominantly from those groups that have been downwardly mobile because of such forces as the movement of jobs overseas. Colonialism of the past and the multinationalism of the present have denied much of humanity the basic necessities of life and any means of improving their condition. It would be a terrible mistake for me to say that psychology is the most useful approach to understanding the existence of fanatical redemptive groups, when economics and politics cause immense and needless suffering.

On the other hand, it is worth considering the psychology of imperialism. In this case, too, the wish to belong to a wonderful group and to pseudospeciate others out of the human race is part of the story. The closest look I've had at conquest and its results came in the decade I spent in the Indian Health Service. Until relatively recent times, the Bureau of Indian Affairs and its predecessors operated school systems designed to obliterate Native American culture and language. This effort was successful enough to have terrible effects in and of itself, but worse yet, it was based on the belief that Indian culture rather than the lack of economic opportunity and self-determination was the cause of reservation poverty.

During my time in the Indian health business, a factory was built with a government subsidy on one of the northern Plains reservations. Subsidy or not, it soon went broke because the employees were not regular in their attendance. The authorities connected with the project explained that it wasn't part of the tribal culture to work every day. Ultimately, new management came in and raised the dismal wages the workers had been paid, and it was amazing how that changed the cultural value system. People showed up for money worth showing up for.

I once made a visit to a Navajo home in company with a Bureau of Indian Affairs official. As we drove into the camp with all its signs of extreme poverty, he said, "Poor people have poor ways." It was important to him to believe that if he lived under the same constraints, he would do better than these poor people were doing.

This country would not exist were it not for the capacity of humans to believe other groups of humans to be less human than they are themselves. The invasion of Indian land and the importation and exploitation of slaves could not have been borne without the luxury of regarding natives of America and Africa as not really human. This attitude is one of the comforts of tribalism, which in fairness I should add was also enjoyed by the natives. There is no Navajo word for Navajo. Like most tribes, they simply say "human being." Members of other tribes are not called people. Words for others shade from the nearly human, "in-law," through the not quite so human, "friend," to the nonhuman, "enemy." Enemies could be raided with no more compunction than would be shown in slaughtering a sheep.

It is appealing to imagine that these distinctions, which are made by all groups in one way or another, derive from the distinction between what may or may not be eaten, a line which is arbitrary and varies greatly from one time and place to another. Since it is not so long ago that there were people who ate people, it represents some progress that now even enemies aren't eaten. In many cases, they might as well be for all the good it does them not to be.

Increasingly over the centuries, pseudospeciation was a necessary but not a sufficient cause for murder, rape and pillage. The inferior group had to do something harmful to the invaders before the invasion was felt to be truly justified. To my distress, the Vietnam War was popular among the Navajos when I was working on the reservation. One exception was my nephew by adoption. One night in a Native American Church meeting, Eddie Lee was praying, and asked God for an end to the war. He said that as far as he could see the United States was behaving just as it had toward the Indians. They appointed chiefs who, in return for the honor, signed treaties with the United States; and when people who didn't recognize the phony chiefs or their right to sign land away broke the treaties, the army came after them for treaty violation.

The applicable parable is Jack and the Bean Stalk. Jack invades the Giant's home, steals his most valuable possession and kills him. The implied justifications for these crimes are that giants aren't human, and that when Jack breaks in, the Giant threatens to kill and eat him. Worse yet, the Giant's saying that he smells the blood of an Englishman can be construed as a threat against the empire, even though there is no indication in the story that the Giant has ever gone down to earth and threatened anyone, English or not. I do not know if the story is popular in India, but I certainly hope not.

Like Jack, England managed to conquer enemies many times its size. Apart from their technological advantages—the bean stalk, the Royal Navy—there must have been other factors that made them and the innumerable other imperialists so formidable. Why were they so sure of themselves, and so violent? I believe that groups which unite against an enemy are filled with a horrible intensity because uniting in that way uniquely aligns many of our most powerful fears and desires.

Situations in which people become enraged can be seen as taking place along a continuum defined at one end by shame, injuries to standing or personal worth, and at the other by the wish for goods, services or safety. Generally, the anger that comes from injuries to worth, which are often symbolic injuries, is the worse kind, sometimes called narcissistic rage. It is more implacable than the anger we mobilize just to get something we want. In the Book of Esther, we read that the king's prime minister, Haman, was shamed by Mordecai's refusal to bow to him. This shame completely ruined Haman's ability to enjoy life, which he felt could only be restored by the destruction of the whole group, the Jews, who also wouldn't bow. On the other hand, anger occasioned by appetites other than pride is more easily ended. If I want the last piece of cake and you take it, I don't want to kill you; I just want cake, and if you give me the piece or maybe just half of it, my anger disappears.

Groups formed by principles of exclusion tap both kinds of rage. We want homeland security and we want revenge. If we can find Osama and do something to him, it will serve both purposes. Revenge is desired as much for the symbolic injury as for the real, even though the real injury was horribly severe. Nobody does that to us! We're the superpower. Losing an embassy on another continent is pretty bad, but a major attack on our largest city is a completely unacceptable contradiction to who we think we are. As long as there are people out there who can do that to us, our sense of ourselves is spoiled and can only be restored by their destruction. Even if we could somehow assure ourselves that defensive measures had made us invulnerable, we would not be satisfied.

One's feelings about cherished self-definitions are like one's feelings about a white dress. An ink spot, even if it leaves ninety-nine percent of the fabric untouched, spoils the whole thing. The existence of Al Qaeda would remain a disfigurement even if they couldn't do anything more to us. They already did something, and if they get away with it our sense of our national identity is unacceptably stained. We have formed ourselves into a newly enthusiastic exclusionary group: United We Stand against those inhuman weirdos. Our fury is of both kinds. We want to be safe up in the air in planes and office buildings, and we want to get even.

In our righteous anger we, or at least some of us, will take great risks or make terrible sacrifices. Our special forces, no less than John Walker Lindh or Zacariah Moussaoui, are willing to give up their lives fighting for something bigger than themselves. Each individual's sense of who she or he is can be infinitely expanded. Devotion to an ideal such as American Freedom or Islam and the Muslim Peoples, and a conviction of all for one and one for all in a fighting group, redefine people's identities as including more than their individuality. As we see almost every day, suicide bombers and others go more than willingly to their individual deaths for the sake of the survival of a greater than individual self.

It is worth noting that absolutely anything can be idealized, and that it is the force of idealization that is the same from case to case, not the force of the thing, idea, or group idealized: abolition of slavery or its continuation, free silver or the gold standard, civil rights or majority rule. Devotion to an ideal can sometimes lead to highly individualized, dangerously unpopular behavior such as Zola's defense of Dreyfus or Scopes's teaching Darwin's theory of evolution; but such self-sacrifice is more common when the ideal is not only popular but also defines a large group.

Few people live more or less continually feeling that their being a part of something much greater transcends their individual identity, but moments when one feels that way are treasured and sought. Experiences range from the mild appeal of clichés about the national holidays and the national sports to a sense of union with the infinite; but in any case, the ability to feel oneself expanded to include like-minded others and noble principles leads to many of the best and worst actions people ever undertake.

The power of exclusionary groups also derives from their being able to combine both of our most basic kinds of fear in a way individuals generally can't do by themselves. We fear being injured and we fear being left. People can be seen as sorting themselves into the classes of those who would rather be hurt than abandoned (who can conveniently be referred to as the depressed) and those who would rather be left than damaged (who can conveniently be called the paranoid). A grand division of humanity like this one is a useful oversimplification. It isn't a question of either/or. People range along a continuum between the two poles, and there is also variation in how accurately people predict either kind of misfortune. Another complication is that people vary from one time in their life to another and from one situation to another, but decisions we make all the time come down to whether we fear one thing more than the other.

Injury and abandonment take an infinite variety of forms and severity. The variety of things meant by *castration* is a good illustration. When we speak of the fear of castration, we sometimes mean simply the real mutilation, but in the bad old days men used to speak of women castrating then by thwarting their sexual or even organizational ambitions and therefore causing them shame.

Usually the idea of castration combines real and symbolic meaning. The loss of a man's genitals would be awful because the loss or damage to any physical part is awful, but especially because the genitals are a particularly cherished part involved in pleasurable and important activities. Beyond anatomy and physiology, they are a symbol of one's standing—one's big cajones. After the World Trade Center went down, there was talk on both sides of the war about the castration of New York, and the metaphor worked well because it captured both the real and the symbolic damage.

Injuries, then, include everything from mild physical pain to the loss of whatever defines one as important—from an athlete's pulled muscle to a general being broken to the ranks. We fear being injured by someone assaulting us, but much more often we fear being injured by someone criticizing us. Anything that invalidates our idea of who we are is an injury. Since I think that what I am writing is correct, if you think otherwise you will be invalidating me to some degree and I will be inclined, as I said last year, to become defensive; but on the other hand, apart from the merits of your critique as I perceive it, I might decide not to risk losing you as a friend and so I would be inclined to agree with you.

Abandonment seems to me the older and more horrible fear, but this probably just says that I am more depressed than paranoid. I do not allow myself to remember clearly the terror I suffered when my parents left me, but I can clearly remember the counterphobic cheerfulness with which I left the house to be picked up by the preschool car, and the way each time I left I said goodbye many times as a precaution. The main way that I can grasp the power of this fear is by a sound always fresh in my memory, the wail of panic my son, then about three, emitted when I started the car one day as he walked around nearby, and he concluded that I was about to drive away without him.

Fear of loss of relationship operates most of the time without specific threats from those whom we don't want to lose. We are moved by fantasies of losing others or their affection, fantasies that start when we consider opposing them in any way. If another person asks us to do something we would rather avoid doing, or criticizes us, or takes precedence over us, or does any of the many other unpleasant possibilities, we more or less automatically imagine what will happen if we don't agree, and we depressed types do agree, while our paranoid brethren refuse.

I think that the crucial time when people go to one side or the other of this divide is at about two years of age when they learn to say no. Ideally, parents welcome the development of their children's independence, and respond with pride and pleasure whenever possible and with gentle but firm opposition when necessary. In such a wonderful case, the child is likely to go through life with a minimum level of both fears, and relative freedom to choose between them.

Unfortunately, no one is perfect, especially not in this particularly difficult parental task, and many people fall far short of perfect. Overindulgence or weak vacillation in the face of temper tantrums is likely to produce a preference for winning even at the cost of love. The same may result from excessive harshness, especially if it is inconsistent. In such cases the child is likely to develop an attitude of angry rebelliousness, as opposed to the imperiousness of the spoiled.

Children who are abused or neglected almost always feel they are to blame for their fate, and try hard to please even unpleasable parents, unless they get some group support from other abused and neglected children, in which case they may become angry specimens of the paranoid type. Parents who are hurt by their children's opposition and control them by the induction of guilt are particularly likely to produce members of the depressive group.

These formulations are schematic and overly simple. One of the infinitely numerous, complicated versions is the one in which parents respond favorably only to the narrow range of behavior that fits their idea of what kind of child will properly confirm the parents' own success and importance. The children are likely to feel that their existence is in danger if they don't fulfill their parents' ambitions, and they may feel throughout life that they have no choice but to maintain their standing at all costs, including the cost of relationship.

The paranoid–depressive character distinction correlates with another basic distinction of motivation. Much of what guides us takes the form either of ambitions or of ideals. Our ambitions drive us and our ideals lead us. Ambitions develop from that early stage of life when our adoring parents idealize us, if we're lucky. Ideals are a complex derivative of the slightly later stage when we idealize our parents. Generally, the preference for status over friendship corresponds with a predominance of ambitious goals over idealistic ones, and vice versa.

An exclusionary group has the unique power to accommodate all these various kinds of people. Al Qaeda united against us, we united against them, and both our groups satisfy the depressive goal of interpersonal security and the paranoid goal of maintaining self-esteem at all cost.

So both sides are fueled by both fears, by both kinds of rage, by both ambition and idealization, and by the appeal and strength of personal expansion to include ideals and an idealized group in each member's sense of self.

With all of these motives strengthening their solidarity and their wish to do violence to one another, it seems unlikely that either side will give up or calm down. If there are no more terrorist attacks, American fervor will probably lessen. One difference between September 11, 2001, and December 7, 1941, is that after Pearl Harbor the United States continued to suffer humiliating defeats for some time. Now, in January, 2002, I read in the paper that terrorism has fallen to number two in the main worries of the American public. It seems likely that there will be more attacks on both sides, and the danger is that we will be involved in an endless feud that can never be won, as appears to have happened in the Middle East. As we see in the case of Israel and the Palestinians, one outrage leads to another in a dismal spiral of disaster.

Sometimes, such wars end in the more or less total defeat of one side, and sometimes the losers identify with the victor and get absorbed into the exclusionary group that defeated them. This happened repeatedly with the Roman Empire and, after World War II, happened also with the American Empire, but imperialism has its limits as a solution to the problem of violence on a large scale.

One thing that I think we analysts should be careful to avoid is giving psychological explanations for the crimes, follies and misfortunes of humanity, when they can be used as rationalizations for ignoring the economic and political causes. Since we are supposed to help people be aware of reality, it is an important goal for us to help people see how their pseudospeciations and other distortions support national and corporate policies that victimize vast numbers of people. We have a tradition of skepticism and thought, and both need to be promoted because people who think deeply about what is going on and what they are told about it are less likely to join up blindly in some horrible crusade.

Psychoanalysis, sociology and cultural anthropology have spent the last century showing that differences among people are more superficial and arbitrary than real and basic, and so we are part of a movement away from xenophobia. Like everyone else, we need to use every tool we possess to bring about change that leads to justice and peace.

It isn't easy to see how this can be done. From time to time, people say that humanity can substitute its common enemies—pestilence, war and famine—for human ones, and unite in trying to defeat them. I don't think it works. The joys of belonging to an exclusionary group can't be generated by excluding abstractions or even viruses. Maybe enemies from outer space would work, as they do in the movies, but we can't count on their showing up and we probably wouldn't like it if they did.

It seems to me that technological developments are helping to some extent, at the same time that they make violence ever more lethal. Movies, television, the Internet and rapid long-distance transportation have all tended to make the world's peoples more acquainted with one another, and more alike. This seems to make it more difficult to see others as inhuman enemies, but it isn't impossible even at close quarters and with similar groups, as can be seen in the Balkans. Nevertheless, it is encouraging to see European nations that have fought one another for millennia growing ever more united. Maybe this can happen worldwide, as we hoped after World War II.

A homogeneous humanity all talking, dressing, eating and, worst of all, thinking the same is not attractive. Maybe some partial set of similarities will come to be. We can at least hope that humanity will learn that all people are more human than otherwise, and that no one should be excluded from the species.

Affects and Motives

A few years after the "Mindless" paper, it seemed to me that I needed to tie up some loose ends in the ideas I had written about then, and I wanted to see what I could do with a problem: I agree with just about everyone I know that we do best when we pay most attention to feelings, but I had come to see feelings as secondary to motives, rather than as motivating in and of themselves. This talk was written before I had become at all used to the evidence piling up of how bad a blunder it was to invade Iraq.

O NE OF MY MOTIVES FOR SUBMITTING A PAPER EACH year for presentation at the Forum is that imagining this congenial audience allows me a fantasy dialogue in which I can sort out my thoughts on some subject that interests but confuses me. Long before I stand before you and see your expressions of understanding or puzzlement, agreement or opposition, and hear your verbal comments, your presence in my thoughts gives me the means of making a series of mental experiments in which I combine words and phrases and see if you get the point.

I want to start with an example to illustrate the complexity of the causes of any action. I had been thinking that I would use some ordinary daily occurrence, but each day as I have become more demoralized by the news of impending war and have thought about the horrible events that would probably begin before the meeting and would be then distracting us, I decided to use an example from another time of war and death.

In 1969, my brother-in-law George, a second lieutenant in the U.S. Army, was in the Mekong Delta commanding a company of the Army of the Republic of Vietnam. Each day George and his men were taken by truck to some place in the marshy countryside, which they explored until they were attacked. They and the Vietcong would fight until enough people were killed on each side, and then the trucks would come back and take them home.

It was an aggravation to George's commanding officer that he was given trucks to carry his troops, while the colonels who commanded American soldiers had the use of helicopters. He devoted much of his time and energy to campaigning for equal treatment.

One day he succeeded. George and his company flew in style into the site of their patrol. Unfortunately, later that day as they crossed a clearing they were met by a much larger contingent of the Vietcong, and were forced to retreat into the shelter of the jungle. Lying low behind trees and thick vegetation, they were able to hold off the other Vietnamese. To George's joy, he spotted a road in the jungle. He called headquarters and asked that trucks be sent on this road to pick them up, but his commanding officer would have none of it. "If I don't use the helicopters, they'll never let me have them again," he said.

George pleaded. The helicopters could only land in the clearing where they, the ARVN soldiers and George, would be fully exposed to the Vietcong guns. The commanding officer said he didn't care, he was going to use the helicopters.

He did, and when they landed, two were destroyed and almost everyone was wounded or killed. George was hit in the thigh, and his femoral artery was severed. He fell and was on the point of bleeding to death, but the pilot of one of the surviving helicopters was his friend and, risking everything, came back for him. He had a cardiac arrest en route, but was resuscitated and is now alive and well in San Diego.

What can I say about the motives of the commanding officer? First of all, they were banal. In millions of places at this moment, people are making terrible decisions for similar reasons. Probably only hundreds of these choices will result in someone's death. Thirty-three years ago, when George told me this story, I had many more idealizations in effect than I do now, and I was shocked. I was aware that doing something stupid out of petty vanity was routine, but I hadn't thought that when it mattered so much it would still be business as usual. Medical school internship and residency should have finished off that illusion, but they had done so only partially.

But to return to the commanding officer: Did he want his men to be killed? Is his decision an example of the inexorability of the death instinct? It could be cast that way, but I think it is more helpfully seen as an example of the inexorability of mediocrity. I could also describe this multiple murder as an example of narcissistic rage resulting from the CO's being dissed by the transport authorities, but this doesn't do much to explain the awfulness of his action, because he was not enraged nor blinded by rage. He was just a jerk doing his stupid thing more or less dispassionately. He had made it one of the important aims of his life to get helicopters—not, I would think, because he had worried since childhood about his penis being too small and weak and therefore loved having powerful things that rose into the air by themselves. I think he was shamed by being assigned Vietnamese soldiers instead of American ones, and shamed by his not being given a status symbol which his colleagues got.

It makes some sense to think that his competitiveness over a symbol was based on a wish to have a larger, better penis than his father and brothers had, but this explanation doesn't get us very far, either, because almost anyone will react strongly to being accorded less status than his or her supposed equals. If I look around at the Forum, for example, and see that the other speakers are drawing much bigger crowds than I am, I will be distressed. Not distressed enough to kill, but maybe just as distressed as George's colonel, who I believe did not think of himself as killing anyone. I believe that the lethality of his shame was due in part to his being in a position in which people's lives lay around him, so that a slight gesture of his could sweep them away as easily as I could knock a glass of water from the podium. I think he killed because of a lack of imagination.

We all are prone to think that everything happens to us. Once I was eagerly awaiting a letter, but as luck would have it there was a terrible riot in the New Mexico State Penitentiary at Santa Fe. Many prisoners and guards were tortured and killed. When the state police and the National Guard successfully concluded their siege of the barricaded prisoners, a large number of cadavers was put into body bags, loaded onto a large truck and taken to the State Medical Examiner's office, which was next door to my office at the University of New Mexico School of Medicine.

The mailman arrived just as the truck from Santa Fe was being unloaded, and the sight made him so sick, he had to go home and didn't deliver my letter. Everything happens to me.

I hope you will think I am joking, and I am but not so much as I would like you to believe. My extreme disappointment that the mail didn't come was in the foreground. Santa Fe was in the distance, and I didn't identify much with the prisoners and guards. If the riot had been in Karachi, even if I had heard of it, I would have given it even less thought, which might be unfeeling but would probably be desirable. Someone I know is unable to see any suffering as distant. If she hears of a sparrow falling in China, she is as distressed as she would be by personal suffering. It makes life much too hard for her and distracts her from her own life.

George's colonel was at the opposite extreme. To him, the loss of some Vietnamese men and a second lieutenant was a small and distant matter compared to the possible disaster of his losing his helicopter privileges. In avoiding that disaster, he had the whole array of human capacities for blinding himself to what was inconvenient to see—he could tell himself that maybe George was wrong, maybe George was a coward and this would teach him a lesson, and so on.

Did this make the colonel a bad man? Yes, but I do not think what made him bad was a seething cauldron of unconscious rage that got the better of his meager defenses. I think that what was wrong with him can be described as a failure to perceive a situation with a larger perimeter than his own immediate interests. No doubt, such self-centeredness is a terrible thing, but it is a common thing. In the ordinary course of life as it is and has been lived in most times and places, people rarely deal with those with whom they don't identify. To the colonel, the ARVN soldiers were gooks; George was a stranger. If it had been the colonel's family and friends in the jungle, he might have made a different decision.

I am afraid the bloodiness of my example will distract you from the point I am trying to make: In order to understand other people's behavior, it is more useful to know how they see the world than to know the basic forces that are driving them. This idea is paradoxical. We have been trained to look for the affect, and indeed in our daily work we are rewarded when we do so by seeing our field of interchange with the people we talk with widen and deepen. We are in the habit of regarding our work as being mostly about emotions. Am I claiming that the facts or alleged facts are more important than the feeling? Sort of. In order to make sense of this claim, I need to discuss the nature of affects.

As always, the rule I make for myself in discussing psychology is that I can use no concept of mind or self or any of their alleged components. I am only allowed to talk about people, their physical components and their activities. I can only talk about people's experience as an activity. Consciousness is a coordination of bodily activities which results in a somewhat unified combination of motions, tensions and other physical states toward a perception of ourselves in the world. We ourselves are not the audience for this perception. Sometimes other people—real or imagined—are, and then the perception is likely to be more detailed, precise and (at least partially) verbalized because we think of the words we would use in telling about it.

The noun *perception* is a useful abstraction, but its verb is closer to reality. Perceiving is one of the main things we do. It is one of the main categories of thought. Thoughts are not things but patterns, in the same way that a song is not a thing but a pattern of sound which is produced by things and can be represented by things. As I sit at the computer, thinking about how to express myself and what you might object to, I am pleased and somewhat inconvenienced by a small cat's insistence on sitting in my lap and purring. My awareness of her presence includes my well-established sense of persons and of cats. It would be fun to specu-late about her awareness, but I only have forty-five minutes so I will leave her subjectivity, as they say nowadays, out of it.

I think of my sense of people and cats, and so forth, in terms of things I could do. Just as from moment to moment I am relying without thinking about it (until right now) on the ability of my fingers to move about the keyboard, in the same way my sense of myself and the cat is a reliance on the ability I have, if need be, to name myself and the cat, to describe what a person is, what a lap is and so on. I don't need to do so, because you all are familiar with people, laps and cats. But many of you are not familiar with my system of mindless psychoanalysis, and so I have to actually do this describing. My descriptions consist, as I type, of imagined speech and actual keystrokes. Freud said that thought was trial action, and this is where I started my mindless career. At the moment now I am moving my fingers, and I am moving my vocal apparatus in a much smaller, quieter way. Maybe I am just moving electrons, ions, and neurotransmitters in my speech and hearing centers and other parts of my brain, but it feels like I am varying the tension in my vocal cords, chest and throat. When I was little, I actually spoke when thinking, and I learned, though sometimes I still forget, to think without moving my lips, much as later I learned to read without moving my lips.

The affective aspect of thought consists of bodily changes corresponding to nonverbal communications which are invisible, in the same way that verbal thought consists of bodily changes that are not audible. For example, I can subvocally shout rather than speak, and I can imagine myself pounding on the podium as I do so. Imagining myself pounding consists of activities in my motor cortex and other brain areas, and tension in my pounding muscles.

I think I have implied, but perhaps I need to state explicitly, that all of this activity called *thinking, feeling, imagining* or just generally *being conscious* takes place in an interpersonal context. We know that an infant raised by a machine (or a machine-like human) providing food, cleanliness and a safe temperature—but no communication—would die. We are also learning the details of how the development of the brain and the organization of its activities depend on interpersonal exchange.

My knowledge that I am a person named Bob, and that what has now jumped off my lap and gone upstairs is a cat named Ashley, were all acquired in interaction with my mother, the other characters of my childhood and (as to Ashleyness) my wife and son. My experience of Ashley getting into and out of my lap was constructed around telling you about it, but any time she gets in my lap my knowledge of the situation consists only of potential communications to someone real, remembered, hoped for or otherwise imagined.

I believe that all of our awareness consists of acts of perceiving; that is, organizing a summation of our seemingly total activity. The activity of my retinas, optic nerves, sensory nerves in my thighs, and so on, is organized into *cat-in-lap*. Most of what we call *affects* are communications to other people, be they real, remembered, or imagined. At the moment, I am feeling sad because my wife just came home and we spoke about the space shuttle crash, which happened a few hours ago. Feeling sad consists of, among other things, my telling you I am thinking about a tragedy, and of a feeling of heaviness in and around my eyes, a sense of heightened activity in my tear glands—subtearful crying—and a downward pull at the corners of my mouth. Just as the words I think and type are actions designed to communicate something to you, the tensions in my face are communications. I am not sure that I will feel sad when I read these words aloud to you, but if I do, you will see my communications of mild distress and of a wish to see that you too feel regret, anger and sympathy.

It seems to me that all people, and maybe all complex animals, have a repertoire of powerful communicative behaviors. Expressions, postures, and patterns of action and sound are all pretty consistently meaningful and available, regardless of culture and to some extent species. Dogs naturally growl and we know what they mean. Crying, smiling and laughing are natural behaviors which arise interpersonally, universally and spontaneously, and have powerful effects. We respond more or less automatically to these behaviors, and we either like or dislike experiencing someone doing these things depending on the pleasing or distressing effect they produce in us. The experience of being sad, angry, impatient, bored, confused (the last two come to mind at the moment because they are what I fear I may see you communicating to me)—the experience of these feelings is the real or imagined performance of these nonverbal communications, plus real or imagined gross movements, such as getting up and leaving, which would express something about one's state.

Conscious emotion is activity. What about unconscious emotion? The notion of feeling something that we don't feel is odd, but can be justified by the common observation that people express emotions without knowing they are doing so. No one can know for sure what someone else is conscious of, and so I can't convince myself that there are unconscious feelings by telling someone that he is angry or sad, or by his saying he hadn't noticed the emotion until I mentioned it. It is convincing to me, however, when someone tells me that I am feeling a certain way and suddenly I become aware of something my face or arms or eyes were doing which I hadn't noticed before.

The reasons for such a state of affairs are complicated and various.

For example, if I am feeling that this talk isn't going very well, I may want to stir your sympathy by telling you that your poor response is making me sad, but doing so would make me ashamed because it doesn't fit my ambition to be, or at least appear to be, mature and somewhat self-sufficient. I might adopt a compromise strategy of not telling you in words how I feel, but visibly struggling to look cheerful, and failing. Then I would get credit for at least not wanting to ask for sympathy but doing so involuntarily because I feel so bad. I could do so because — as I just proved — I can imagine telling you about it. If such behavior seemed so awful to me that I couldn't imagine telling anyone about it, I couldn't think it, but I could still do it and then you would know something I wouldn't know myself about my affective state.

Sometimes we impulsively say things that a moment before we thought we weren't going to say. More commonly, we show a nonverbal sign that we want to think we didn't mean to reveal. The reciprocal situation can also occur. I can be aware of my fantasy of looking sad, but manage not to give in to the wish to do it, and so I would know that I was sad, but you wouldn't.

But there is another kind of unconscious emotion. For example, if I had been brought up in a military household (to continue my obsession) where weakness was never tolerated, I would not only be unaware of my wish to evoke your sympathy, but also I wouldn't do it. Speaking with me after my talk, one of you might mention to me that I looked distressed as I was speaking, and then with shame and anxiety I might recognize that I had wanted to touch you or scare you, or something. Here, finally, I have got back to the question of how following the affect leads to an understanding of a person's situation as he or she knows it. I would be aware, and might say that I was disappointed that people didn't like the paper.

The example brings us to motives. What does it mean to say that I wanted to scare you? In addition to feelings that are real or imagined communications, there are experiences which we also call feelings that are tensions of one kind or another.

My grasp of current neurophysiologic research is rudimentary, but I think it would make sense psychologically and physiologically to say that at all times our brains are receiving an enormous amount of data from various sensory organs, internal and external, and synthesizing patterns from them. I suppose that these patterns are largely formed cortically and are then scanned by various other parts of the brain, cortical and more central. When more central portions of the brain recognize significant patterns, they signal the cortex as to what kind of response is in order.

The significance of each pattern is determined by a combination of innate and learned values. For example, *need to eat something* is innate, but *there in the store is something good to eat* is a combination of innate and learned.

As I imagine this system, an enormous number of patterns are formed all the time, and almost all of them are dismissed as unimportant, and give rise to no further activity. Some, however, give rise to a signal of danger or desire. Signals can be mild or emergent: from *that would be okay*, to *have to have that*, or from *avoid that*, to *annihilation is imminent*.

My hypothesis is that under stimulation from below, the cortex forms various patterns of action which are sent back to the midbrain, which evaluates them and generates new signals that amount to thoughts ranging from *that won't work*, to *do that at once*. There must be a great range of such signals varying not just in intensity but in urgency, ranging from *get your hand off that hot thing instantly* to *must bend every effort to getting that eventually*.

The patterns formed in response to tensions of need or desire amount to theories and plans. Theories are competing beliefs about the world and our place in it. If I am frightened, for example, because someone seems likely to do something to me that I would hate, I will generate various versions of the situation which differ, among many other variables, as to the degree of the other's ill-will and our relative strengths. Various parts of my brain compare these versions to past events and to my sense of my own capacities.

What we call *mood* is largely the tone of optimism or pessimism of the brain centers that estimate our chances. New experience of success or failure can modify our sense of what we can accomplish. So can biochemistry. My observation of people taking SSRIs or other antidepressants is that they feel the world is less dangerous and they have a greater standing in it than when they aren't taking drugs. Cocaine and the amphetamines have a similar effect. It appears to me that mania and severe depression are similar, in that some force other than immediate experience is influencing the tone of whatever part of the brain evaluates a person's chances.

However well or badly that part of the brain is working, the possible kinds of action it can select are fight, flight, surrender, hope for mercy, and so on. If I think I am sure to win, I will feel calm and commanding. My planned and then my actual behavior will be confidently assertive. If I think I have a chance but it isn't a certainty, I will feel angry and anxious and will be more desperately active: threatening, guileful, assaultive, or in some other way combative. If I think I will lose, but have a chance to avoid the conflict, I will feel terrified and run like hell. If I think I will lose and escape is impossible, but submission will lessen the pain, I will feel depressed and probably guilty and ashamed, and will plead or propitiate, or something like that.

In the worst case, if I feel I will lose and there is no possibility of escape or propitiation, I will panic. I don't mean just that I will be quite scared, but that I will feel I am about to be destroyed even if actual death is not threatened. This situation is the traumatic state in which unbearable tension to do something is present along with no possible course of action, and the baffling counter-tensions disorganize one's ability to perceive oneself and the world. As our ability to do so is destroyed, so are we. We may reconstitute ourselves afterward, but we will be changed by the trauma.

Each experience of such horror remains as an unbearable presence, really or potentially felt. A less-than-traumatic bad experience can be thought about and worked on. If someone tells me these ideas are stupid, I can decide that the critic is stupid and wrong, and simply be angry and dismissive. If he or she convinces me that I am being stupid, I will hate it, and will go through all the ordinary stages of mourning: denying that the unpleasant words were said or that I care about them; trying to figure out how to have them taken back; imagining that I never wrote this paper; and so forth. When I see that none of these maneuvers works, I will finally simply be angry and sad that the experience can't be escaped, and after some time I will be resigned.

When George was lying in the jungle, bleeding, he was in the traumatic state. Today he can give a somewhat detached account of the events of that day, but I don't think he will ever be able to think his way back into the terror without becoming panicky, and he will never be resigned and forget. It will often be out of his thoughts, but it will come back when he is reminded, sometimes when he is asleep, or if any situation approaching helplessness occurs.

George remained sane, but if severe and repeated trauma occurs, many do not. Trauma can occur in what appears to another person to be a benign situation. Many adolescents, for example, because of their beliefs about what behavior is acceptable, get caught between their emergent sexual needs and the need to survive psychologically. They feel they have to find some intimate relationship and some sexual satisfaction, but are so insecure that they are convinced they will be so rejected as to produce annihilating humiliation, and they are therefore in an inescapable dilemma. When the need is great enough and the fear just as great, then they will have an awful experience of disorganization they can only escape by reconstituting themselves in simpler, cruder terms, and giving up on the process of checking the reality of their perceptions by the reactions of others.

We all know that it is hard to treat people who have sustained real trauma, particularly if it is repeated and early. The precariousness of their ability to perceive their situations as bearable makes it inevitable that an intense relationship like analysis or therapy is bound to include numerous occasions when some—often unavoidable—failure of the tact or gentleness of the therapist recreates the traumatic state. Tolerance of the often furious response of the person, and efforts to understand what happened in an atmosphere of acceptance, can sometimes slowly bring the original damaging experiences into a safe interpersonal world where they can be borne and finally worked through.

This kind of work is a particularly clear example of the advantages of focusing on the situation instead of the affect or, worse yet, the drive. If the analyst interprets the other person's need for care and tact as a demand for control of the treatment or an attempt to destroy it, retraumatization is likely to be made worse. If the analyst can demonstrate how the person's reaction is the only possible one to have in the situation that occurred, there is a chance for progress.

Besides mourning when people have had awful experiences which can't be undone, there is another basic way that we help them. Traumatic and other undesirable experiences influence the optimism or pessimism of the systems that judge whether trial actions in thought will succeed or not. Any person's array of possible perceptions of her or his interpersonal situation is determined by past experience. Almost everyone's repertoire of versions of the world includes ones in which other people are friendly and receptive, and ones in which others are hostile and rejecting. Versions of one's own social standing can have a similar range from attractive and powerful to ugly and weak. The degree to which any version seems likely depends on past experience, among other things.

Here is another crucial example in which following the affect leads to knowing the situation that explains how the other person is feeling and behaving. Emotional outbursts or, more commonly, tiny hints of a disavowed feeling can lead us to direct the conversation to the terrible beliefs that limit the other person or lead to trouble. Even more importantly, they can lead to almost undetectable hopes. As Joseph Weiss and Harold Sampson point out, people come to therapy with the unconscious plan of disconfirming their pathogenic beliefs.

I want to return to the way brain centers generate tension signals. The principles that determine what kind of a signal is generated can be described as *fears* and *appetites*. Many lists of both have been formulated. I doubt that any list can come close to covering all the possibilities, but here is my adaptation of various versions of fear I know: primary fears of death, the stimulation of the pain fibers of sensory nerves, abandonment, control by others, loss of social importance and influence, injury, shame and guilt. The last two should perhaps be disqualified as not primary, because they are affects derived from fears higher on the list. Shame is the experience of the failure of security, and guilt the threat of punishment. Freud and others argue that guilt becomes independent of fear of punishment by becoming fear of the superego. Since mindlessness doesn't allow for mental organs like the superego, I prefer to say that we refine our fears from the expectation of being punished by our parents to beliefs in such things as a just God, Hell, or some more abstract moral force of the universe. It has been my experience that many more people give up their belief in God than their belief in the Devil and Hell.

Here is my list of appetites: air, water, food, warmth, secure attachment (ranging from love to less intense affiliation), sexual pleasure (including orgasmic satisfaction and levels of tension leading toward it), and security (by which I mean knowledge that one's importance to others is strong and reliable either as a worthy individual or as an individual associated with a grand person or group or a great ideal). I also include knowledge and understanding on the list of appetites, but not victory in competition as a primary appetite, because I think of it as a form of security. I am having a hard time deciding whether to include mastery. The release of the tension to avoid a danger or achieve a goal seems to be rewarding in a way that is greater than the simple diminishment or cessation of the tension.

We are equipped with neural structures that give rise to yet another innate emotion: pleasure. Just as the brain can generate a signal of fear or desire, it can also generate a signal of pleasure. Life in its complicated forms has persisted because sex—which makes no particular sense from an individual point of view—is accompanied by intense pleasure. Perhaps orgasmic pleasure is unique in kind, but I think it is only unique in degree. I think there must be a way that the release of any tension must also stimulate pleasure centers.

If so, mastery deserves a place on the list. This conclusion is supported not only by the pleasure we feel when we reach any objective, but also by the way we seek tensions we can master in such things as games and various entertainments. I think music is the best example. A piece of music starts out somewhere definite that either is or becomes familiar. It leaves that home base and goes further and further afield, only to come back again in the exciting conclusion. This seems to be one of the essential rhythms in a satisfying life: separation and reunion.

In real life, moment-to-moment motives are far removed from the basic fears and appetites, except for the appetite for mastery. We are in the habit of talking about derivatives, that is, substitutes for what is more deeply and unconsciously desired, and we say that the satisfaction of these derivative desires is a watered-down substitute satisfaction of the real desire. I think this version is helpful and accurate only some of the time. Life is hard and complicated enough that we can rarely head directly toward what we want, or away from what we fear. We are constantly making elaborate plans to lessen our tensions.

Once after my friend's car had broken down on Stone Way in Seattle, I was desperate to get change for a dollar so I could use a pay phone to call a taxi to take me to an admissions interview for the Seattle Psychoanalytic Institute. I was determined to get there as close to on time as I could so that I would not make a bad impression on Mike Allison, the interviewer, so that I could resume my analytic training here; so that I could combine the realization of a long-delayed ambition with living in the same city as my friend whom I hoped to marry. The wish to marry and the ambition to be an analyst could also be traced back more or less ad infinitum to other goals, but I pursued the quarter single-mindedly. At that moment, a quarter was the only thing that mattered to me.

Similarly, the colonel didn't want to kill George. He wanted helicopters.

Someone standing in the way of the colonel's getting helicopters, or my getting a quarter, would have been subjected to a dose of rage. Rage would not have been the motive in either case, but an activity brought into play to get us what we wanted. Rage isn't a drive. It's a capacity.

When I was an intern at the Cincinnati General Hospital, in those days a dreadful medical slum, I met a woman who had suffered almost every disaster which could attend the removal of a gall bladder. She was understandably angry and, by upbringing, also tough.

She endeared herself to us, the house staff, on one of those rare occasions when we saw an attending physician, the pompous chair of the Department of Surgery, make rounds once a week. When he came to this Ms. C., without greeting her or saying any other word to her, he pulled her bedclothes down and her gown up and palpated her abdomen.

She said, "Get your hands offa me, buddy."

The great man continued to palpate silently.

"I said, Get your hands offa me," she yelled.

When he continued to feel her stomach, wounded and sick as she was and from a supine position, she decked him.

Some days later, I was working in the evening when it was time for the nurses to turn the lights off. It was a sixty-bed ward with one light switch. Ms. C. waited until many of her fellow patients began to snore, and then, I suppose just to do something about how much she hated the place, she began to bellow. The nurses rushed to her bedside and in whispers tried to quiet her, but each attempt was followed by a new bellow. I walked over and said, "L. C., shut the fuck up!"

"You can't make me!"

"If you don't shut up, I'm going to give you a shot that will knock you out."

She shut up. The next morning, Ron Moline, who was her intern, came to work and went around to see all his patients. When he got to her, she said, "You know that Bergman?"

"Yes," Ron answered.

"He really knows how to talk to people," she told him.

I was no longer angry after Ms. C. became quiet, and if I had needed to yell at a store clerk to get my change, I would have been quite satisfied after I got it. The colonel might have had to yell at someone to get his helicopters, but he would have been calm after he got them.

There is rage that is different, however, because it comes from a different sort of motive. For example, I suppose that the colonel envied and hated the people who gave or withheld his aircraft. The fact that they could humiliate him like that was an unbearable flaw in his sense of himself and his standing. Getting helicopters no doubt helped; but since he was afraid, when George asked for trucks, that the helicopter bosses would never let him have a helicopter again, he was still weak and they were still in a position to humiliate him. They were a thorn in his side, and his envious hatred would not have been satisfied until they were removed. If they were killed or broken in rank, or he promoted to be in charge of them, then he would have been relieved. Even an apology, an acknowledgement of the injustice he had suffered and a promise to give him what he wanted in the future, might have been good enough, but probably none of that was forthcoming, and so he probably continued to long for their destruction even more than he longed for better troop transport.

This kind of tension and its allied affects are the scourge of the world.

Because of the effect of the news on my mood, I want to finish with an even worse example. It comes from *Wartime Lies* by Louis Begley. It is near the end of World War II. The inhabitants of Warsaw, expecting the arrival of the Russian army, have risen against the Nazis. But the Russians haven't arrived soon enough, and the Germans have regained the upper hand and, with their Ukrainian allies, have gathered the people in the center of town and are shipping them to Auschwitz, raping many of them in the process.

> Just ahead of us stood a tall and strikingly beautiful young woman with a baby in her arms. I had noticed both her beauty and her elegance.... A Ukrainian grabbed her by the arm and was pulling her out of the column. At first she followed without protest, but then she broke away from him and ran toward a German officer standing some two meters away. I had also noticed this officer before. He had a distinguished, placid face and a very fresh uniform. The boots hugging his calves were polished to a high shine that seemed impossible to maintain in this street covered with chalky dust and debris. His arms were crossed on his chest. Could the young woman also have been dazzled by the boots? When she reached the officer, she threw herself on her knees at his feet, held the baby up with one arm and with the other encircled these superb black tubes. A cloud of annoyance mixed with disdain moved across the officer's face. He gestured for the Ukrainians to stand back; a silence fell as he decided on the correct course of action. What followed the moment of reflection was precise and swift. The officer grasped the child, freed his boots from the young woman's embrace and kicked her hard in the chest. With a step or two he reached an open manhole. There was no lack of these, because [the resistance] had used sewers as routes of attack and escape. He held up the child, looked at it very seriously, and dropped it into the sewer. The Ukrainians took away the mother. In a short while, the column moved forward.

Like the American colonel, this one had suffered a blow to his pride. His country was losing the war, and people that he believed to be not only less than he, but even less than human, had humiliated him by their success against him. The continued existence of the vermin who dared to attack him is intolerable, and so they are about to be put out of existence. One of them appealed to him, and was very appealing. He might have felt some attraction, pity and tenderness, but attraction to what is contaminating produces disgust, and pity for the disgusting becomes contempt.

The most dangerous and awful element in his psychology, I believe, was his ability to see his situation as one in which he and his countrymen were human, and others were not. He had the support of a whole nation, and one of the greatest propaganda machines ever created, in his belief that he was basically a different species from the young mother and her child. I think that the capacity to deny the humanity of other people is the most dangerous element of human nature, and that the greatest challenge to all of us today is to work toward the time when everyone sees all other people as the same as themselves.

Autonomy, a Memoir

The summer before I gave this paper at the Forum, I wrote the beginning of an account of my childhood. I'm not sure if it had merit simply as a memoir, but I found myself using those recollections as a way of exemplifying how bad it is for us to live for other people's ambitions.

I WILL BEGIN WITH SOME PIANO STORIES. MY GRAND-mother was born in 1870 in Geneseo, Illinois, a small town near the Mississippi. When she was three, she surprised the family by sitting down at the piano and playing with both hands, reproducing music she had heard. In a few years she had surpassed the local piano teacher, and at eight she was giving piano lessons. Her prodigious talent was the talk of the town, and when she was fourteen, the people raised a fund to send her to Boston to study.

Just before she was to leave, she came down with typhoid and nearly died. It took her a year to recover and somehow, for reasons I have forgotten if I ever knew them, the chance to go was lost. She was a very good pianist all her life, but without advanced training. As an adult she played piano and organ in churches and movie theatres. She was determined that her only child would not lose the opportunity that had been denied her. The only trouble was that my mother had little if any musical talent. Some time in her adolescence she gave up trying to play the piano and decided to become an opera star. She took voice lessons from then until the Depression, when she could no longer afford them. After all those years she still couldn't sight read, and to my childish ears she couldn't sing very well either.

My sister is seven years older than I am, and some of my earliest memories are of hearing her practice the piano. She sounded pretty good to me, but our almost invariably sweet mother frequently interrupted her playing, screaming that she had made a mistake. Occasionally the screams were accompanied by slaps. Forewarned, I resisted piano lessons, but got them anyway. I had a serious learning disorder. In four years of lessons, I never learned to read music. My resistance somewhat baffled my mother, but still she insisted on helping me with my piano practice. Even though I had seen the precedent, I was astonished when she hit me. In spite of this mistreatment I still liked music and followed my mother's example by giving up on the piano and switching to an instrument she didn't know much about. As I had hoped, she quit assisting my practice. At last I learned to read music and learned to play as well as an untalented, only occasionally industrious student can. My sister plugged away at it until high school, and being more adept than I, became an acceptable amateur.

Our downstairs neighbor, Arthur, who is two years older than I, was like my grandmother at a slightly lower level. His family had little interest in music, but he had a lot; he played by ear at an early age, and by the time he was eleven or twelve was an accomplished pianist. I can remember with great immediacy standing in the stair hall admiringly listening to him play Grieg's Piano Concerto.

He wanted to be a concert pianist and/or a composer, and he studied music in college. His parents, however, were determined that he give up this useless, nonlucrative pursuit and become a doctor, even though they could easily have supported him for the rest of his life if he never made a dime as a musician. Ultimately, Arthur obeyed, doing so well as a premedical student that he got into a fine medical school where he was first in his class from the end of the first semester until the day before graduation, when he dropped out. It was the world's longest, hardest practical joke, but poor Arthur was too anxious and conflicted to enjoy it.

One more story. The elderly mother of a friend in Vancouver told me her family's history. Her father, the son of Jewish immigrants on the Lower East Side of Manhattan, had a knack for business. At an early age he moved to Canada, where he made a fortune. My friend's sister was yet another child prodigy of the piano, but unlike my grandmother and Arthur, her family provided well for her career. She was taken to another city where she lived with her mother so that she could have the best teacher in Canada. Before she was an adolescent, she was giving highly successful concerts and was famous. Her teacher advised that she should next study with a great man in Germany, and despite the political situation, this Jewish family moved there and stayed until 1936.

Much to my friend's annoyance, everything in her world revolved around her sister's career, which came to a sudden and unexpected end just after her triumphant return to Canada. She announced that she would play no more, and she didn't. It was Arthur turned inside out. Arthur and my grandmother were autonomous in wanting to be pianists. My mother, my sister, my friend's sister and I were not. Arthur's medical career and the Canadian piano prodigy's concert career were not autonomous but quitting them was autonomous. Autonomous ambitions come from the heart. Other ambitions are attempts to please or satisfy someone else. I think the Canadian pianist was a mixed case. She must have loved playing in the beginning, but her mother took it over and it turned into the family cause.

When I was a kid, psychoanalysis was a hot topic. Everyone talked about it and we heard and read about all the famous people who were being analyzed. Everyone knew that psychoanalysis was a powerful anti-cultural and anti-family force. People got analyzed and broke with their parents, divorced their spouses and left their religions. Analysts at that time believed that analysis of the Oedipus complex was the main goal of anyone's treatment, but the public thought the main goal was rebellion. I think the public was right.

Psychoanalysis, Marxism and cultural anthropology together released western civilization from its traditions. Nowadays, many of us long for some certainty about how to proceed with the details of our interpersonal life. I think that a hundred years ago, people not only knew what they were supposed to do but also didn't particularly think about why. The first anthropologists wrote about exotic cultures and assumed that they were primitive way stations along the path of the evolution of society to its great peak in nineteenth century European culture. Even at that stage, there was a hint of cultural relativism. Even if European culture was the best, the contrast to other versions revealed that culture is a system of roles and rules that were not the only possibilities. Marx showed how the structure of society was to the advantage of a powerful minority and a disadvantage to the rest of us, and argued that revolution was inevitable and desirable. Freud avowed no such program and at times seemed to be arguing for the necessity of the subjugation of basic desires, but the satiric song of fifty years ago, "Dr. Freud," not only expressed common knowledge, but was even right:

> He forgot about sclerosis
> and invented the neurosis
> and a thousand ways that sex can be enjoyed.
> He adopted as his credo
> "Down repression, up libido"
> and that was the start of Dr. Sigmund Freud.

Many features of analytic theory lean in that direction. The contention that various sexual impulses are a normal part of every human and the renaming of the conscience are two good examples. As soon as we started calling it superego, we were undermining the notion that the promptings of conscience are always right.

These liberating trends of theory and practice have largely remained disconnected and implicit. As with so many features of psychoanalysis, the best analysts always dealt with the important issues, but they did so because they could read the truth between the lines of theory. What they were doing was not explicitly written or taught.

For example, the first person to whom I was ever referred for analysis, Bernard Kamm, was trained in Vienna in the twenties. In our first and only interview—he turned out not to have free time after all—he asked me what my parents did for a living. I said that my mother was a ghostwriter, and he shot back, "Did she ghostwrite you?" The question impressed me at once, but it took me years to realize just how shrewd it was. I don't know how he would have helped me to answer it.

Three analysts I ended up actually working with dealt with it, but not very well. The first of them, Paul Kramer, a contemporary of Kamm's in Vienna, summed up the version that was essentially adopted by all three by saying that I had a paternal superego but a maternal ego ideal. Among other troubles with this way of putting it, the ghostwritten script is much more in the area of ambition than of idealization.

I eventually figured out a different formulation following the work of Heinz Kohut, who I think developed self psychology to escape a mother who had ghostwritten him. From having known him a bit at the time he was first elaborating his new ideas, from studying what he later wrote, and especially from reading his biography by Charles Strozier, I formed the idea that his first analyst, August Aichorn, like Bernard Kamm, understood these issues and helped him, but that his American analyst, Ruth Eissler, did not. His third analysis, done by himself and reported in his paper, "The Two Analyses of Mr. Z," didn't really get underway until deterioration in old age made it undeniable that his controlling, invasive mother was crazy. Even then, his model of the personality and his suggestions for clinical practice dealt with the issue somewhat indirectly and in a way that is not at all easy to see clearly.

I will attempt to illustrate how I think Kohut thought it works, or at least how I think it does, by telling something about my mother's ghostwriting. The attempts to get me to be a great musician, the ghost composing perhaps, didn't work at all well. I think they wouldn't have worked even if I'd had talent. My mother was too tormented and confused on the subject herself for her efforts to be anything but heavy handed and clumsy. Her more successful efforts were literally about writing.

As I have said, her first effort to escape her mother's program for her was to sing. Her second and more successful one was to write. Writing wasn't playing the piano, but at least it was an art, and she did have some talent for that. What crystallized it was her admiration for a writing teacher in her senior year of high school. She always had a strong tendency to idealize people. Her father died when she was three. Her mother's father did about as a good a job of replacing him as could have been, but the loss wounded her for life.

Then, when she was sixteen, my grandmother remarried. My mother hated her stepfather. He lived in Chicago, and so she had to leave my great-grandfather's house in Louisville. The writing teacher fitted into the vacant niche, and he liked my mother's work. From then on she wrote. It seemed second best to her, but she loved it. She moved from the laboratory high school of the University of Chicago to the college where she studied English, not music, and for all four years wrote for the school paper. She was managing editor of the University of Chicago's student newspaper, *Maroon* in 1917–8. To give a quick example of the effectiveness of the ghostwriting, I was news editor of that publication in 1954–5, and probably would have gone on to be managing editor except that in 1956 I met my former wife and, by latching on to her, escaped maternal influence to some extent.

I would not be sitting here writing this now if ghostwriting were all there was to it. My mother's writing was fairly autonomous and she loved it. As a baby—just as now—I talked a lot. I believe it was simply something I was inclined to do by temperament, and my mother responded enthusiastically. I like to make a distinction between primary and secondary ambition. The primary version is autonomous, which is not to say that it is uninfluenced by the parents. If my mother had not been so thrilled with my talking, I probably would have talked a lot anyway, but since she was thrilled, I have always loved words and stories.

She responded well to other interests of mine even when they weren't so much the same as hers. For example, I have been fascinated all my life by going away and coming back, because, I think, I was separated from her at birth and lived the first two weeks of my life in a hospital nursery. We lived near the railroad and I loved the trains. My mother often took me to watch them and she gave me lots of books about trains and airplanes. My loves of long-distance running, cycling and rowing are latter-day versions of this primary ambition.

The primary ambition to tell stories remained uncontaminated for several years. I can remember that before I could write, I narrated my life to myself with the expectation of writing it down when I could, a plan being realized at this moment. Trouble arose from several sources. One of them was that my mother never got famous as a writer. The part of her writing that was secondary ambition was the need to be famous. Family myth had it that my grandmother would surely have been famous had she been able to go to Boston. My mother loved to write, but she had to prove something about it by being a famous writer. She did all right at being employed as a writer and earning money all her life, and before I was born she was pretty well satisfied by being the editor of the *Chicagoan*, a rip-off of the *New Yorker*. She wrote all kinds of things for the magazine that were well received, but she longed to sell something to the *New Yorker* and over many years accumulated hundreds of rejection slips, and no sales.

Part of the trouble was that the death of her father and other disasters had left her basically rather depressed and a bit bitter. Unfortunately, she defended against that mood by a brittle cheerful optimism. She avoided anger and criticism of anyone except my sister and me. Her fiction, therefore, was bland and upbeat. There were exceptions to this rule. During the depression, after her magazine folded, she wrote lurid (for those days) fiction for *True Story* magazine, and once, rather late in her life, she got so mad at a relative of ours that she wrote a story about what a son of a bitch he was. It won a national prize. Similarly, she wrote much more freely when writing under someone else's name, thus the ghostwriting.

But she needed me to have the fame she was missing, and she wanted me to be a child prodigy like her mother. The first outbreak of her ambition for and through me was when I was required by my religious school to enter an essay contest. Each year, all of us students had to write an essay on the subject of world peace to compete for a prize established at the temple in honor of a dead relative of ours. I had little interest in writing an essay or winning a prize, but the version of my mother who helped with piano lessons appeared in a new realm. Every year I entered, and every year I won—not a great achievement, because there weren't that many contestants; the others were no more interested than I, and most of their mothers didn't help them. My mother's help was part coercion and part cheating. She applied considerable pressure to get me to write, and then she gave me editorial assistance, a phrase I take from an acknowledgement at the front of someone's autobiography: "Thanks to Ruth G. Bergman for editorial assistance." The assistance was that she wrote it. She didn't exactly write the peace essays, but she sure rewrote the hell out of them.

When I was eight my grandmother died, a disaster for me, because she had lived with us all my life, and had been as much a mother to me as her daughter was, and I loved her dearly. But beside that, my mother never got over the loss, and immediately became much more involved with me. A few months after my grandmother's death I read a piece in *My Weekly Reader*, a publication of Scholastic Press, an outfit that never published anything of the slightest merit until they lucked into Harry Potter. The piece I read suggested that it would be fun to produce a neighborhood newspaper. I think the idea appealed to me because I had a healthy identification with my mother—the Paul Kramer part of my motive—and more importantly, I knew it would excite her. It did. For five years, I slaved away producing something like 250 weekly editions of *Neighborhood News*. Any time I tried to stop, my mother would rage and grieve. I only escaped when high school with lots of homework approached.

This is where I stopped writing yesterday evening. I went to sleep worrying about what to say next and woke up in the night struggling with the question. It turns out to matter to me much more than I had expected that you realize that the newspaper was not wholly a fake—that I was not a fake as a boy editor and publisher. I suddenly realize now why it always has meant so much to me that even though my two unpublished novels are very amateurish, I did type all those hundreds of pages. The hard truth is that I did not type all those hundreds of pages of *Neighborhood News*. The myth was that my mother was doing it for me until I learned to do it myself, and all those years I was studying typing. I learned how eventually, but according to my mother, with my eager agreement, I never learned quite well enough. What was worrying me in the middle of the night was that you should know that I did compose the prose that appeared. I dictated it to my mother who took it down on the typewriter in newspaper-size columns.

The paper came out on Saturday. On Thursday, I cut up the stories and pinned them onto two dummy pages, and working from those, my mother typed two mimeograph stencils. Friday evening, I turned out the hundred or so copies on an old machine given me by a friend of my father's. Running and maintaining the mimeograph was my favorite part of the enterprise because that and delivery were the only parts I did by myself. The editorial assistance consisted of my mother's teaching me what news is and how to write a lead, a story and a headline. It is still one of the things I can do with ease. There was real news in the neighborhood because, shortly after we began publishing, the area suddenly changed from middle-class white to working-class, mostly black. Our landlords, Arthur's parents, turned their many six-flat apartment buildings into eighteen-flat slums. I wish I had covered the apartment conversions a bit more aggressively, but I did cover them.

Why am I bothering you with these details? I didn't really want to be a boy journalist, but it mattered to my mother and therefore to me. We were both thrilled when a couple of times, my city-wide rival, the *Sun-Times*, printed feature stories about me and once reprinted as a guest editorial one I had written and published. Telling you that makes me unpleasantly tense. Even after all these years, it matters to me that you be impressed and at the same time I hate myself for caring, and worse yet the experience is hollow. The hollowness comes from two sources: I'm not sure if my accomplishment was real, and the impetus for it didn't come from my heart. I will use the need for a contrary case as an excuse to brag some more. If I tell you that I used to run marathons, I am a little pleased and a little ashamed of myself but the tension is much less and the claim seems solid. No one suggested I be a marathoner. No one helped, and I know for sure that I really ran 26.2 miles in various times I can remember or look up in my runner's diary.

I'm not sure if it is still true, but in the heyday of psychoanalysis, everyone knew the phrase *inferiority complex*. The *New York Times* even made it a part of the headline of Freud's obituary. I suppose that it was so strongly associated with analysis that the writer didn't check to see if it was really one of Freud's ideas. I think that almost everyone hearing the expression for the first time knows immediately what it is, and fears or knows that he or she has one.

My fear that I wasn't really responsible for the paper and my eagerness to prove that I was, is a specimen of the universal experience of having a double image of oneself: inferior and superior. I have that feeling about *Neighborhood News*, but not about this talk. In both cases your reaction is vital, but I want to prove something about the newspaper, and don't have to about the talk. My mother's need for me to have been a child prodigy still acts on me strongly enough that I feel I would be in some sort of danger if I let her down, and the shame and doubt as to whether there was any reality to my supposed achievement still plagues me. But in giving a talk I want to entertain you and interest you in ideas that interest me. I am enjoying writing it and hope you enjoy hearing it. If you don't, I will be disappointed and ashamed, but I won't feel as though I were exposed, the way I did one day when Arthur's older brother Gibby told me that everyone knew my mother wrote the newspaper.

I flatter myself that my enjoyment of talking like this is similar to Kohut's. Few people have been more of a nonstop talker than I, but he was one of them. On some occasions he made a bad impression by going on and on. My colleague, Mike Allison, has told me of a time when the self psychologist appeared at an international meeting. Kohut said that the group would have a free and open discussion, and then talked the whole time himself.

When he was before an audience that expected him to do all the talking it wasn't objectionable. The Chicago Institute Lectures was a series of seminars, most of which began with a single question. The answer took the rest of the hour. I often heard him do that, and it was a pleasure because what he said was new and complex, and expanded the area of human life I could grasp psychologically, but also because he took such pleasure in his ideas and in discussing them. It clearly was an autonomous activity.

I didn't know him during his more conventional days and so I don't know if he seemed different then, but I think that he probably did. I think that his mother's demand that he be great combined with his inherent gifts resulted in his rise to prominence. In Chicago he was called "Mr. Psychoanalysis," and he became president of the American Psychoanalytic Association. His success was partly based on his seemingly complete acceptance and mastery of the psychoanalytic dogma of that time. I think that he felt he had to live up to his mother's ambitions for him. He later wrote that a capacity for joy was a result of successful analysis of narcissistic fixations. It seemed to me in 1965 that he took quiet joy in his ideas. I doubt that he was like that when he was slaving away to be successful enough to satisfy his mother.

Kohut's mother needed more than prominence and, in at least one weird way that I know of, he complied. His mother was ashamed of being a Jew and converted to Catholicism. Kohut, who in general seems to have been a model of personal honesty, successfully convinced me that he was a gentile.

I don't know why Kohut didn't make the bad effects of parents imposing their own ambitions clearer and more central in his writings about self psychology. He was hesitant about self-revelation. I think he probably hoped his Mr. Z disguise would be impenetrable, and similarly he put his problem with his mother in a corner of his theory instead of in the center, and even then he emphasized a result and not the cause. In his discussion of the grandiose self and the mirror transferences, he points out that there are two defenses against the awareness of the intense and usually unrealistic ambitions resulting from early fixations. These are the vertical and the horizontal split.

The horizontal split is repression, the vertical, disavowal. Some grandiose ambitions are conscious but disavowed. For example, a bossy person may be perfectly aware that he tells people that he knows better than they how to do things, but he denies that there is anything about this activity that implies he is superior. "If I happen to know how someone can do things better, I have the obligation to help them out. I don't think I'm better than anyone else."

Kohut advises working first to undo that denial so as to deprive the analysand of that source of ambitious fulfillment and therefore increase the need for what is repressed to come to light. He implies that the expression of the repressed grandiosity is desirable in its being more deeply felt and more amenable to continued development into realistic and fulfilling plans and activities. Almost as a footnote he points out that the vertically split-off portion of a person's grandiosity is a product of parental demand.

I believe that this feature of personality appears in many theories under many names. For example, it is the false self. Perhaps a more accurate title for this talk would have been "Autonomy Versus the False Self." I wasn't really an editor and publisher; my mother wasn't an opera star, but in contrast my Canadian friend's aunt was really a great pianist and Arthur was almost a real doctor, but it didn't feel real to them and they quit.

In his book, *The Restoration of the Self*, and the paper, "The Two Analyses of Mr. Z," Kohut shows a way to escape from needing to be something that one isn't: identification with the other parent. That was my way out of journalism. My father, who had been treated with not-so-benign neglect by his mother, spent his childhood and adolescence on the streets of Chicago having adventures with his friends. The adven-

178

tures often involved inventing and building things such as sailing carts that they traveled about on. He grew up to be an architect, competent, down-to-earth and unassuming. I grew up watching him work on buildings and, more immediately around our house building furniture and model airplanes. He made fun of the pretensions of big-shot famous architects whose buildings wouldn't actually have stood up without people like him who kept an eye on the details and demands of the real world.

Through the eight grades of elementary school, most of which coincided with my years as a newspaper publisher, I didn't bother much with schoolwork. My mother and I knew that I was above all that. I didn't do badly in school, but my grades were mediocre because I didn't try. As the ninth grade approached, I got the idea that grades were going to count and that I would have to do lots of homework. Before the ninth grade started, I made up my mind that I was up against something real and difficult and that I would approach it with my father's method and diligence. I did, was moderately successful the first year, and more so in subsequent years as I got comfortable in the new role. I suppose one way of looking at it is that in high school I identified with my father in the way that theoretically I should have at the beginning of elementary school.

I think one of the most valuable of Kohut's contributions is his understanding of the ego ideal. He describes normal development of narcissism as having two main components: the grandiose self and the idealized parent imago. I have just had a conversation with a friend that alerted me to the need to be clear about something here. We finally figured out that we were at cross purposes because I was talking about idealization in the Kohutian sense which is second nature to me, while she was talking about idealization in the more usual way as a distortion and a defense. Kohut did write about idealization in that sense, but it didn't interest him as much as what he called primary idealization. The idealized parent imago is not realistic from anyone's point view but the child's. The narcissistic economy of toddlers is disturbed by the recognition of their limitations. They restore their balance by taking their big and competent parents into their sense of themselves. The process is one of mistaken overestimation and gradual—if all goes well—disillusionment, rather than of overestimation as a reaction formation against the wish to tear down. As kids advance into childhood they gradually become more realistic about the people who are their ideals. At first, children think that they are great simply because their idealized people are, and they are a part of them. Later they think that they are not great yet but that they want to be, and they strive toward being like those they admire. In the best case, the actual people who have been used as models and sources of self-esteem are replaced by ideals. When I was in the ninth grade I was trying to be like my father. Since that time I have largely replaced him as a criterion, but I still strive to have some of his good qualities.

Some theorists' versions of the ego ideal are demanding and shaming. Kohut certainly includes that kind of shame and demand in his theory, but leaves it in the realm of ambition. The ambitions of very young people, and of people who got stuck early in narcissistic development, are indeed peremptory. Failure to live up to them produces intense shame.

We are driven by our ambitions, but we are led by our ideals. Our ambitions are important but we love our ideals. I often fail to live up to the conscientiousness, thoroughness and realism that I learned from my father, but then I feel sad and long to do better.

No wonder it occurs to me at this moment when I am aware of how wandering this thing I am writing has turned out to be, but I think maybe I'll do a little better next time. I am glad to think that I will still value those qualities. That I pursue them makes me feel that I am an all right person. The fearful fantasy that you won't get or like what I am saying gives me a little jolt of signal shame. If I thought you would scoff at *Neighborhood News* as my friend Gibby did, I would feel anxiety as well as shame because, as I said, to this day I still have some of the old feeling that if I wasn't a special child, the version of myself that my mother and I made up will disappear and I with it.

That version of myself did largely disappear at Hyde Park High School and in my first year of college. Oddly, my literary ability also disappeared. To my disgust, I failed an exam that would have allowed me to skip freshman composition, and I didn't do too well when I took the course. On one occasion, an assignment fit something I wrote when I was eleven (and that I had not dictated to my mother). I submitted it with a new essay that I thought was better. The old one got an A-plus and the new one a B-minus and a question from my instructor as to why the difference. I didn't know then, but now I think that my father's approach was well-suited to my other courses but a little too methodical to produce good writing.

Then my father died in a strange and horrible accident. I was repossessed. I blamed myself for his death and didn't think that I deserved to be like him. The completeness of my reversion still seems astonishing. In place of my old paper, there was my mother's. I joined the staff of the *Maroon* and it was the only thing I worked hard at that year. My grades fell off. I was back to feeling that class requirements were irritating trivia that I should be above. The only thing that improved was my writing. I retook the English Composition Comprehensive Exam and raised my B to an A. I was in a mess, and it took an early marriage and lots of psychoanalysis to get me out of it.

It's not easy to say how the analysis did the job. I don't think that interpretation was the main force that worked. Paul Kramer, my first analyst, did make vital interpretations about my guilt, but I don't think either of us had a clear idea of how my false-self relationship with my mother worked. Nevertheless he helped me leave home—my mother's home. I was at least partly reunited with my father and his good qualities, and the work solidified by idealization of analysis.

I chose my profession back in my first newspaper days. Like anyone's choice of profession it came from many sources, such as my undoing of my separation anxiety and my wish to help others undo theirs. I was also prompted by primal scene curiosity; identification with my mother's favorite cousin, who stayed with us during my childhood when he came up from Cincinnati to be a candidate in the Chicago Institute, and most important for this context, the fact that it was a condensation of my mother's love of the humanities and my father's love of technology and science. I don't know what would have happened if I hadn't become myopic when I was ten. I really wanted to be an airline pilot.

Anyhow, in analysis I gradually was able to stop being such a nervous wise guy. (Am I now a calm wise guy?) Fortunately, the Vietnam War further pulled me out of my Chicago orbit. Going to be part of another culture in the Indian Health Service combined the escape to the streets I had learned from my father with having to learn to make my way as an analyst where almost no one had heard of such a thing. No one in that culture would enter into any collusion with me that psychiatrists were special and great. That sentence strikes me as obscure, but I can't figure out how to redo it. So I will expand. When not in my guise of boy newsman, I was out in the street mixing it up with kids who were completely different from my parents, especially my mother. Child prodigies were not highly regarded, and I learned to make my way anyhow.

The part about collusion will take more space. Psychoanalysis is a selfobject of mine. There is always a danger for any of us that it will become a *falseselfobject*—I mean an object of the false self. False selves, like real selves, involve more than one person. We constitute ourselves out of our relationships. My relationship to you, the people who attend this Alliance Forum, is a real relationship dating back about nine years. I always write something for this occasion, and it is most of the writing I do. As I think about my ideas, I always have at some level of awareness the thought of putting them into words and telling them to you. Your attention and your discussion help define who I am as an analyst and a member of this community.

My false self as a boy publisher was constituted mostly by my mother and me. We had various false ideas that we supposedly believed, such as that I was doing this because I wanted to. I occasionally would assert that I wanted no more newspapering, and my mother would react more or less the way George W. Bush does when people say that the present war was unnecessary.

These beliefs are falseselfobjects. Hell hath no fury like someone whose falseselfobject is scorned. (Try burning a flag sometime.) Anyhow, like any group we are in danger of being false and of colluding to shore up falseselfobjects.

If we do that simply in the face of our fear of the insurance companies' cost-cutting care managers it isn't harmful, but we also do it when our customers make us anxious, and that is harmful. Aside from my exhibitionism, one of the reasons that I have written about myself instead of one of the people I see in my office is that I have become aware of how we use our falseselfobjects to make ourselves falsely secure at the expense of our patients. When one of them complains about my inadequacies, I am tempted to think of us psychoanalysts as skilled and knowing people who have to put up with a lot. I retreat into the fantasy of telling colleagues about the negative transference, the negative therapeutic reaction or some such collusional dogma. I have become particularly cautious about my tendency to tell little anecdotes of the terrible things that happen to me as a clinician so as to get sympathy and some votes on my side of the dispute.

That caution has made me worry about presenting cases. Where this subject started, if you will think back, was with my claim that a value of being among the Navajos was that there was no one to collude with in this way, or at least not for some time until the mental health program enlarged. Even then, since many of my coworkers were Navajo, it was hard to put on psychoanalytic airs. The patients were gratifyingly ready to give me a chance to show that I knew something, but they didn't feel the slightest need to pretend that they thought I did, just because I was a doctor. I cherish the memory of a man I saw early in my Indian days with whom I thought I had had a particularly good first interview. At the end, he said with some enthusiasm, "Thanks a lot—if it works."

False selves are not restricted to people like me who had ambitious, controlling mothers. I suppose we are actually in the minority. Certainly many people I have known have suffered from a terrible necessity to prove this or that about themselves not because their parents needed them to but because their parents responded so little and so unsatisfactorily to whatever they did. In reaction, these people tried to figure out what would impress their parents, and then tried to be that.

I often hear people described by their therapists with such epithets as narcissistic or entitled. I think that most of the people they talk about are trying to use their suffering to be important, and they have the awful sense that if they aren't important they won't be anything. Important may be slightly the wrong word. Recognized as important may be more like it. My mother and I were quite focused on my fame, my wide acceptance as a prodigy. That was one of the maddening things about the situation. I was much more driven to have people see me as a marvel than to be one.

Years ago, my Canadian friend's son—the great nephew of the pianist—was writing a novel even though he was only a child. He had a big handwritten manuscript that he carried everywhere with him, especially to dinner in restaurants with his parents and their friends. When inspiration struck he had to be able to scribble away, and so his family made special accommodations for his artistic needs. I recognized that number at a glance. He knew I was onto him and didn't mind because I never blew his cover, though he and I talked a little later about how he never wrote without an audience. Had the two of us been the same age there might have been trouble, because for both of us, being good didn't matter so much, but being unique was essential.

People like him and me are sometimes mistakenly called competitive. Entering a writing competition was the last thing on our minds. This morning when I was out rowing I encountered another sculler going the same way I was, and I thought perhaps I was faster than she. I tried hard. I don't know if she was trying too, but by golly I was faster. My pleasure in that somewhat unusual result was the gratification of a mild primary ambition. Most scullers are faster than I am, and that seems a sad fact to me. If I had been raised by parents who absolutely had to have a champion athlete in the family it wouldn't be sad. It would be disastrous. Competition is often a wonderful thing for people burdened by false self needs because it is a way of escaping the fantasies and entering the real world, as I did when I went to high school.

Psychoanalysis or psychotherapy can also be an escape from the dictatorship of the false self. When we can interact with someone in a way that makes it safe to say anything, and when there is an atmosphere of mutual respect and enjoyment, free play of heartfelt ambition and meaningful pursuit of cherished goals can replace desperation to appear one way or another.

Blue Notes: Poetry and Psychoanalysis

The editor of the newsletter of the Seattle Psychoanalytic Society and Institute asked me to write something about poetry and analysis. The invitation gave me a chance to write about my favorite poem, something I had been wanting to do for years.

IN T. S. ELIOT'S "FOUR QUARTETS," A FRAGMENT IN Part I, "Burnt Norton," reads:

Words move, music moves
Only in time; but that which is only living
Can only die. Words, after speech, reach
Into the silence. Only by the form, the pattern,
Can words or music reach
The stillness, as a Chinese jar still
Moves perpetually in its stillness.
Not the stillness of the violin, while the note lasts,
Not that only, but the co-existence,
Or say that the end precedes the beginning,
And the end and the beginning were always there
Before the beginning and after the end.
And all is always now. Words strain,
Crack and sometimes break, under the burden,
Under the tension, slip, slide, perish,
Decay with imprecision, will not stay in place,
Will not stay still.

Poetry and psychoanalysis strain words to their limits. Poets, analysts and analysands need to express the almost inexpressible. We try to convey the essence of our experience, including the pertinent facts, the associated memories and the passions. An approach to a complete account of any moment in the life of one person, let alone two together, would require hours of saying or chapters of writing unless some method could force meaning upon meaning into a few symbols.

Music is wonderful in that way. Beethoven's 16th quartet op. 135, or Louis Armstrong and His Hot Seven playing *West End Blues*, compress whole worlds into sound. The limitation of music, though, is its leaving out the concrete details. Richard Strauss did claim that he could describe anything, even the taste of lager beer, in music, but even he needed the poet and librettist, Hugo van Hofmannsthal, to supply some of the specifics.

Words are wonderfully specific. Sentences like, "Turn left at the third traffic light and go two blocks," are perfect in their lack of ambiguity, but it is the very lack of ambiguity that cripples speech in its attempt to express anything like the subtlety, contradictoriness and many-layeredness of actual life. Words are like pianos, organs or xylophones that can only play tones that are exactly a half-step apart. Voices and many instruments can produce an infinite gradation of pitches, but our system of notation is like the piano: the worlds of sound between the lines are hard to express.

The African ancestors of jazz include quarter-steps or simply unstable tones, and so jazz players need to find ways of producing blue notes, the ones that occur in the crack between two piano keys. Sometimes pianists hit those adjacent keys together to render something like the note between them. When we speak and write, to get the whole palette of existence we have to somehow hit the notes in the cracks between adjacent words, because words tend to be stuck in place without the give that, say, a trombone has. One of the simplest ways of hitting the meaning in the crack is through the simple juxtaposition of words that are on either side: for example, an oxymoron like *make haste slowly*. Other tropes are more complicated, but each is a method of locating meaning between, around and over the words as tent poles and stakes hold a tent in place but are not the tent.

Fortunately, we have practiced this sort of expression every night of our lives. All people are poets when they make their dreams. Writers can do it when they are awake, too. Freud seems to have had relatively little appreciation of one of his great achievements: the recognition of dreams as poems, and the resulting expansion of the freedom of written poetry to be dreamlike. Nine years after the publication of Freud's *The Interpretation of Dreams*, T. S. Eliot wrote:

Let us go then, you and I,
When the evening is spread out against the sky
Like a patient etherised upon a table.

What few early readers the poem found mostly said that the lines meant nothing, as many people before 1900 had said that dreams meant nothing.

In demonstrating that dreams mean something, Freud needed only to demonstrate single meanings. He appreciated but did not emphasize that dreams are little things that mean a lot. Eliot and other poets of the early twentieth century broke loose from the custom of having any obvious meaning, and so were able to write poems whose dreamlike nature emphasized how many more things than one they meant. In "The Love Song of J. Alfred Prufrock," the word *evening* is stretched beyond its usual limits by its including the concept of sunset along with many other connotations. We often use sunset to imply evening, but not commonly the reverse as here, where clearly what is spread is the last light spreading from the sun to clouds all along the horizon.

But then there is the startling simile of the anesthetized surgical patient. Prufrock announces at the beginning of his love song that he sees everywhere a torturous pull between beauty and the customs and qualities of the machine age. He is timidly stuck in a role determined by his place in an affected and artificial society, but longs for real contact with the natural and the transcendent. He is helpless against the forces at work on him, and can only long for something more genuine and vigorous: "I should have been a pair of ragged claws / Scuttling across the floors of silent seas."

The strangeness and ambiguity of everything from the start forces all kinds of questions: What kind of love song is this, and to whom is it addressed? Among the answers that satisfy me is that it is a song of someone to himself, someone afraid to sing out loud. Eliot lived his life backwards. When he was young he seems to have been like the timid old Prufrock, and when he was old he became the vigorous lover of his young wife; and instead of writing about the wasteland he wrote about quite energetic cats. In his uncertain youth he must have feared never being able to say what he meant and be understood, and of not being able to appeal to others as one who heard them well:

> And I have known the eyes already, known them all—
> The eyes that fix you in a formulated phrase,
> And when I am formulated, sprawling on a pin,
> When I am pinned and wriggling on the wall,
> Then how should I begin
> To spit out all the butt-ends of my days and ways?
> And how should I presume? ...
>
> It is impossible to say just what I mean!
> But as if a magic lantern threw the nerves in patterns on a screen:
> Would it have been worth while
> If one, settling a pillow or throwing off a shawl,
> And turning toward the window, should say,
> "That is not it at all,
> That is not what I meant at all"

He was intent on writing in a way that could not be formulated, and created a great work that still leaves us finding new significance almost a century later.

In my opinion, formulations are the bane of psychoanalysis and criticism of poetry. Though I don't like Archibald MacLeish's poem very much (because it has a tendency to mean) I agree with his famous lines: "A poem should not mean / but be."

Neither poems nor dreams are ciphers to be decoded. Someone conveys some part of existence in a form that someone else can appreciate;

that is, the audience when fully responsive to the created expression has a similar intuition of experience as the writer/dreamer had. Art does not relate to existence as hat-check relates to hat, but as soup relates to soup bone. One is not a token of the other but is an essence of the other. It is useful sometimes for an analyst to say about a dream or some other creation, "I think one of the things you mean is ...." but to imply that only one thing is meant not only misses all the other points but worse yet, implies that the analysand has put his meaning into code only to avoid facing something squarely. Of course, we do disguise our meaning for that reason all the time, but that is not the only thing we are up to. Every dream, joke, memory and so forth expresses so much that a full analysis of it would be similar to the whole analysis of which it is a tiny part.

Our analytic heritage tends to lead us into the error of formulation. Freud had what seems to me an odd idea that he expressed in *The Interpretation of Dreams*. He said that dreams were largely visual images which could be translated into verbal dream thoughts, and that the original dream thought existed in words in the dreamer's mind before he or she translated and disguised it in pictures. This cumbersome theory implies that unconscious primary process is in words even though words are poorly suited to expressing the sorts of thinking we infer primary process to be.

If the dream thoughts were in words originally, then we would be justified in seeing dreams as coded messages, not as works of art. It seems to me much more lifelike to assume that our moment-to-moment experience exists in every sense modality we possess. Some of our experience is verbal thought and is in words or thought summaries of collections of words, but much of what is on our minds is experienced in touch, taste, nonverbal hearing, bodily tensions and movements and so forth. Dreams, poems and other creations cram all sorts of experience into something that expresses them, and a reader or an analyst needs to respond to many levels of meaning at once.

When we respond we are an appreciative audience, which is satisfying in and of itself, and when it is the creation of an analysand that we are appreciating, the other person's perceiving us as understanding her or him, is part of what is therapeutic. But beyond that we are in a position to be a useful critic. I do not mean someone who points out what could be better in a work of art, but someone who helps others to appreciate the work. Great poetry is not obvious or easy to grasp because it means so much. A good critic is perceptive and practiced in responding to art. Critics need historical knowledge so that they know what various parts of the poem (or dream) refer to. As skilled readers of poetry, we can help others to know poems. As analysts, we are sometimes in the odd position of being the critic who helps the artist to appreciate her or his own work.

By our appreciation we also increase our analysands' skill as poets. Some come to us already skilled. Many years ago, I heard a schizophrenic young man say that as he was beginning to fall apart he would go into his family's cornfield, where he could see only corn and sky and imagine that he was hiding there, "the last survivor of a defeated army." But many people who come to see us think at the beginning that they need to tell us the facts in simple and even hackneyed ways. If we can make it safe to say anything to us and respond in ways that are appreciative and, if possible, poetic and playful, analysands will reward us with beautiful evocations of their experience. These can be dreams, images, memories or almost anything. When things are going well, these bits of poetry become leitmotifs that run throughout years of the analysis.

Someone I work with told me years ago that one of his favorite movie scenes is from *Monty Python and the Holy Grail.* In order to be allowed to cross a bridge, a traveler must be able to answer questions put by the troll who guards it. A wrong answer is punished by being plunged into the abyss. The hapless member of the group is relieved to be asked an easy question, "What's your favorite color?" "Blue," he answers." "Wrong!" the troll shouts, and down he goes. This person's parents consistently acted as if his own idea of himself was wrong, and when something comes up about his believing or not in the validity of his own experience, one or the other of us is likely to shout, "What's your favorite color?"

First memories, as Harry Stack Sullivan pointed out, are poems on the subject of who people believe themselves to be. My second psychotherapy patient was an enormous and muscular but anxious young man. When I asked his earliest memory, he said, "A big yellow chicken." Many other memories can be poems expressing a great deal about a person's basic perceptions and dilemmas. Someone told me that her mother, who was highly skilled in generating her own glamorous appearance but had little regard for her daughter, and especially for her daughter's appearance, was wonderful at costumes and makeup. One year when this person was in elementary school, she begged her mother to do her up as a witch for a Halloween party. It was unusual for the daughter to ask for anything, and it took a lot of asking before the mother finally gave in and made her into a wonderful and frightening witch. But when they got to the party, the little witch was struck shy and, much to the mother's dissatisfaction, could not bring herself to go in. We often hear shorter but still eloquent figures of speech. An analyst with whom I consult told me that her patient, reporting on the onset of a new bout of her terrible self-doubt, said that she had just encountered "the first emissary from the pit of pain."

Besides eloquence, poems and poetic expressions have a certain stillness to them. A work of art is not propaganda or cries of pain or lust. (Even though there is some truth in the remark that the operas of Verdi are battle cries and the operas of Pucinni mating calls.) Making art out of experience distills the experience and puts it into a form that can be contemplated. Two people engaged together in that contemplation is analysis at its best. At its worst it is the intrusion into the private experience of one person of the formulating and destroying voice of another.

> I have heard the mermaids singing, each to each.
> I do not think that they will sing to me.
> I have seen them riding seaward on the waves
> Combing the white hair of the waves back
> When the wind blows the water white and black.
> We have lingered in the chambers of the sea
> By sea-girls wreathed with seaweed red and brown
> Till human voices wake us, and we drown.

Some Thoughts on
Psychoanalysis and Justice

It has always seemed to me that psychoanalytic understanding supported a view of responsibility and justice different from the ones that are in common use. Long ago I had some experience with evaluating the mental status of criminals, and the system seemed crazy. Then, after John Hinckley's attempt at assassinating Ronald Reagan, the system changed and became crazy and tyrannical. Some case in the newspaper tipped me into writing this.

ONE WINTER NIGHT IN THE LATE '70S, A SQUARE block of downtown Durango, Colorado, burned to the ground. A firefighter was killed. Investigators learned that the old apartment hotel where the fire started had been badly neglected and that violations of the fire code had been ignored by a building inspector who was bribed by the owners. The prosecuting attorney of Montezuma County was considering indicting the inspector when the police arrested a fire-setter. There had been a number of clumsily attempted arsons, none of which had done significant damage. Patrolmen saw a well-known town character, Gilbert Martinez, trying to light a small amount of wood he had piled next to a porch.

Mr. Martinez was a crazy homeless man who usually dressed in women's clothes and hung around downtown. Detectives asked him about the earlier little fires. He said he hadn't done any of them, and added that he also hadn't set fire to the hotel. That was the first time that anyone thought the hotel fire had been deliberate. The investigators had concluded that it had started in the building's defective wiring.

Little further questioning was needed to obtain a confession. Mr. Martinez said that friends of his had rented a room, bought some wine to drink and were having a party, to which he hadn't been invited. He tried to join them, but they wouldn't let him in. Humiliated and enraged, he took paper and boxes out of the hotel trash, piled them against the locked room door and set fire to them, thinking that the door would burn down. The place was such a firetrap that soon everything burned down. Since the firefighter died as a result of his arson, Mr. Martinez was indicted for felony murder.

At the request of Richard West, the public defender, I spent several hours with the defendant and testified at his trial that he was chronically schizophrenic and receiving no treatment and that being excluded by people he thought were his friends caused him to fall apart more than he already had. I said that he felt that he would be destroyed by his unbearable feelings unless he took decisive action. The prosecutor hired three other psychiatrists who testified that Mr. Martinez was mentally normal. The proceedings ended in a mistrial when the jury failed to reach a verdict. Eleven jurors voted for acquittal by reason of insanity, but one adamantly refused to agree because throughout the trial God had been speaking to her, saying that Mr. Martinez was sane and guilty.

There was a change of venue to Breckenridge, Colorado. The cases put on by the two sides were much the same except for a couple of details. The public defender asked one of the prosecution's experts, who was making a lucrative career out of such court appearances, if he ever determined that any defendants were insane. He perjured himself by saying that it was about fifty-fifty. The prosecutor made the odd mistake of addressing the jury as "sensible, simple mountain folk." They were twelve with-it residents of a fashionable ski resort. They returned a verdict of not guilty by reason of insanity, and Mr. Martinez was sent to the state mental hospital in Pueblo.

A few months later, I heard from Mr. West that the doctors there wanted to discharge the arsonist because on medication he was much improved, and also because he caused a lot of trouble. Other patients were fighting over his sexual favors. Mr. West was trying to talk the Pueblo authorities into keeping him. He said, "I don't like the idea of Gilbert coming back to town with a book of matches in his hand."

I don't know what happened, but I was familiar with the problem. Several years earlier, as the psychiatrist for the Mescalero Apache reservation, I had repeatedly gone to Las Vegas, New Mexico, to talk the doctors at the state hospital out of discharging the most dangerous patient I had ever met. In those days, the paradox of psychiatric defense was that if it could be shown that murderers were severely and chronically insane, and therefore likely to remain dangerous, they were often released in a short time, while people who killed in an unusual, extreme situation that was unlikely to occur again were locked up for years.

Psychoanalysis made a large contribution to the creation of this odd situation. Analytic thought made one of its early courtroom appearances in 1924 in Clarence Darrow's defense of the so-called thrill killers, Loeb and Leopold. In fact, Darrow attempted to engage Freud as an expert witness. The great defense lawyer advised the young men to plead guilty, and he undertook to save them from hanging. He did present psychoanalytic expert witnesses who testified about the underlying causes of the murder, and then he argued that the crime was not the result of the workings of the young men's free will but was determined by complex forces. He said, "Nature is strong and she is pitiless. She works in mysterious ways, and we are her victims." The plea was successful, and in the subsequent several decades, as psychoanalysis became influential and the idea of psychic determinism became well-known and fairly widely accepted, the nature of the insanity defense was liberalized.

In the nineteenth century, when the insanity defense originated, it was necessary to prove that defendants did not know the nature and quality of their actions, or that if they knew them they did not know that they were wrong. Many other standards were introduced over the years; for example, the policeman-at-the-elbow test. If criminals were sane enough that they would not commit their crimes with a policeman standing next to them, they were not criminally insane. The trouble with that test was that lots of people are crazy enough to commit awful crimes but sane enough to wait until the police go away.

In the public enthusiasm for psychoanalysis of the '40s and '50s, it was widely accepted that odd or bad behavior could be explained scientifically and understood as a product of trauma or other unfortunate experience. It was not to be condemned, but pitied as a sickness. (When this opinion was new, the word *sick* had not yet deteriorated from a euphemism to a dysphemism.) A trend in the formulation of tests of criminal responsibility moved toward the position that one was not responsible for a crime if it were the result of mental illness or defect. Insanity defenses became more feasible and therefore more frequent, and the public tended to change its attitude toward the treatment of criminals. A number of analysts argued for this change, most notably Karl Menninger, whose book, *The Crime of Punishment*, was widely read. To a large extent the goals of revenge and punishment were discredited. Confinement and the death penalty were seen as deterrents to crime, and many people saw the goal of penitentiaries to be rehabilitation.

The fate of those found not guilty by reason of insanity was affected by another seemingly liberal development. Books and movies about psychoanalysis and psychiatry were popular, and often included portrayals of the horrible state mental hospital system. It was true that large numbers of people were incarcerated in institutions that were easy to get into and hard to get out of. Before the advent of the phenothiazine drugs in the mid to late '50s, little or no real treatment occurred and hospitalization usually made people worse.

Psychoanalysis had made psychiatry popular after World War II. The advent of psychiatric drugs and the beginning of the community psychiatry movement kept it that way. Congress established the community mental health system and provided what now seems like opulent financial support for psychiatric research, education and treatment. Young lawyers and psychiatrists (including me) attacked the involuntary treatment system. Patients' civil rights were protected, and it became a right to be released promptly when treatment had been successful. These changes worked pretty well as long as the money for community treatment lasted. It was a wonderful thing that patients could be treated near home, where their families could be involved, and continuity of care could be ensured after hospital discharge.

The Community Mental Health Center Act provided money for centers only for a few years. Congress and the Great Society national administration assumed that states and counties seeing the benefits of the mental health centers would continue and increase their budgets. This assumption was wrong. However, expansions of civil rights that save tax dollars are popular. In the name of patient rights, the states were happy to let the patients out of the hospitals, where even deplorable conditions cost a lot, and so for decades chronically mentally ill people have been spared long-term institutionalization and have been given the privilege of living—and dying—on the streets.

The situation was worse in the cases of many criminally insane people. Ever more poorly funded public hospitals were eager to give such patients their right to prompt discharge when they improved. Gilbert Martinez, my Apache criminal, like many others improved pretty promptly when the demands and complexities of his life were reduced by living in Las Vegas and when he took his medicine—something he never did at home. The hospital staff argued that he had a right to discharge because he was better, and that even if they could be sure he would deteriorate back home they didn't have a right to keep him. They were happy with that idea because discharging him saved work and money, and anyhow he wasn't so much improved that he didn't need to be humored to prevent dangerous outbursts.

The latter tendency enabled me to succeed in arguing against discharge. I would ask to interview him. He and I liked one another, and the conversation would go fine until he said, "I'm going to be discharged."

"No. I don't think that's a good idea," I replied, and he would blow up.

"I'll kill you!" he shouted. "And I'll kill so-and-so and so-and-so too."

The whole thing changed in 1981, when John Hinckley shot Ronald Reagan. The Hinckley family, like the Loeb and Leopold families, could afford skilled lawyers and expert witnesses. They put on a long and careful case for a finding of not guilty by reason of insanity, and a conscientious jury deliberated at length before returning that verdict. Many people and many state governments reacted strongly. The insanity defense was limited in most states and abolished in three, and there was also a shift in the public attitude toward the goals of the criminal justice system. People felt cheated of their revenge on Hinckley, and revenge again became a widely accepted goal. It seems to me that this trend has increased over the years so that punishment is widely accepted as a benefit that society owes the victims of crime, who are represented as being cheated if sentences are not severe. It seems to me that analysts were discouraged by the change in public attitude and have become deplorably silent about it and the underlying issues of personal responsibility and accountability.

I think that our daily practice is based on assumptions about these philosophical and ethical issues, but we don't make our assumptions explicit or discuss them. Do we as analytic therapists believe that human behavior is determined, or free? What do we think the consequences of bad behavior should be? Determinism was one of the legs on which Freud stood his argument for the meaningfulness of the psychopathology of everyday life and other symptoms, and for the existence of the unconscious. For example, he rejected the claim that slips of the tongue were mere accidents, on the grounds that biological systems, like the rest of the universe, operate on the basis of cause and effect and are not random. In a way, it therefore seems he was saying that we do not have real choices, but that our actions are the inevitable results of a web of causes. But in another way, he was saying exactly the opposite.

People who make mistakes in speaking have often claimed that the mistakes are random accidents, but Freud replied that mistakes are caused by unconscious intention, and from that point of view, people who misspeak are doing so by choice. But is an unconscious choice truly a choice? In our daily experience, we know that it had better be treated as a choice. If someone tells us that he meant to bring us a check, but forgot, we may not be well advised to argue the point, but we need to adopt some strategy that will get at the motives for delaying payment of our bill. Much of the motive for neurosis is the concealment of choice.

Many obsessional people are seemingly convinced, and try to convince the rest of us, that they have wonderful intentions and that the harm they do is accidental and beyond their control. Years ago, I met a devoted wife who carefully washed any food that she bought for her beloved husband. She feared that her purchases might carry a radioactive atom or two and that it would emit a ray which would hit one of her husband's genes and cause a mutation which would result in cancer and his death. She washed the food so much that it disintegrated and went down the drain, so that her husband had to take her out to dinner every night. She knew that her food-washing was intentional, but she didn't want to know what was really behind it. She couldn't believe she was an acceptable person if she wished her husband would die and thought he ought to feed her instead of the other way around.

Hysterical people disguise choices as the results of illness over which they have no control. Simple examples of hysteria are rare in big-city practices nowadays because Freud's work is so widely known that few people can convince themselves or others that such a symptom isn't a choice, but in the Navajo Nation when I was there in the '60s and '70s, hysterical seizures were every bit as common among young women as they were in Vienna in the 1890s. In the Navajo way, it is particularly bad form for an adolescent girl to make demands or cause trouble in the family, but epilepsy was widely known and feared as a sign of incest. They had that idea before Freud did. So someone could cause great consternation, demand special treatment and make an accusation by having a fit, and no one thought she intended those results.

Intention is a concept that is important both to psychoanalysis and to law, but the two disciplines treat it quite differently. Lawyers attempt to prove or disprove that malefactors cause harm intentionally or unintentionally, and it makes a big difference, for example, in determining whether someone has committed first-degree murder, second-degree murder, or manslaughter. No one denied that Loeb and Leopold planned to kill someone, but a man I evaluated, who killed seven people in a bar fight, claimed not only that he had no idea that he was going to do such a thing, but that he couldn't remember having done it. I think that if he had only killed one person he might have been charged with manslaughter, but under the circumstances he was tried for seven counts of second-degree murder. He had learned martial arts and practiced using the traditional Japanese weapon, nunchucks, with fantasies of being a great warrior. Then he took his nunchucks to a bar in Gallup, got drunk and lethally fought members of a traditionally enemy tribe. His planning might have been unconscious, but I think the general nature of what he did had been planned.

But is intention the same as free choice and the opposite of determinism? Perhaps choice and determinism are not incompatible. I have been thinking about this for a long time, because when I was a kid, Louis L. Mann, my cousin the rabbi, liked to brag about his debate with Clarence

Darrow on the subject. He claimed that he challenged Darrow's denial of free will by pointing out that he did believe in free choice, because he had asked Judge Caverly to make a choice, the lesser possible sentence. According to my cousin, Darrow had given a great shrug and retired from the scene of the debate. He shouldn't have. What he should have done was to answer that the judge's sentence was determined by complex causes, an important one of which was Darrow's argument. He should have added that his argument was the result of an almost infinite number of causes, including his inherited temperament and capacities and all he had experienced. In our work we influence the people we work with, and vice versa, and we accept both that we and they are making choices and that the choices are determined by factors which we try to understand.

The experience of choice is notoriously misleading. The hypnotic phenomenon, among the first influences on Freud to recognize that there are unconscious mental processes, continues to be striking. A hypnotized person is given a suggestion of what he or she will do after the trance ends—for example, opening an umbrella immediately after the hypnotist coughs. It often works, and if the hypnotist asks why the person has opened an umbrella indoors, the answer will almost always be a rationalization such as, "I thought I saw a hole in it and I wanted to check before I went outside." The rationalization will be given with great conviction, but everyone else present knows it is incorrect. The real motive, of course, is complex.

There are a variety of reasons why people choose to go along with a hypnotist's act, a common one being the gratification of a wish to surrender control, and therefore blame. Having frequently seen such performances, and many more or less clear-cut instances in which I believed I knew more about why someone was doing something than he or she did, has left me skeptical of my own ability to know for sure why I do what I do. I also notice that there is social pressure to know why I do things, and that pressure contributes to the likelihood that, if asked, I will have an explanation; but I have found that saying I don't know why I did something causes me less trouble than I used to expect. Of course, I spend most of my time among people who are used to the idea of being "Sunday riders," even those who haven't heard Freud's story of the poor horseman who, when asked where he was going, said, "I don't know. You'll have to ask the horse."

But how does the horse decide? My neurophysiologic hypothesis is that at all times the cortex is patterning itself in response to the organs of external and internal sense, and that the midbrain is scanning those patterns and recognizing them as indicating such conditions as threat or opportunity, relaying back to the cortex a demand for patterns of possible action. The essential elements of decision-making are the cortex's ability to generate a large number of patterns and the midbrain's selecting among them on the basis of a balance between need and danger. The outcome is the result of all we are and all we know — and it is inevitable. As Bruno Bettelheim used to say, "If I saw things the way the other guy does, I would do exactly the same as he does."

The conclusion I draw from this picture is that our actions are determined, but we are constantly influenced by the world around us, and especially by the world of human relatedness. It is not that we are forced to do what we do, but that we constantly decide and inevitably make the best decision we can given all the information we have.

I do not believe that I am more or less responsible for my behavior than Gilbert Martinez and the corrupt building inspector were, but that I usually have better information than they did. I never knew the building inspector, but I did know Gilbert Martinez, and I think it's likely that one of the reasons that I have a more complete and accurate picture of myself and the world than he is that my cortex and other parts of my central nervous system work more efficiently than his. His schizophrenia is probably largely the result of the DNA he has had since conception. My schematic version of what that means is that he has a smaller and less flexible repertoire of patterns of cortical activity than most of us do.

Of course, some of the information we have isn't true. I say this in order to address the danger that the information-based model of human behavior is leaving out passion, such as the passionate desire to keep eating every day.

Obesity, especially severe lifelong obesity, is difficult to treat by any means, and there is ever-increasing evidence that it is an inherited condition. At least two neurohormones stimulate eating, and clinical experience has convinced me that when they are active, the midbrain sends a signal that starvation is imminent. Rational thought is often not sufficient to overcome this information, no matter how erroneous it is. Nevertheless, from the outside, and often even from inside of an obese person's experience, it is obvious the problem is simple and consists of a failure of willpower. Every ounce of fat that any of us carries is made from food we once swallowed. All we have to do to lose weight is to stop swallowing things until we have used up as much body fat as we want. Many of us watching greatly overweight persons eat or shop for food are horrified, and want to ask how they can do such a thing as to eat more when it is obvious that they don't need to, and are only making an awful situation worse. Some people actually do ask strangers about it, and so many people think that the huge person's size is voluntary that obese people sometimes are subjected to being touched in public by curious and derisive strangers.

When I have worked with such people, it has seemed to me the first priority was the alleviation of shame, because they have been told for as long as they can remember that they must control their eating. They agree, but cannot do it because their midbrain is supplying them with the conviction that starvation is imminent. It is often said that overweight people need to learn to respond normally to normal sensations of hunger and satiation. That is easier said than done, because many of us, even if feeling stuffed, want to eat as long as the food supply lasts. I used to think my own wish to do so was a result of my separation from my mother in the first two weeks of my life, and that other people had similar sources of the fear of abandonment and starvation. Now I am not so sure, because so many studies have shown that the best predictor of weight is the weight of a twin, no matter how different the twins' lives have been. It makes sense that this inherited trait is common, because food has regularly been available only recently.

The ten thousand years since the last ice age and the beginnings of agriculture are only a small fraction of the time since our species evolved. Native American tribes of the desert were once marvels of long-distance running, fueled by diets so skimpy as to seem to defy the laws of thermodynamics. Since the advent of pickup trucks and McDonalds in the communities of Sells and Phoenix, Arizona, they have become some of the fattest and most diabetic groups on earth. For longer than the rest of us, and probably more strongly, they had Darwinian selection pressure to carry the trait of desiring to eat, immediately, all the food one ever found.

DNA is only one source of misinformation on which destructive action is based. As I have pointed out, perhaps with tedious frequency on these occasions, we are constantly engaged in trial actions that we call thoughts. As I decide what to write next, I imagine the day of the Forum and you listening to me. I try to discern what you will find understandable, convincing and interesting. Since I have spoken at the Forum so many times, there may be a good chance that I am imagining you correctly, but I'm sure that some of what I think is wrong. In less familiar circumstances my accuracy is lower, and I say and do things that don't work.

Since my life, after the first two weeks, has been remarkably fortunate, and particularly since my mother and grandmother were so receptive to almost anything I said, I have confidence—more than is sometimes justified—that people will be interested in what I say. That is one of the reasons I am sitting here at the computer, and in a few months will be standing before you. Lots of people who are smarter and better read than I am don't give talks, because the results of their trial actions are determined by early lives in which they were listened to poorly, if at all. Disastrous trial actions are usually partially or completely out of awareness. For example, many people cannot remember stories. They experience this inhibition as a failure of memory. If wonderful experience convinces them that they are in the presence of someone who enjoys hearing them, their faulty memories miraculously improve.

Bad early experience not only distorts the outcome of trial actions, it also produces faulty information—passions—that doing certain things is necessary.

For example, some people continually show off and brag. They are always desperate to be impressing someone. This is a hard problem to remedy therapeutically, because it is often shattering to let them know that trying so hard has the reverse of the effect they desire. It works better—if it can be done—to correct the misinformation that they will be nothing unless they are marvelous.

Whatever the source of our need to accomplish something, it will result in our doing whatever seems best to us—unless we can't think of anything to do. In most such cases, we will feel one of the emotions of dissatisfaction: anger, depression, and so on. In the most awful cases, the need seems absolute and immediate, even though every trial pursuit of it ends in disaster. The need and the person's ideas of who she or he must be are incompatible. The result is a horrible, terrifying paralysis and a sense of imminent or universal destruction: the traumatic state. The experience is so unbearable that it soon results in some action, such as the restructuring of the personality into a psychotic form and/or suicide. I testified in the courtrooms in Durango and Breckenridge that Mr. Martinez was threatened by that condition and escaped it by trying to burn the door down. It seemed to me that his horrible experience made it impossible for him to do otherwise. I still think so, but I no longer believe that only those in such awful circumstances do what they have to do. I think it is true of all of us.

We analytic therapists believe that it is possible to understand why people do the things they do. I think most of us believe that people choose their actions, and that those choices make sense when seen from their point of view. This idea implies that people could do otherwise than they really do, but they wouldn't because it wouldn't register as being the best choice. I believe that the reasonable position on the question of determinism is not exactly that we couldn't be any other way than we are, but that we wouldn't, given the picture of ourselves and our world that arises from the interaction of DNA and history. We tell people that their destructive actions make sense, and that is different from saying that their actions are not their responsibility. We have all done terrible things because we chose to do them. If we are lucky, we will learn enough to make better choices in the future.

Free will—like many other concepts—makes no sense when viewed intrapsychically, but makes perfect sense when viewed interpersonally. Free will, like freedom, depends on free access to information. The horrible behavior of genocidal nations results in part from their leaders controlling the press and other sources of knowledge. Psychoanalytic treatment improves behavior by improving the range of information one uses to guide life. Simple enlightenments can illuminate whole segments of life which have been unknown. We try to help our customers to know more about the impulses that animate them. This helps them learn that they want to do something they concluded was disgusting, sinful, and so on, but, more importantly, find out that we continue to think they are decent human beings even though they have such wishes. They can then undertake trial actions that were previously blocked and will learn that there is a whole range of possibilities, some of which may be productive.

Tough customers may continually denigrate us and the other people in their lives, but if we are successful in forming a friendly collaboration, they will learn that people don't necessarily hate them, and they can stop hating others as much. Let me repeat an example I have used before in a talk here. Years ago, when I was the psychiatrist for Carlsbad, New Mexico, one day a week, I brought such a person back to Albuquerque for hospitalization. A few weeks later, she had a leave from the hospital and I took her back home for a daylong visit. When we returned to Albuquerque, it was too late for her to get dinner in the hospital. So I invited her to eat at my house. She was aghast. "But I'm the bitch of all times," she said. The freest possible persons would be the ones with the widest, most accurate knowledge of themselves and the world and of all the ways of being that would be accepted by the others in their lives. Such people are not criminals.

So what should our government do with criminals? For a start, I think our present policy of seldom allowing an insanity defense should be expanded. We should never allow such a defense, and at the same time, we should recognize that all criminals are guilty by reason of insanity, since a fully sane person will not commit a crime. In that sense, none of us is really sane, because I think any of us will commit crimes under certain circumstances, which for those of us who are lucky occur rarely, if at all. Justice consists of treating everyone the same. Since each of us makes the best decision we can on the basis of the world as we know it, criminals shouldn't be punished for doing what we would have done in their place. They, like the rest of us, are living their lives as reasonably as they can.

Though I think criminals should not be punished, I think there should be a major response to their behavior. I do not think that revenge is a proper goal of the justice system, but there are a number of proper goals. We need to protect ourselves from continued criminal behavior by those who have been tried and convicted. We need to establish conditions that discourage crime. We need to satisfy victims, and society in general, that we have let criminals know that we will not tolerate their crimes. We need to insure that criminals make all possible reparations to their victims, and we need to assist them in doing so. We need to do all we can to help criminals to have better information about themselves and the world so that criminality will cease being a reasonable result of their experience.

When we find that someone has harmed others, we need to evaluate the likelihood of their doing so again. One of the things that analytic work indicates most strongly is that people are likely to do the same things over and over. Unless the circumstances of the crime are unusual and unlikely to occur again, it can probably be assumed that criminals will continue to be criminal unless something affects them strongly. Being locked up in a penitentiary probably affects all prisoners strongly, but there is considerable reason to believe that the effect is likely to perpetuate, and possibly worsen, criminality. People who feel that they are suffering because we have been trying to get even with them will be likely to try to get even with us if they get the chance. Many other factors tend to have the same result. Being segregated with other criminals and treated with vindictiveness and disrespect promotes a sense of being a member of a group that is an enemy of society, a group to whom it seems reasonable to treat ordinary citizens as enemies.

In spite of these bad effects of incarceration, most criminals will have to be kept away from the rest of us until there is reason to believe they are safe. It is even arguable that killing certain criminals could be justifiable. Napoleon demonstrated his ability to escape imprisonment and cause thousands more deaths. For that reason, the British surreptitiously killed him. If Hitler had not killed himself, most people in the world would have wanted his execution as revenge, which I think would have been wrong; but on the other hand, his continued life might have inspired his followers to carry on his hellish activities, even if his confinement for the rest of his life could have been insured. The serial killer Ted Bundy was particularly skillful at escape, and he killed people between his confinements. For that reason, I think it could be argued that his execution was justified. Indefinite confinement of such supremely murderous people seems the proper choice. We need to be inventive in ways to prevent their escape and also to continue to evaluate them to see if they continue to be dangerous, since dangerousness seems to me to be the only justification for keeping someone locked up.

Sexual criminals are another group that presents a special problem. We know that sexuality is so strong a force as to be unlikely to be permanently resisted. We have also learned that some people have rather a limited range of sexual fantasy and activity that is at all satisfying to them and that the specificity is almost impossible to change. Fortunately, most people's essential sexual wishes can be fulfilled with satisfaction to others and without harm; but to be safe on the loose, rapists and pedophiles either must give up sexual satisfaction or change what it is that gives it to them. Neither change is likely. Heavy pharmacologic treatment or indefinite incarceration are serious steps, but they may be necessary until someone finds something better.

If our safety demands that people be held against their will, and punishment is not a legitimate goal, we need to make confinement less punitive. Our attitude should be that it is a misfortune to be criminal and to have to be locked up, and the extent of that misfortune should be minimized as much as possible. Some steps are already taken in that direction; for example, conjugal visits. Many new steps could be invented. To a large extent we could replace huge fortress-like prisons with smaller, more specialized ones in which prisoners could be as free as is safe and as much as possible in contact with people, jobs and schools that would enable them to fulfill their ambitions and abilities to the extent they are able. Unfortunately, such steps have been more unpopular in the present revenge-seeking climate of public opinion, and therefore it seems to me that we should again raise our voices against revenge.

We rightly regard revenge exacted by crime victims as another crime. I think revenge carried out by the courts is equally wrong. The new director of our state's prison system pointed out that many of the system's problems are due to our locking up the people we're mad at in addition to the one's we're scared of. One of the reasons that private revenge is against the law is that it leads to cycles of revenge for revenge, as in gang warfare, for example. Revenge exacted by the state has the same effect. But I frequently read newspaper accounts of crime victims and their families saying that they have been denied justice if they have been denied the full measure of revenge they think they are due. Prosecutors also claim that severe punishment is necessary in order to do justice to victims.

In our daily work, we don't encourage revenge. We encourage forgiveness and reconciliation wherever possible, as have the governments of South Africa and other countries that have established truth and reconciliation commissions. Victims are not benefited by the suffering of their tormentors, but they are benefited by acknowledgment that they have been wronged and by whatever amends can be made. I am thinking about the therapy of a man who was severely abused sexually and physically early in his life. Recently he said, "I don't want revenge. I just want my family to admit it happened and that they are to blame."

Criminals would benefit from an extension to them of the nonjudgmental attitude that is one of the foundations of our profession. The theologian Paul Tillich said that it was the same as the good news of the New Testament, that people are entitled to acceptance no matter what. We should emphasize more the more Jewish prescription for being forgiven: acknowledging our wrongs to those we have harmed, and asking their forgiveness. Alcoholics Anonymous makes that principle one of its main foundations, and we and the justice system have a lot to learn from AA. The central six of the twelve steps are a process of acknowledging wrongs done to others and making amends. Both criminals and those they have harmed benefit from that process, and if the courts owe something to crime victims, this is it.

Gilbert Martinez did acknowledge that he had done terrible harm, but nothing was done about his making amends. The building inspector did neither. If Mr. Martinez could have stayed in Durango and received good psychiatric treatment, and if ways could have been found for him to work within his limited abilities for the betterment of the family of the dead firefighter, everyone would have been better off. The same would have been true for the inspector and those who bribed him; presumably, they had greater abilities to devote to making reparation. The fact that the inspector was never prosecuted is an offense to all the victims of the fire, and to society, because the events showed that public officials can be corrupt and be corrupted with impunity.

Proper reparations would be more satisfactory than punishment in the case of many serious upper-class crimes. There is satisfaction for the millions of us victims of Kenneth Lay in the thought of his falling from his great height into a federal penitentiary, but his jail time won't do anybody much good. We are all benefited if he and Lawrence Fastow lose all chance to do the same thing again, but I'm not sure that there is any guarantee of that. It would help if there were more laws that restricted the professional and business activities of such criminals in the same way that we have our licenses restricted, suspended or revoked for unethical professional conduct. But it would be even better if Lay had to give his entire fortune to the public utility companies he swindled, so that those whose electricity went off and those who had to pay exorbitant rates could pay a little less for a while. In addition, it would be good if both Lay and Fastow, his smarter partner in crime, were made to devote the rest of their lives to improving the energy system. It seems to me that it would be proper that reparations be even more demanding than the present set of punishments. People who do great harm would benefit by making reparations, but we would also benefit if they were required to devote a lifetime of time and energy to the good of their victims and of the public in general.

More humble criminals would also benefit from such a system. Many of them are not very capable. The illiteracy rate among prisoners is much higher than in the population generally, and many of them have few skills with which to make a living honestly. A program that would train criminals to do a job and earn money with which to make payments in restitution would benefit everyone. Even now, in some western states young prisoners are formed into wildfire fighting teams, and in some instances have distinguished themselves as brave, strong and skillful. The group morale based on shared experience and pride in toughness devoted to public benefit seems in at least some cases to have undone previous criminal identities.

The life of Nathan Leopold, one of the murderers in the infamous Leopold and Loeb case, is one of the finest examples of transformation based on service. In prison he studied and taught. He mastered twenty-seven languages, and organized a school for inmates in his prison and correspondence courses for prisoners elsewhere. When Americans fighting in the Pacific in World War II needed better treatment for malaria, trials of new drugs were performed at the Joliet Penitentiary. Leopold not only volunteered to be infected and to take experimental drugs, he also helped to design and carry out the research. He ultimately studied to be a medical technician, and for years worked as one in prison. His exemplary conduct led to his release after thirty-four years. He moved to Puerto Rico where he worked in a clinic until his death.

Leopold was an unusually talented and energetic person. To promote such results in more ordinary cases would require elaborate new systems. Here are some of the utopian details I imagine: Trials would be conducted as they are now to determine guilt or innocence. After a conviction, at least as much attention would be devoted to evaluating the defendant's needs and abilities as had been devoted to the original trial. Boards with extensive professional staff would assess dangerousness, the nature of the personal characteristics that led to the commission of the crime or crimes, the damage done to victims and their resulting needs, the capacities of the criminal to be productive in the service of making reparations, and the criminal's social circumstances. The board would then formulate a detailed plan for the treatment of the defendant. Defendants would be placed in the least restrictive circumstances that would provide community safety. Many could stay at home with close monitoring, by electronic as well as ordinary means. Staying at home would need to be on the condition that it would be possible to separate the defendant from antisocial groups in the neighborhood.

Whenever possible, the criminal would be brought together with his or her victims and together they would be helped to work out acknowledgment of responsibility, amends, and ultimately reconciliation.

In cases of severe mental illness, treatment would be arranged with the least restrictive safe confinement. The plan would be approved by the court and carefully monitored by the board. Any restriction would be periodically evaluated for its effectiveness and its necessity. New methods of evaluating dangerousness would be developed and constantly evaluated. Any new offense committed by a criminal in the program would be studied to improve methods of evaluation. Great ingenuity would be required to devise plans of reparation that would be as just as possible and make the best use of the criminal's abilities. When it would not be possible for reparations to be made to specific victims, reparations to the community would be designed in accordance with what the person could do or learn to do, and what the community needed.

The political problems of establishing such a system would be even greater than the problems of designing and operating it, but I think it is time for us to resume our part in the discussion of criminal justice and bring to it all the wisdom, good will and influence we can muster.

Pomposity and Insecurity:
The Need to Be Better than Others

Talking publicly about not being defensive made me self conscious enough to notice some of the ways I am pompous. I am still self important enough to do my self analysis in public and in writing.

HAVING TYPED—IF THAT WORD CAN STILL BE USED —such a title, I have become anxious just sitting here at the computer. I expect I will be even more scared when I am reading this out loud. I am setting myself up. Perhaps my insecurity will protect me from foolishness. I think it is possible to be pompous while aware of one's insecurity, but for the most part extreme pomposity is a defense against that awareness, even if everyone else present is aware that the pompous person is insecure. I am attempting to protect myself by being open, which is crucially different from being transparent, a frequent characteristic of pomposity. Now that I have attempted to stave off the charge that I am being the very thing I am attempting to discuss, I will make some arrogant claims.

Pomposity abounds everywhere, and that includes us. It is annoying in a speaker or teacher, but it is often self-defeating in a therapist, especially when meeting an insecure and suspicious person. A few years ago, I was consulted by a woman who explained that she had rejected a large number of prospective therapists because they were too "textbooky." I think she might have stuck with a therapist whose speech was simply stilted, but besides being stilted, what she heard was doctrinaire. We in this business are prone to anxiety, especially when seeing a new customer, let alone a tough one like her, and often we try to reassure ourselves by relying on the symbols and customs of our profession.

In doing that we are playing to the wrong audience, to each other instead of the person in the room with us. We fear or can see that we are making a bad impression, and instead of talking about how things don't seem to be going well, we may inwardly blame the customer, don a stereotype of therapeutic demeanor, and think of colleagues who would see that we are doing our job just right. For many years, many people in Chicago regarded Lou Shapiro as the best analyst in town. His name is not familiar in Seattle because by and large he didn't write anything, but he did do a great many second analyses of analysts who realized that their training analyses hadn't been good. According to local lore, a rich young socialite looking for the best analyst was given his name. Shapiro came into the waiting room, rumpled, short, Jewish and not perfectly shaven. He looked at the impeccably turned out young man and saw his face fall. "So come in anyway," he said.

At about the same time, I was doing the opposite. We doctors in the Indian Health Service were commissioned officers in the United States Public Health Service and we were in uniform—essentially navy uniform. I once had an occasion to visit the San Diego Naval Hospital. I was panicky because I had no experience with what is called "military courtesy." I was afraid I wouldn't salute properly or stand up straight enough and would be scorned if not arrested, but it went fine. Hordes of sailors of both genders were walking down the street. They all saluted me and said, "Good morning, sir!" I was treated with greater respect than I ever had been before. I calmed down and began to like it. By my second visit, I was noticing people who didn't sound enthusiastic in greeting me, and even one who didn't salute at all. I wondered if I should have him arrested. I discovered that I loved unearned respect. The essence of pomposity, it seems to me, is exhibiting cues that are meant to elicit unearned respect.

I expect you will have noticed that the San Diego story is a metaphor for our professional situation. We are saluted all the time. The "unobjectionable positive transference," as Freud called it, is objectionable if it goes to our heads. One of the people I see is almost the only non-analyst in her family. She warns me not to put on airs about my importance to

her. I do not know if her imitation of her relatives congratulating themselves on how terrible it is for their patients when they go on vacation
is accurate because I don't know her family, but it is accurate of me —
before she told me about it — and of friends of mine before and since. We
play to captive audiences of one, and no doubt if some of them hold us in
high regard and we become vital to their security, it is partially earned
by our not getting in the way and even by good things we say or do, but
as we all know, and quickly forget, it comes with the role. On occasions
when I find myself impressed by someone's thinking that I am an analyst
in a million, I try to remember hearing the clientele of other people who
seem kind of average to me saying the same of them. It doesn't always
work. At the Naval Hospital I did remember that the sailors were salut-
ing the uniform, but I couldn't get away from some sense that I must be
pretty wonderful to be wearing it.

I think that pomposity is a failing that we often neglect as therapists
and supervisors. It is hard to point out without injury to one or both of
the people involved, and I think that our clinical theories of its origin
are poorly developed. I try to avoid using the word *narcissism* because I
believe it has come to mean so many different things, and because it is
used pejoratively and often tautologically. Narcissistic people are said to
be that way because of all the narcissism they have.

(I am afraid that my verbal quirk has become a pompous pain to
my associates. The grandson of Alexander Graham Bell wrote that the
inventor didn't want people to answer the phone by saying hello. He
wanted them to say "Hoy hoy." The grandson reported that in answering
the phone he often said, "Hello; I mean hoy hoy, Grandfather." My loyal
friends use the "N word," catch themselves and apologize.)

Narcissism, as I understand it, can be a factor in unpleasant self-
importance, self-involvement, selfishness and so on, but the ordinary
adjectives convey more information. Besides, narcissism can be a factor
in pleasant and productive qualities such as enthusiasm or devotion to a
pursuit such as psychoanalysis. Freud was one of the framers of twentieth century culture who succeeded in removing pejorative connotations
from the word *sex*. Heinz Kohut tried to do the same for narcissism,
but failed, which is a pity because it is no more good or bad than sex,
thought, fantasy or anger. The consequences of any of these, and of many

more forces, can certainly be terrible or wonderful, but should no more be praised or blamed than should fire.

I have just paused in my typing and got panicky. I went back over what I had written so far to try to straighten it out, and especially to try to remove as much of the pomposity as I could, but then I lost momentum, and I hear your critical voices saying that my descriptions of us are wrong—except perhaps of me—and that I had better have something more substantive than this to offer. Then I grasp at the straw that this panic is what I have to offer. If I hadn't been so scared when I drove up to the hospital, getting used to being saluted wouldn't have been so enchanting. Insecurity doesn't get enough respect, and it is partly Freud's fault. He liked Alfred Adler fine until Adler rejected his main idea and suggested a new one of his own. Both men seem to have been pompous enough to claim that what they thought of was not only the best idea, but the only one. Adler ended up denying the existence of the Oedipus complex, and Freud ended up saying, "Psychoanalysis knows nothing of an inferiority complex." It did us a lot of harm.

To this day, many of us focus much more on what we want to do to others and fear they want to do to us than on who we fear we are. As W. H. Auden wrote in his poem "September 1, 1939": "Lost in a haunted wood / Children afraid of the dark / Who have never been happy or good."

Whatever the cause of that horrible sense of ourselves, we spend much of our time and energy trying to get away from it, and most of our efforts are ineffective or destructive.

What I think is useful about Adler's word is that it emphasizes not only the unfavorable contrast we make between ourselves and others but also our feeling that it is our fault. Certainly, when we feel inferior to others we often believe them to be at fault, as can be heard in the Scottish ballad, "Johnny Lad": "The Queen was playing football with the lads on Tinkham Green / The forward for the other side was scoring with great style / The Queen she called a policeman and had him thrown in jail."

We naturally want to get away from the feeling that we have a terrible inherent flaw, and often do so by deciding that someone who reminds us of our inadequacy is doing something bad to us, on purpose, and ought to be punished. But, to continue to blame Freud, decades of denying the importance of feelings of inferiority has distorted much of psychoanalysis to this day. The wish to arrest the rival star player has been the center of attention instead of the terrible feeling of not being a good-enough player oneself.

Most of us have focused on envy at the expense of insecurity. The Adlerians, it seems to me, have the opposite distortion, as have their successors, the followers of Harry Stack Sullivan and of Heinz Kohut. Early in the development of self psychology, Joseph Kepecs pointed out that Kohut was reincorporating a long-despised term into analysis, and Kohut included it mainly by implication. I think that insecurity and envy are two ends of the same thing. The imbalance I am trying to describe consists in always picking up one end rather than the other. Melanie Klein, who I think usually picked up the envy end, advanced our cause by pointing out that the thing, whichever end you picked up, came into being when life did, without waiting for sibling rivalry or the oedipal period. To vary the metaphor, insecurity and envy, like the closely related concepts shame and anger, are chicken and egg; deciding which came first is best done on the basis of clinical usefulness.

My fear in San Diego in 1970 was based on my sense that I hadn't measured up. In an intellectual way, I convinced myself that I wasn't in the armed forces fighting in Vietnam because I thought to do so was wrong. The problem was that I had been a little kid during World War II when all the young men were in the fight and admired for being there, and I still have some basic sense that being in a war is a natural and inescapable part of the life cycle. So a military base was populated by people who had developed in an important way that I had not. They were brave, aggressive, knew how to stand up straight and wear a uniform, and I was a cowardly, geeky peacenik, poorly disguised in a quasi-military uniform.

My fear of inferiority seems a good starting point for understanding my pompous excitement when I seemingly triumphed over my insecurity. But what came before that? Was I still feeling inferior to my father, whom I could never displace from my mother's life? To some degree I think so, but there was much more to it than that. My father was forty-six when I was born, fifty-one at the beginning of the war, much too old for the army. He had been in World War I—not very real to me. Everyone else's father was in the war. I was worried this contrast said something bad about him and, by extension, me.

In addition, my mother and grandmother were constantly telling me that I had every possible talent and accomplishment. That idea was exciting and pleasing but also frightening and awful, particularly when experience with other people showed me that it wasn't so. The memory that comes to me as I write is of being three or four, with my mother at the front window of our apartment, across the street from the school. My mother has called me there to watch the patrol boys march into school from their posts. She points out the boy who is the captain of the patrol, and I know that she is sure that someday I will be that boy.

In fact, I wasn't. My best friend Eugene was, a fact that still bothers me and I am sure did in San Diego in 1970. If I had beaten out Eugene, I am sure I would have been rather a pompous safety patrol captain.

Even though I want to look at insecurity as generally being at the root of pomposity, I don't mean to imply that insecurity is a bedrock part of human equipment, even if we all have it. Adler thought it came from actual physical defects. Sullivan thought it was contagiously spread from the mother, whose anxiety about herself and her infant became the infant's original anxiety. Subsequently her forbidding gestures became a signal that the unpleasant situation of being with an anxious mother was about to recur. Kohut's account is much more complicated, and I think a bit incomplete, but more useful, partly because of its complexity. For some years at this meeting, I have been describing my version, which I think is an explication and extension of Kohut's. I am emboldened in continuing down the path by the research results of the attachment theorists and neuropsychoanalysts, though I prefer my own theoretical formulations.

Teleology is said to be the mistress of every biologist, publicly denied but privately cherished. In the same way, blame is the mistress of every psychoanalytic theorist. Just as the biologists are right in trying to escape from the tendency to explain phenomena as the result of intelligent design, we are right in trying to escape our tendency to blame someone besides the unintelligent designer for the flaws in human nature. Nevertheless we all give hints that we are blaming someone: the parent, the child, the analysand, the analyst. Psychoanalytic case histories can almost always be classified as either being analysand idealizing or analysand debunking: "The patient, a brilliant biochemist…" "The patient, a highly self-centered and entitled young man…"

Almost alone among us insecurity specialists, Adler, like Freud, was an analysand blamer. Most of us are parent blamers. But, naturally, I want to deny that I am. In my defense, I will claim that I don't blame anyone. Everyone does what she or he sees as necessary or best on the basis of the world as it appears to him or her. I think my mother's ambitions for me caused many of my troubles, but I don't blame her for that because her fantasies of me resulted from her mother's ambitions for her, which resulted from her mother's having come down with typhoid at exactly the wrong moment, and I can't blame my grandmother for that.

This must be the most apologetic and defensive paper I have ever written, but I will press on.

Freud saw our troubles as inescapable because our instincts were opposed to the nature of reality, and especially the part of reality called *civilization*. Kohut saw our troubles as inescapable because no one's parents are good enough. For example, he thought the Oedipus complex was a breakdown product of normal desires brought on by parents who didn't understand or appreciate their children's normal sexual and competitive wishes, but since parents who understand and appreciate do not occur in nature, the happy, successful oedipal situation, as opposed to the complex, is like what Candide said: "The only good place in the world is El Dorado, but no one can get there."

I believe that if every interaction between infants and children and their caretakers were perfectly attuned, insecurity would vanish from the world. We would all be playfully and productively competitive, and realistically fearful and aggressive. It would be very bad for business, but fortunately we don't have to worry.

Most of the troubles that keep us busy, and virtually all of our pomposity, arise from the set of personal goals that I—in splendid isolation—have been calling secondary ambition, a concept derived from what Kohut calls vertically split-off grandiosity. It came as a shock to me to realize that the difference between the theories of Kohut and Otto Kernberg were not as great as I had always thought. Vertically split-off grandiosity is almost the same in manifestations (though not in etiology) as Kernberg's pathological narcissism. Melanie Klein's manic defense is a subset of it. Primary ambition is the El Dorado version, or would be if it occurred without the secondary version.

Kohut said that our desires are organized by the supraordinate motivational poles of ambition and ideals. We are driven by our ambitions and led by our ideals. If we fall short of our ambitions, we suffer shame and anger. If we fail to live up to our ideals, as almost always happens, we are sad and long to do better, but are consoled by our still cherishing our highest goals and by the hope that we will come closer next time. To the extent that we don't expect to be able to achieve our ambitions we are insecure. To the extent that we expect to fall short of our ideals we are humble.

Ambition is rooted in the beginning of life. Its earliest form is the need for reciprocal, echoing, mirroring interaction with our caretakers. The reason Harry Stack Sullivan was right that babies catch anxiety from their mothers can be seen in Regina Pally's videos. Infants whose expressions, postures, and sounds occur in harmonious back and forth influence with a secure mother aren't catching anything but joy. Infants who are out of harmony with an anxious mother are clearly anxious. Infant observation shows how our sense of ourselves is interpersonal from the beginning. I think that it is reasonable to call the baby's need for reciprocity *ambition*, because it has the same form as do desires that more clearly fit that term. Babies who want their mothers to smile back at them when they smile are not so different from governors who want to be president. The governors just want the response on a grander stage. Even seemingly solitary ambitions, such as mine to row around Lake Union faster than I ever have before, are basically desires to occupy a certain niche in my interpersonal world. Even if I never told anyone—a likely story—a personal record slightly redefines all my relationships.

Primary ambition develops smoothly from the earliest happy communications if the people in children's lives continue to appreciate and participate in what they do. The basic fantasies we want to live out are determined collaboratively with our caretakers. Those things that come easily and naturally to us and that make the most sense to the adults around us are the ones that we strive toward all our lives. A child who is an early, fluent talker in an intellectual family may evolve gradually into a scholar. In a political family, such a child may evolve into a public speaker. Children's wanting to be something that makes sense to their parents is a result of natural and largely unconscious parental influence. Such ambitions are heart felt and seem to us to be the basic elements of our character.

Ambition in the earliest stages relates only to those who respond to us, but gradually a comparative element is added, and ambitions are relative to competitors. I don't think anyone knows for sure if this trend is inevitably determined by our DNA. I don't know of any cultures without it. Anyhow, it comes natural to us to tell our babies that they are just the best ones in the world. They get the idea. When my daughter was two, I would say, "Helen, you're so beautiful." She would smile graciously and say, "I know it."

Potential trouble arises around the beginning of the second year. Toddlers need interaction, but they also need to have it more on their own schedule and at their own initiative. As D. W. Winnicott pointed out, they need to be alone in the presence of their mothers, able to concentrate on their own experience, and to take for granted that if they need what Margaret Mahler called refueling, they can get it. Another challenge is the toddler's recognition that there is plenty that he or she can't do that the bigger members of the family can. If things go well, idealization comes into being. The children's security is now based not only on their own cherished abilities but on the abilities of their cherished family, whose greatness is the children's own through identification.

I do not see this idealization as a defense against envy. Insecurity/ envy arises when the connection with the family fails. That misfortune is most likely in relation to older brothers and sisters, but is far from automatic. In the summer of 1966, my then only child was a year and a half when we moved from a culture where sibling rivalry was regarded as inevitable and even desirable to a culture where it was rare and deplored. When Helen was born in the spring of 1967, we had picked up enough Navajo ways and opinions that the children have always been, by white standards, unusually loving and harmonious. Even when older children are competitive and mean to younger ones, the little ones often show a capacity to admire and cherish the older, and feel secure because they have such big, capable siblings.

Worse trouble comes as children become more capable. What an infant does spontaneously is almost never dangerous, because the parents see to it that possible dangers are out of reach. But a toddler can and does do all kinds of undesirable things, and needs to do things that the parents direct. As Winnicott says, if the child's murderous rage doesn't kill the parent off, a new kind of love for the parent comes to be. If the battles of this stage can be negotiated without either parent or child becoming a tyrant, the child will probably always be secure and autonomous, but this is the time when some degree of secondary ambition develops.

In the worst cases, the ground is already prepared by failures in the evolution of primary ambition. Babies whose parents are out of whack because of anxiety, depression, exhaustion from other problems, or who otherwise don't play their necessary parts, are insecure, as has been convincingly demonstrated experimentally. They aren't capable of thinking there is something wrong with their parents, but they gradually develop a more and more refined opinion that something is the matter with them. When the battles of separation-individuation start, they are poorly equipped to stand the strain. They frequently panic and, depending on the family response to their tantrums, they develop a characteristic style of fight or flight.

If the parents are also panicky or out of control, a lot depends on whether the parents win or lose the fights. The child of a parent who uses excess force, moral or physical, to ensure victory over the small enemy is likely to develop a masochistic style; insecurity is defended against by a determination to always fight on despite always losing in order to demonstrate moral superiority, and by being the most injured person as an unsatisfactory substitute for being the most successful person. The child of a parent who panics and loses is likely to develop a paranoid style: insecurity defended against by a determination never to give ground to a perceived adversary, and to withdraw from relationship rather than to risk personal diminishment. If the insecure child is met by a more controlled parent, but one who insists on winning without compromise, the child is likely to develop a depressive style; insecurity defended against by trying to please, and a preference for sacrificing one's own standing rather than give up relationship.

I'm afraid that this description is much too abbreviated and over-simplified, but I hope it serves as a rough guide to the different types of secondary ambition. I use the term to draw a distinction between simple, basic drives for achievements that seem wonderful in and of themselves and, on the other hand, drives for achievements that are not originally our own ideas, but ones based on our knowledge or illusion of what our significant others want, so that achieving them will prove to them that we are not nothing. In many cases, including ones like many of us in this business and the people we serve, our secondary ambitions are a more or less accurate transcription of our parents' ambitions for us. People who are like this are almost always on the depressive side of the spectrum, wanting to please more than wanting to be impressive.

There is a confusing subgroup; those who are trying to live out the ambitions of paranoid parents. Generally, to whatever extent we are moved by primary ambition, we are secure and make decisions based on our wishes, and conversely, to whatever extent we are driven by second-ary ambition, we are insecure and make decisions based on our fears. That description strikes me as a bit bloodless. Lots of us have horrible, if intermittent, convictions of ways that we aren't as good as others. Even slight hints that we can't be better will feel like a sudden blow, or even just a touch, to an exquisitely sore boil. The pain is so great that we fall apart. It is an emergency that must be ended by some extreme measure, frequently a furious attack on whoever did something, even so little a thing as a mild expression of doubt about one of our opinions.

I want to make one more distinction among types of secondary ambi-tion. Some people who are trying to be what their parents wanted them to be are volunteers. Others were drafted. I know a volunteer, one whose mother seems to have paid little attention to her baby and imposed on her a rigid system of caretaking; for example, bottle feeding on a strict schedule and later feeding solid foods regardless of what the baby liked. If she wouldn't eat what was provided, she didn't eat, and the same food was offered until the infant gave up and ate it. The mother thought that her child's crying was abnormal and bad. At later ages she labeled any expression of dissatisfaction a bad mood and, instead of attending to the complaint, demanded that the girl get over it. During the second and third years, the child gave up crying and became terrified of disturbing her mother. She was often sleepless and terrified during the night, but no one ever came to comfort her, and not only did she not dare to ask for help, she was also frightened of disturbing them if she had to get up to go to the bathroom. The father was generally unavailable, and though the daughter admired him greatly, both parents told her that he was much too important and busy for her to bother him, and so she lost the chance to develop security based on an identification with a wonderful person. Neither parent had a detailed program for what she should do or become except rigidly well-behaved.

This woman tried hard to find achievements that would please the parents, but the mother was usually competitive and denigrating and the father unresponsive. She grew up convinced that she was stupid, fat and ugly despite being intelligent, thin and attractive. She has felt all her life that only constant effort at the highest possible level could ever hide her deficiencies from everyone. Her work and personal life are dominated by her over-conscientiousness. What she does is almost always admirable and she is liked and admired, though she doesn't believe it. She does believe it when anyone is dissatisfied and angry with her and sees it as proof of her inferiority. She is not pompous, unlike people whose parents drafted them into a life prescribed in detail and who are much more likely to be so.

For example, a man I know was named in accordance with his parents' particular grand ambitions for him. For as long as he can remember, it was assumed that not only would he pursue a particular profession, but also that he would pursue it at schools his parents picked out at or before the time he was born. Thirty years later he is right on plan except that he rebelliously chose a different branch of his profession than had been specified. However, he is eagerly pursuing advancement to the high position in his profession that was specified. His need to show that he is the best at more or less everything, as his parents expect results in competitive success, but also a tense and driven bragging about it that is quite pompous at times. I said that he *needs* to show he is the best, despite my generally being reluctant to describe motives as needs. I usually prefer to speak of wishes because so often people claim they need rather than want in order to escape responsibility for a desire which they fear others will disapprove of. Conversely, 'need' is sometimes used as a pejorative implying that other peoples' reasons for their actions are primitive: "Why did you need to do that?" instead of, "Why did you decide to do that?" But I think the man whose life is following his parents' plan really does need to be the best, because it feels to him that if he isn't, he won't be himself by his parents' definition of him, the only one he really knows.

Other insecure people also need to be better than others even if their parents didn't exactly specify that was what they had in mind for them. They may not spend as much time and energy on competing, but their lurking sense of inferiority is so threatening that, if someone, e.g., their therapist, implies that he or she knows better or is better in some way, it triggers an emergency response because any hint that someone finds them inferior is too painful to be borne. This sort of situation is one in which a therapist's pomposity can be quite a menace. Our own insecurity may make us need to be better than the customer—not only to know better but to have only good intentions. So if customers dispute our claim that we know something about them that they don't, and accuse us of trying to undermine them, we are sometimes tempted to point out that we do know better, that we are actually being helpful, and the customer is only angry because he or she needs to control us. I think accepting the possibility that the customers are right and finding out more about their version sometimes is unacceptable, because in our insecurity—and working with a tough customer can certainly make us insecure—we, too, can't bear not to be the better one.

Even when we therapists are quite secure and calm in the face of the storming of vulnerable people, perfectly reasonable theoretical formulations may lead us to be less than helpful. If I offer an explanation of some problem and the other person experiences my calmness and capacity to think as a reminder that he is distraught, and worse yet, his inability to think while in a panic convinces him that he really is basically as stupid as he always fears, he may complain bitterly and insightfully about my not only failing to help, but on top of that making him much worse. Often enough such an attack is so effective that I become distraught, unable to think, and feel basically stupid. Undeniably projective identification is a valid concept for understanding these events, but unless used with extreme care it will lead to interventions that make matters worse, because they are likely to include ideas such as the person's destroying our capacity to think out of a deathly need to be as good as or better than we.

These suggestions, no matter how helpfully offered, amount to an indictment that is unlikely to be thought through and truly accepted. The person instead will need to exonerate himself or compliantly plead guilty. I think the former is more frequent and results in plenty of murderous rage on the part of both people, and sometimes results in a prolonged stalemate. Various colleagues have told me that it is well known that I have difficulty in accepting the negative transference. My idea of the truth of that criticism is that I fail to see the usefulness of generating and maintaining antagonisms. It is true that many of our customers need help in healing splits and transforming rage into ambivalence, but you don't learn to swim by drowning. In some ways rageful defensiveness is preferable to compliance, which is likely to lead to a new layer of secondary ambition. The analysand may adopt the analyst's goal of fighting narcissism—his own and everyone else's.

In another talk at this meeting I developed the notion of the *false-selfobject*—not a false object but a selfobject of a false self. I believe that Winnicott's notion of false self is secondary ambition viewed as structure. The sense of hollowness derives in part from the insecurity that secondary ambition attempts to stave off. What also feels false is that the person's desperate needs for victory come not from the heart, but from someone else's needs and values. Just as primary ambition consists of the wish to be in a certain relationship with another or a group—a true selfobject, secondary ambition consists of a need to disprove inferiority by being in a certain relation with someone or a group—a falseselfobject. The compliant acceptance of an indicting interpretation is like a conversion experience: "I was lost and frightened until I was born again into the church of psychoanalysis and learned to fight my narcissism." My favorite of colleague Ivri Kumin's papers is the one on the effect of incorrect interpretations. He points out that often, rather than being cast aside, they may become imposing monuments covered with mother of pearl.

I hope I have adequately disposed of my straw man, projective identification formulation, in this example. A version that I think works better is that the person is just as intelligent as I am, but terribly insecure. Like someone in a fragile, unstable boat, any little wave will swamp him, and I'm the wave. His panic over his pathologic belief that everyone is actually smarter than he is impels him to try to disprove it by showing that I am just as stupid. I am satisfied up to a point with the notion that I am just as stupid as he is, because he's not stupid at all. Beyond that area of agreement, I am ready to believe that there must be some truth in his complaints, and I try to engage him in a detailed examination of the whole interaction in hopes of finding out what happened. Probably we will discover something like a condescending tone in my original remark, and if all goes well, which happens a small percent of the time, when I own up to my condescension he may think about his own fragility, a quality that is easier to accept in himself than a wish to destroy my mind.

If we can restore our equanimity, the whole episode may go a small way toward increasing his security by invalidating his more basic pathologic beliefs in his stupidity and inability to get along with anyone. Once in a while, the repair of one of these difficulties can produce a joyful burst of mutuality in which both people abandon all efforts to be one up. I think that good result is what Emmanuel Ghent has called surrender (as opposed to submission). It is also the result of a successful completion of the first two steps of Alcoholics Anonymous.

As tricky as it is to work with extremely insecure people, often the trickiest part is to address their pomposity directly. After several years of analysis, I made my first effort to address the way someone's grandiose behavior caused her trouble. The effort was ultimately successful, but so distressing that the next day she told me that she had been awakened in the middle of the night by a bomb going off in her house, and even as she was telling me, she was not completely convinced that there hadn't really been a bomb.

The reason that Kohut called it vertically split-off grandiosity is that the grandiosity is conscious, but treated as though it doesn't exist or is something else. Its nature is denied. My favorite example of that is Frank Lloyd Wright. Called to testify in a trial, he was asked to state his name and occupation. He said, "World's greatest architect." Later when his wife expostulated with him, he said, "But my dear, I was under oath." Wright's mother had decided before he was born that he would be the world's greatest architect and worked hard from the time of his birth to see to it that he would be. I think what was unusual about his story is that it worked.

Many a person is programmed to do what he or she can't, but exceptionally talented children sometimes make their parents' wishes really come true. Many great leaders are in that category: Wellington, Grant, Churchill, Franklin Delano Roosevelt, MacArthur and Truman. The interaction of the last two is particularly interesting. Douglas MacArthur's paternal grandfather was the youngest and one of the most heroic generals in the Union Army. MacArthur's mother was disappointed in the military career of her husband, but determined that her son would live up to or surpass the great example of her father-in-law.

Janine Chasseguet-Smirgel has written about mothers who tell their sons that they are far better than their fathers and reassure them that they needn't compete with them. Unlike some of them, MacArthur's mother did expect her son to compete in the world in order to prove his superiority to his father. She indoctrinated him with her fantasies of his exceptional qualities and great destiny from the beginning of his life and involved herself in every detail of his growing up. Even when he went off to West Point, she lived for four years in a room across the road from his dormitory so that she could watch his light each night to make sure he stayed up late enough to study more than anyone else. When he was the virtual ruler of the Philippines in the 1920s, he learned one day that his mother was about to arrive on a surprise visit. The great man panicked and hastily arranged for the concealment of his living arrangements, and especially of his Filipina concubine.

Harry Truman's mother was similar. He ended each day in the White House writing her a letter to account for his actions. She was different in not having quite so detailed a plan for her son's greatness, and indeed, she imbued him with her own version of humility. The combination of conviction about his own correctness and ability with an unassuming, down to earth presentation of himself as an ordinary citizen was one of the most striking features of his character and one of the sources of his success. It seems plausible that, when the great collision of these two men occurred, the general underestimated the president in accordance with his mother's view of his relationship with his father, and that he overestimated the power of his popularity with the public because it seemed to him like a new edition of the adulation of his mother.

Freud's observation, that the first son of a loving young mother feels like a conqueror, fits well in this context. His remark can probably be read best as having to do with the development of his primary ambition, of which he clearly had plenty, but that isn't the whole story. Freud was of the first assimilated generation of his previously traditionally Jewish family. His parents made great sacrifices—and demanded his sister sacrifice her piano—in the interest of his making it in the gentile world. Some of his unfortunate personal qualities, such as his pompous rejection of Adler, may have resulted from the insecurity that came with the fairly high degree of his secondary ambition. The fortunate irony is that his great work resulted in a counter force to secondary ambition. Even when psychoanalysis seemed to be focused on the resolution of the Oedipus complex, it was functioning pretty effectively in the furtherance of separation individuation. I was young when analysis was at its most popular, and it seemed as if everyone was either in analysis or at least enthusiastically discussing it. In those days, it was simply assumed by most people that analysis was primarily a way of escaping parental influence. The intellectual climate of that time was anti-maternal. Phillip Wylie introduced the term "Momism," and it was widely popular.

Analysis has thrived among Jews, and the widely accepted target of treatment and the analytic outlook was the Jewish mother. I believe that there was some truth in the stereotype that Jews wanted their children to be doctors and to stay closely connected to a family which they would thereby make upwardly mobile. The Jews of the early twentieth century seem to me to be an instance of a general phenomenon. Oppressed ethnic groups, as they escape persecution and encounter economic opportunity, naturally have an explosion of expectation and ambition. Parents and grandparents who slaved away just to stay alive, and who expected each generation to help the previous one to make ends more or less meet, tend to expect their children and grandchildren also to devote themselves to the family good. But in new times and/or a new country the goal is not just survival but social and economic advancement. Those who have been oppressed push their children to excel in the new culture. They imbue them unapologetically with their own goals. In the first decades of the last century this strategy was so successful that Jews appeared in university, and especially medical school classes, in such disproportionate numbers that the gentile authorities took measures to limit them. To get over having been pushed, lots of the educated Jews got analyzed and many of them became analysts. That phase of Jewish life has largely passed I think, but there is a new and much larger group moving into that niche, namely Asians. I was told, I think on good authority, that a common joke among young Asian-American doctors is that their white friends won't believe that their parents still listen in on their phone calls. As Heinz Kohut used to say when he heard of an unfortunate child, "Work is being prepared for the next generation of psychotherapists."

It may be that it is just my old person's preference for the conditions of his childhood, but I don't like the way middleclass childhood is now conducted. In the good old days when we weren't in school, we went outside to play and lived in a society of children that ran itself until our parents called us in to dinner or to bed. Parents weren't concerned with quality time, and if anyone had asked us kids, we would have said that quality time was when our parents let us alone and we could do what we liked. The kids I know now are so scheduled by their parents that they seldom get to direct their own lives. The scheduled activities seem to be designed by the parents to get their offspring into the right primary school so that they can get into the right secondary school so that they can get into Harvard. Work is being prepared. But it's rewarding, interesting work, and I'm glad there will be customers for all the smart young Asian psychoanalysts I think we will soon be training.

Faith and Gullibility

When I was in the Indian Health Service, I used to publish papers and talk at meetings about Native American religion. When I first attended Navajo religious services, I thought I was going as an observer in order to learn about the people with whom I was working. Pretty quickly, though, I realized I was going in order to worship, and I became a member of the Native American Church. After that change, I felt a conflict of interest between the believer and the observer and, worse yet, between the member and the person whose professional career was being advanced. Had I been Indian myself, it wouldn't have mattered, but there have been too many people who have learned from the Navajo and not helped them. There was another problem; as I went around giving my talks, I drew fairly good crowds. (This was the '70s.) They took me seriously and believed what I told them. I was pleased until I realized that these people would believe anything as long as it wasn't conventional, corporate, American popular culture. I quit. I was in the middle of a paper about the use of humor in the Native American Church, which still seems like an interesting topic to me, but I vowed, to paraphrase Chief Joseph, to write no more forever. The Northwest Alliance lured me back by announcing that they were publishing an issue of their newsletter that would feature essays on faith. Since the problem of distinguishing faith from gullibility was at the heart of half of my problem, I decided to have a go at it.

ONE DAY EIGHTEEN YEARS AGO WHEN SOMEONE WAS late, I was leafing through *Newsweek* in my office waiting room and was startled to find a picture of my brother. The story was that Marcellus had made it snow. After one bad snow year, and at the start of what was predicted to be another, Copper Mountain Ski Area in Colorado had hired him to do something about it, and he had. I wasn't surprised that Marcellus had made it snow, but I was a little put off by his doing it so publicly, in the white world, and wondered if it weren't sacrilegious to use medicine power for the benefit of a big commercial enterprise.

Some years before that, I had played a role in his crossing over from prominence in the Native American world to fame in the immigrant American one. I had been invited to a conference in Council Grove, Kansas, an annual event back then, put on by the Menninger Clinic to bring together healers from many cultures. In those days I was going around giving talks on Indian medicine based on my ten years of work with indigenous practitioners. I had grown uneasy about doing that because I was an observer rather than the real thing. Most people I knew who were the real thing were not able to speak English or were not comfortable speaking it publicly in white person format. Marcellus Williams was. He is a traditional Creek medicine man, a ceremonialist in the Native American Church, has a degree in theology, another in cultural anthropology, and year after year takes part in the medicine ways of various tribes and learns new skills. The Menninger's people happily accepted my suggestion that I bring him with me, he impressed everyone there, and one thing led to another.

He and I are brothers because of the Native American Church (NAC). In 1966, when I was assigned by the United States Public Health Service to be the psychiatrist for the Navajo Nation, the NAC was the most rapidly growing movement there. It was also illegal. White missionaries had lobbied the tribal council more than twenty years earlier when it had first appeared there and had convinced them that a religion that used a mind-altering drug was an immoral menace. The council was amenable to the idea more because they disliked a new medical/religious way becoming a rival to traditional Navajo ways than because they minded psychedelic drugs, since Navajo medicine had those. But there had been a shift of Navajo opinion.

As David Aberle shows in his wonderful book, *The Peyote Religion Among the Navajo*, the destruction of the old herding economy, and with it the coherence of the extended family system, made traditional Navajo religion, with its huge ceremonies that demand the support of lots and lots of relatives, always difficult, and sometimes impossible. In addition, demoralization and loneliness called for new solutions that a pan-Indian redemptive religion offered. It also offered the construction of new extended family through adoption and help with the overwhelming problem of widespread alcoholism.

My other brother, Tom Nez, came back from the Korean War a drunk. Members of our family nabbed him on the street in Gallup, New Mexico, and dragged him home to Wide Ruins, Arizona, and put him through some sweat lodges and a peyote meeting. The meeting was run by Jack Koshaway, a Sac and Fox "roadman," as NAC ceremonialists are called. He had been invited to come to Navajo by early converts who needed an expert to teach them. He and various members of the family had taken each other as brothers, and so a new family extending among different tribes was created. Such a development was a big change from age-old Navajo chauvinism, but one that was strengthening for people who were in danger of drowning in the mainstream of American life, as it was then often called. Koshaway introduced Marcellus, a much younger man, to the south-central Navajo, and ultimately Marcellus took his place. In the meantime, Tommy quit drinking and progressed in the NAC, and after some years Jack Koshaway gave him his "fireplace," as we call it when one roadman trains and ordains another. Tommy and Marcellus, the leading roadmen of the area, took each other as brothers.

In 1966, all I knew of this was that there were a lot of Navajos regularly ingesting a plant that was rich in mescaline and other powerful drugs. At the time, the popular press and the allegedly scientific literature was full of alarming accounts of people going crazy because of psychedelics. I thought I should learn something about it, but all the people I asked said they knew nothing. A few years later, it was fun to be part of the secret group and to join in the pretense of ignorance when what might be the law was around. But, for a year, people thought I might be the law.

I met Tommy in the spring of 1967 when we both played on the Gallup Indian Medical Center softball team. One day, toward the end of the softball season, I ran into him at the hospital where he worked as a driver-interpreter for the Trachoma Team. He greeted me in Navajo and I replied. He asked how I was and I said fine, thus exercising almost all I then knew of the language. In English, he said that he had heard that I was asking lots of people to help me attend a peyote meeting and asked why I wanted to do that. I said that many of my patients were going to them, and I thought I ought to know about it so that I could understand them better. He said that he would take me.

Saturday night and Sunday morning of the next weekend were one of the big turning points of my life. At first I was terrified, and then I was terrified and sick. Then I was paranoid, thinking that these twenty or so people in the hogan with me had come to see me suffer. About the time of the "midnight water"—one of the main events of a meeting—I calmed down and realized that I was incorporated into a group of people to whom I was completely open, who were completely open to me, and that our communion with one another was based on our complete openness to the presence of God.

I had never experienced such a thing since my early childhood, and then it had happened only fleetingly because most of the time the people around me in temple were only going through the religious motions. As a child I was a serious Reform Jew. It still hurts my feelings that many Jews regard that phrase as oxymoronic because to them reform is by definition not serious. I believed as a child that we Reform Jews were the most serious because our elimination of the countless details of Jewish observance left us in unobstructed touch with the Essential. In my adolescence, however, I was disappointed. The people around me seemed not to actually be worshipping when that was supposedly what we were all doing, and the whole organization of the temple appeared to me to be serving ulterior motives which largely were based in egotism. I dropped out and became confused about what it was I believed in.

For a while, I believed in psychoanalysis as though it were a religion, in doing which, I think I was the same as many others.

I was impressed during my residency when a fundamentalist patient balked at being interviewed by one of the faculty in front of a roomful of us beginners. She said she would proceed only if he believed in God. The interviewer, Mike Serota, said, "I believe deeply in my profession," and she was satisfied. I think Freud's generation of scientists believed in science as earlier generations had believed in God. That was, I think, wearing a bit thin by the middle of the twentieth century, and in any case, by the time I went to my first peyote meeting I was feeling queasy about according science that much importance, and was even wondering if psychoanalysis was a science. So that first meeting was like coming home, and that community became my home.

Over and over, I have had the joy of being out in the great space of the desert night with my usual walls gone—the walls of my individual self—and all of us present, united with the whole of creation.

That is the main thing, and oddly, the miracles that I have seen are almost a distraction, not that they aren't wonderful. One night, long ago, Tommy, running a meeting, came into a mood that I can come closest to describing by saying that he was playing—with us and with God. It was a brilliantly starry night with no clouds, and on a whim he said, "I think I'll ask the Creator to make it rain." He did, and it rained.

Traditional Navajo medicine/religion is a lot more like psychoanalysis than the NAC is. Before I went to that meeting, I met a man name Daghantsaaza, a famous *hatathli*. The *hatathli* are the highest order of Navajo medicine people. The word is usually translated as "ceremonialist." They preside at seven- or nine-night ceremonies with a fixed liturgy that includes the recitation of myth and prayers, dancing and sand painting. What the *hatathli* do is like performing the whole of the *Nibelungen Ring* by memory.

I heard about Daghantsaaza when I was going to visit Navajo schizophrenics. One of them, along with her family, told me that she no longer was ill, and they were right. She said that she had been cured by a ceremony Daghantsaaza had performed. So I found him. I told him that I thought maybe we were concerned with treating the same kinds of conditions. He said he wasn't sure about that, but that he would tell me the most important thing he had learned from his grandfathers: "There's a part of the mind that people don't know they have, and it's that part that determines whether they remain well or become sick."

For some years, I spent days talking with him and with other *hatathli*. Like psychoanalysis, their work is based in a prescribed procedure and it is within the strictly defined limits of their practice that people have a healing experience. I believe that the ceremonies are often successful because the Navajo system is designed to find the one that conforms to the conflicts that are at the heart of the difficulty. The experience of the patient with the *hatathli*, when it works right, resolves personal and familial dilemmas. Every part of every ceremony is based in Navajo cosmology and theology, about which some people are literal-minded and fundamentalist, but most are not.

The cosmology and theology of the NAC are a good deal more vague than those of Navajo tradition or those of most western religions, and its practice, though orderly and well-defined, is far less rigid or detailed than the ceremonies or the liturgy of western religions. The *hatathli*'s account of reality is handed down by authority. NAC faith, when things are working right, is based on the experience one has in the meeting.

In my opinion real faith is based in experience. Gullibility is coerced pseudofaith, reaction formation to doubt, the desire for membership in a special group or for self-enhancing magic. When I was first speaking in public about Native American healing, I was gratified by being well-received. Not long afterwards, I realized that my audiences were gullible. They were ready to believe and admire almost anything as long as it wasn't conventional. Many of them were particularly eager to believe in magic, and when I talked with them, I found that they were adherents of schemes that I thought were farfetched quackery. I didn't think I was fooling them, but I could have easily done so.

What made me particularly queasy was the idea that I might be one of them: an outsider so eager to believe something special and wonderful that I had been tricked or had tricked myself. I was reassured by continuing real and convincing experience back home on the reservation and by my fellow speakers on these programs. They were advanced teachers of various non-Western disciplines and religions: Sufism, yoga, Tibetan Buddhism and so on. Almost all of them were down-to-earth and impressive. Their accounts of their practice made sense and their personal presence conveyed their accomplishment in connecting with forces beyond their individual selves. I wanted to know more about their ways so that I could be more like them. For the most part, they were more interested in growth and development than in any system of belief.

Systems of belief that organize people's lives seem to be accepted more often than not for ulterior motives. The other day I heard a National Public Radio story about a Democratic candidate for the U.S. Senate. He routinely asks the voters he meets to remember him in their prayers. For all I know, he may have true faith based on his own awareness of God, but since the Republicans are basing their appeal on their fundamentalist Christianity, I suspect that the candidate is more moved by a desire to undercut the opposition than by an eagerness to be prayed for. That idea was enhanced when I heard him say in his stump speech that he came to religion the old-fashioned way—"My parents made me go to church." Even if he is sincere in his request for prayer, I suspect that his faith is based on identification with the aggressor and that he would feel guilty if he didn't believe, try to believe, or at least say he believes.

Adherents of Indian religions are often similar. Two sisters I knew once consulted a Navajo diviner of the kind who looks for visions in a hanging drop of water. One sister was an MSW in our mental health program and, from college on, had been a fervent advocate of preserving Navajo culture. It was her idea to go to the seer. Her sister had not gone on in school beyond Bureau of Indian Affairs boarding school, where she had been taught that Navajo religion was dangerous superstition. The social worker was disappointed that, no matter how hard she tried, she saw nothing in the water, and her sister was a bit embarrassed that she had a vision. I think that one was trying to believe but did not because of her identification with non-Indians who had been her teachers and were her friends, and that the other was much more open to Navajo experience because her schooling had not changed her identity much.

It is decades since the government has attacked Indian tradition. Everyone supposedly supports it nowadays. Right now there is a campaign for Navajo tribal president going on, and the candidates are acting like the senatorial candidate, letting everyone know that they are believers not only in traditional Navajo religion but also in the NAC, which hasn't been illegal since 1970.

I was lucky in becoming a part of the NAC when it was still underground. It took courage to belong in those days and it had in no way become bureaucratized or conventional. I think I came to psychoanalysis too late. In the early days it was disreputable and iconoclastic. The early analysts were convinced by their own introspection, and by the experience of being analyzed, and of analyzing, that Freud was onto something. Luckily for me, even though when I first heard of it psychoanalysis was at the height of its public acceptance and people were jumping on the bandwagon, my first real encounter was reading *The Psychopathology of Everyday Life* when I was a kid. It was completely convincing because as I read it, I could see the evidence in myself and everyone else I knew. A few years later, on the other hand, when I read *Totem and Taboo*, I tried to believe it because it was what the team I wanted to join believed.

In the long run, what I am convinced of in psychoanalysis is all and only what I have experienced, and that is quite a bit. Like the Indian rituals I know, the analytic procedure, when it is working right, overcomes the isolation of our separated selves and, in the best of moments, when two—or more—of us can be free to say to each other what is really happening, we are not only in touch with each other but, through that touch, are aware of our connection to Everything. That expression of the experience may sound strange because we live in a secular society in which religious experience goes politely unmentioned or is aggressively trumpeted as an attribute of superiority. Anyhow, I don't care what any of us call what I take to be a connection to the Infinite. It only happens occasionally, but we know it when it does, and we know that it is what we're looking for. It is and isn't miraculous. It isn't the flashy kind of miracle when the usual rules of nature are suspended, but a better kind in which they are most fulfilled.

Flashy miracles are a poor substrate for faith because it's so hard to know the real from the fraudulent, but being out in that desert night is convincing in and of itself—and so is psychoanalysis when it's working right.

I have been gulled often enough. Both Marcellus and I—along with most of the other people at Council Grove—were thrilled by some wonders that two people performed there, but a few years later both were exposed as frauds. I don't think that Marcellus and Tommy are frauds, and things I have seen them accomplish are amazing coincidences if they aren't miraculous—and there have been a lot of them. Even though I do think that it is a mistake to base my faith on that kind of miracle, those wonderful events are valuable because they force me to face the truth that there are facts that I can't explain and that contradict my usual beliefs. They force me to be modest about my understanding of creation.

Marcellus' snowstorm was so vigorous, lengthy and unexpected that it stranded many motorists, including him, in the mountains. *Newsweek* was not alone in covering it. He was on television in Denver the next day. The interviewer asked him how he did it and he said that he hadn't. He said that he was an intermediary who passed on the wish for snow to the Creator, who had decided to grant the request.

"How does it feel to do magic?" the announcer asked.

"It wasn't magic."

"What was it then?" the man asked.

"Snow," Marcellus answered.

Enthusiasm and Meaning

My friend and colleague, David Sargent, died tragically young. He was a geriatric psychiatrist. I am not, but I inherited one of his patients anyway. She inspired this paper.

RECENTLY I HAVE BEEN SEEING E, A VOLUBLE AND passionate woman in her eighties, who has led an eventful life. She is, by and large, satisfied with the past but not with the present because she is weak and has difficulty walking. She is furious about the future and has no intention of "going gently into that good night." I always enjoy spending fifty minutes with her. (I would have said "an hour" except that I know she would give me a hard time about it.) She and her therapist many years ago, the late Dr. Ann Becker, inspired this paper. As a young woman, E suffered from crippling fear of being out in public. Working with Dr. Becker cured her, and she says the essence of the cure was enthusiasm. The enthusiasm that Dr. Becker advocated and demonstrated was infectious and has endured throughout E's life.

We all start out enthusiastic. Infants are frequently enthusiastic, a condition most apparent when they laugh. Most toddlers are entranced by what they can do, by the world of people, and by objects they discover. Separation-individuation takes a toll so that by no means all people in their third and fourth year are free to be joyous—or at least not frequently. This dismal decline continues so that the average level of enthusiasm gets lower with age. E and other fortunate people are exceptions.

When my six-month-old great-nephew sees me waving my arms and chortles, and when I make a face and he makes the same one and says "Ah!" his pleasure and excitement are the same as mine. I also am conceptualizing the interaction at many levels that he does not yet know. His ability to stick out his tongue when I stick out mine doesn't depend on his knowing what tongues are, but I don't have to use my conceptual abilities either. Since I can think of tongues and mouths and fun, the interaction has a kind of meaning for me that it doesn't for him, but that kind is less important than the biologically determined significance that we have for one another while we are playing. That kind of significance is the crucial sense of the word *meaning* when used to indicate affective importance as in, "You mean everything to me," or, from Macbeth, "A tale / told by an idiot full of sound and fury / signifying nothing."

I think that our work as therapists is often about restoring or creating meaning. One of the first people I was responsible for as a resident working on an inpatient unit was a woman, a bit younger than I am now, who was severely depressed. She spent most of her time wringing her hands and saying over and over, "I'm hopeless and helpless. I'm hopeless and helpless."

I had a hard time getting her to say anything else, but one day I asked her about the work from which she had recently retired. I knew that she had worked for a museum. I asked what she had done there.

"Do you know the Saturday morning movies?" she asked.

"Yes. I always went to them when I was a kid. I loved them," I responded. "Do you remember the brochures?" she inquired. "Yes." I told her, adding, "I collected them in a loose-leaf notebook."

"I wrote them," she said. The excited conversation we had about the illustrated natural history lectures for children was completely different from anything else that had happened between us, and seemed to be the beginning of her recovery. It meant a lot to her that her work had meant a lot to me, and the incident meant so much to me that I have remembered it forty-four years later. Its meaning to me will be maintained if it means something to you, and will be diminished if you don't think it means much.

When I was ten or eleven, sitting in my pediatrician's waiting room looking at a children's magazine, I read the first lines of a short story:

My brother had the ability to see the value in things when I missed it. We would be walking along, he a few steps behind, and he would stop and pick up a stone or something that I had passed without a thought, and I knew that there was something special about it.

At that point, the nurse came and got me. I don't mind that I didn't read more because I think it might have been disappointing, but the image of the two boys has remained a constant symbol of what I have always thought is one of the greatest skills one can have. It is the basic skill of the artist. It is a form of enthusiasm which artists seem to possess even when they are feeling awful or when they are focusing on something ghastly.

When Shakespeare caused Macbeth, in his despair, to say that life signified nothing, he must have been partially identifying with the disgusted king, but his genius was to know exactly what was special about the situation and to show the rest of us vividly what it was. Artists have these two basic abilities: to experience the world directly and passionately, and to make something that conveys the experience to an audience. People with an impaired capacity for enthusiasm find little meaning in anything, even their misfortune. They feel empty and see other people and creation in general as insignificant. I think that having the enthusiasm of the brother in the story tends to move one toward being an artist. Those without talent for expression of some kind, or those who don't develop that talent, are artists of a sort, often gifted conversationalists whose life always seems interesting to the rest of us even if the facts of their life are rather ordinary. The reverse is also true. Those whose lives should be fascinating but who do not have enthusiasm can be awfully dull. Talent for some sort of expression without a passionate interest in the world can produce sentimental works, or even dazzling ones, but not meaning or art.

Great art, if we can comprehend it, opens us to a fuller participation in life, but only a few works are so accessible that a small child or another audience unfamiliar with the artistic form can immediately appreciate it. For example, I would need instruction and practice before I could grasp Chinese opera. Great artists are original. What they know is new and leads to new ways of expression. Frequently, the rest of us have to have help in learning to perceive it. None of Van Gogh's paintings from Arles sold until well after his suicide. Now they sell for tens of millions. What happened?

New art becomes accessible through the work of critics. They are artists of art, with a superior ability to experience it, and then tell us of their experience in a way that allows us to see and hear what we previously missed. Sometimes all that has to happen is for us to be convinced that we should pay attention. A huge price can have that effect, though it can also produce either an Emperor's New Clothes phenomenon or an equally unenlightened scorn for those we presume are pretending to be smart in order to dupe us. The role of critic is particularly important to us because that is one of the main things we therapists do. We hear poetry all day: dreams, historical accounts, impressions of this, that, and us, and it's our job to help the poets appreciate their own work. We need to hear with enthusiasm. But all sorts of things can go wrong.

Enthusiasm can die in the cradle if no one is there to make the baby smile and laugh and be delighted in return. The small person will not take delight in the world and won't try to express him or herself to anyone else. As adults, such people have little confidence in their ideas or feelings or in their ability to tell anyone anything. I have noticed that about half my customers will sometimes say, "I had an interesting thought." The others never do, or at least not until we have done a lot of work, and they are the same ones who never tell jokes—indeed can't remember jokes, since to remember a joke you have to be able to imagine telling it to someone who likes it. They can't even dream of that.

Some years ago I was seeing two people who were of these opposite types. One of them was unusually talkative and gregarious, and the other laconic and shy. The latter was an accomplished person and professionally active internationally. His accounts of himself should have been interesting, but weren't. One day, I said that he feared that if he talked about what he was doing, I would be bored. He replied that he knew that I wanted him to talk like X, and he could, but it would be awful. He tried to prove the point by speaking for ten or fifteen minutes in the voice of the other person. It was a lively and engaging account of his travels the day before. He was greatly improved but wouldn't believe it, saying that what he had told me was a mass of trivia. It was years before he was as lively as that again. Fortunately, most shy people have a few private or even secret enthusiasms, precious activities or places or possessions that keep them going, but which they protect from ever being seen and spoiled by someone else's scorn.

These people who missed enthusiastic interaction when they were babies often overvalue others. Instead of confidence in themselves and what they have to offer, they want others to be their guides. Some of them latch on all too quickly and naively to some new acquaintance only to be terribly disappointed. Then they quickly find yet another new person to latch onto. Some use rules instead of actual human authorities and lead life as though from a cookbook, making few or no changes in the recipes. The luckiest ones have parents who, though not good at responding to their babies, are reasonably accepting, are reliable and admirable enough people that their children can value themselves by feeling a part of the valuable parents. If all goes well thereafter, in the normal course of childhood and adolescence, the children are gradually and manageably disappointed in the actuality of their mothers and fathers and, in place of idealization, develop cherished ideals—abstractions much more reliable than any living human. Such people are often especially valuable members of society because they modestly but effectively advance the causes they cherish. They are often called selfless, and have a conviction that their lives have meaning, and help others to feel that they too can be meaningful.

The trouble is that most of the time parents who aren't enthusiastic about their babies aren't reliable and admirable enough in the rest of their dealings with their toddlers and preschoolers to be of use through identification. Speaking of preschool, I think many people nowadays are saved, or at least partially saved, by going to a good one. It used to be, and still is in much of the world, that children were the responsibility of lots of adults, so that if the mother and father weren't good enough there was a mother's sister or somebody who was adequate. Many families in this and other Western countries went through a few generations of living in nuclear families at a time when mothers could stay home. Now that American downward mobility has made us all two income families, an accidental side benefit is that some children are saved from having exclusively bad care. But preschool can only do so much, and inadequate parenting especially in the critical year or two starting at about eighteen months can do serious damage to the young person's enthusiasm and ultimate ability to find meaning.

To paraphrase Tolstoy, the good outcomes are alike and the bad ones more various. If all goes well, children and parents battle, everyone survives, and they love each other the more for having fought and survived. The children continue to want to please the adults, but they know that it is their choice to do so, and what pleases the mothers and fathers most is the children's enthusiasm for their own aims, which are now modulated within the limits of necessary restraint. Even though the children restrain themselves, or sometimes accept parental restraint without too much *Sturm und Drang*, they are making their own choices based on their natural inclinations.

The bad outcomes can be divided into two groups. Some parents manage to impose their ambitions so that, to a greater or lesser extent, the children feel that they must try to fulfill them. It feels as if life depends on continuing to be themselves in the parents' eyes and that their parents will not see them if they pursue independent goals. It's not unusual that such parents will admonish behavior that doesn't follow the program by saying such things as "That's not you." But even if it isn't said overtly the point is that the parents get to be the ones who define the children. In extreme cases the children cannot distinguish their own will from that of their parents.

I never quite grasped what this was like until I once said to a woman in her forties, "You can't believe you're right unless you convince your mother you are." She looked at me with astonishment. What else was possible?

Some children with slightly more independence than that feel compelled to do something different from what the parents want. They haven't learned that they can have the same idea as mother without agreeing that they are mother's slave.

The second kind of bad outcome occurs when the parents aren't pleased by much of anything the children do, and don't bother to impose their ambitions because their ambitions are limited to wanting the child to do some work and not make trouble. Such parents are often dissatisfied with their offspring's work performance and frequently tell them that they are useless and never get anything right. A father I have heard about was in the habit of telling his daughter that she was as useless as a bottle of piss. The girl had the gumption to complain that he never said he was pleased with anything she did, and he told her, "If I don't say anything, that means everything's all right."

Usually, neglected and abused little people feel there is something basically wrong with them and strain every fiber to right it. They try with more or less success to figure out what their parents' ambitions for them might be and try to live up to them. It doesn't come natural to them to think that they are all right and that their parents are at fault. I think one reason they don't is that, if it is in fact all their fault, they have hope of fixing the intolerable situation through their great efforts. If the trouble is with the parents there's nothing to be done. The children of psychotic parents are sometimes an exception from this generalization, especially if the parents' craziness is recognized by the neighbors. Other adults blame the parents and enable the kids to do so too. Many criminals also become exceptions to the generalization, when in the course of late childhood or adolescence they band together and reinforce each other's discounting of their parents. Thereafter one of the motives for their bad deeds is the wish to prove they don't care what parents or other authorities think of them. Their long frustrated longing for an admirable leader is not only the fuel of the defiance with which they ward it off, but also accounts for their readiness to idealize gang leaders or the leaders of antisocial political parties.

All of these consequences of poor parenting decrease the possibility of enthusiasm and a sense of meaning in life because they all promote the development of false selves. A false self, as I understand it, is protection against insecurity. The real self has to be encased and largely put out of operation because the parents' bad response or non-response to it causes unbearable shame. A woman I saw some years ago was touched by D. W. Winnicott's statement that sometimes the false self can only protect the true self by killing it. She quoted him to me as the person who could see best—better than I—how desperate her situation was. As a girl in a large family with negligent and abusive parents, she had attempted to enlist her sister in a pact to beat each other so that they would be accustomed to it and would not be so fearful of their mother. Long after she left home, she still was injuring herself regularly, and sometimes

I triggered her doing it. If I gave her true self any grounds for hope that I could see and appreciate her, that hope was so dangerous that it had to be beaten—or cut or burned—out of her. What was much worse was my seducing and abandoning her—by seeming interested and appearing to understand, only to fail to grasp what she was telling me.

We are all familiar with dramatic examples of this kind, and as awful as they are, I feel somewhat better about them than about people whose false selves function more smoothly and less dramatically. Those people look a lot better put together, but are suffering in ways they barely know because the emptiness of their lives feels so natural. They live to prove that they are *not* nothing. Some are just scraping by, demoralized by repeated failures to live up to the parental ambitions that would seemingly get them recognition. They feel lifeless and empty except when some rare success buoys them up and the full force of their ambition to impress the parents or somebody at last bursts out and they become expansive and frantically active. Events like that often get them diagnosed as Bipolar II (if not I) and put on mood stabilizers, which indeed may smooth them out. I am not saying that the bipolar diagnosis is meaningless. I think that many people who become manic or hypomanic have inherited a neurological defect which interferes with the normal dampening of mood changes, but I also think that many people whose character armor sometimes gives way are incorrectly diagnosed as bipolar.

Some false selves appear to be doing much better than just scraping by. Those with talent and an energetic and determined constitution can be conspicuously successful and really fulfill the ambitions of their pushy parents, or the ambitions that they rightly or wrongly believe their negligent parents harbored, but they are never successful enough to fill up the void they feel within and relax. They can appear to be enthusiastic and to have an enviable and obviously meaningful life, but, like Richard Cory in Edwin Arlington Robinson's poem of the same name, they may be in such despair that the false self does commit self-murder. Richard Cory was no braggart (the most successful false personae are not) but plenty of them brag all the time, since disproving nothingness is so important and feels so impossible. Some of the worst behavior comes from the struggle to escape feelings of inferiority.

Shakespeare portrayed many horrible characters, and Macbeth is not his worst, but Lady Macbeth must be his worst woman. Like Iago, whom I would take to be the worst, the wife of the Thane of Cawdor induced someone else's murderousness. Maybe Shakespeare blamed the women—I am including the witches—in order to rationalize Macbeth's villainy, but I think there is a deeper meaning. Macbeth seems to be a decent and even heroic person when we meet him, but the witches excite him with their prediction, and then his wife demands he murder in order to fulfill it. Lady Macbeth is a bad mother par excellence, not just as the one who allegedly incites patricide, but I think also, and perhaps even more importantly, as the one whose ambitions can dominate over real and meaningful ones. Anyhow, I think that is why the king reacts to impending doom not just as a disaster but also with despair because life seems meaningless.

The absence of meaning suffered by many people—most of them much better characters than Macbeth—results from their lives being organized around vacancy. Their efforts, no matter how passionate, to be the king, or director of the analytic institute or whatever, are not propelled so much by a love of the prominent position itself, or even a love simply for prominence, as by the need to feel that they aren't the nonentities they felt they were in early life when no one responded from the heart to the things they did from the heart.

Fortunately, most of us aren't that bad off. We have elements of both kinds of character organization. I know an artist whose grandfather made a fortune in manufacturing. The generation of his parents, aunts and uncles was divided among those who ran the family business and those who became physicians. The extended family culture valued the doctors far above the business people. The artist's father was one of those who continued to manage the factory but was ashamed that he wasn't a doctor and seemed to try to make up for it by a rather flashy way of life. His son showed his artistic interests and gifts early and his mother appreciated and supported them, but the family's ambition also had a major effect. He happily goes to his studio and paints every day, and he is delighted by finding new materials and new methods for making art but is dogged by a conviction that he is a failure because his MFA is so inferior to a degree he thinks he ought to have, an M.D. from Harvard or a Ph.D. from MIT. His cousin did follow the dictates of the family ambition and has spent his life working as a doctor, and feels his life has been empty and meaningless.

When we trap ourselves in pursuits that are more to bolster our self-esteem than to enjoy doing something we love, we may have times of enthusiasm, or at least excitement, but not joy, because self-esteem can never be bolstered enough.

One of the many parables of this problem is the fairy tale, "The Fisherman and His Wife." The husband catches a magic fish and releases him when he speaks. In return the fish offers to grant him a wish. The fisherman says he doesn't need a reward because he never would have killed a fish who could talk. The wife is furious and demands that the husband return to the shore and ask for a cottage. When the wife gets a cottage, she decides that it isn't good enough and demands a mansion. Through a series of ever-increasing and always-fulfilled demands including to be queen and then pope, she reaches the wish to rule the sun and the stars. The fish then returns her to her original hovel.

The *New Yorker* once ran a cartoon showing a dissatisfied couple driving in a sports car. The husband is saying, "We thought a fine car would bring us fulfillment. Maybe we should recarpet the house." One can never keep up with the Joneses. But are the Joneses trying to keep up with the Smiths? I think usually they are, and often there is the irony that the Smiths are also trying to keep up with the Joneses, but sometimes people who are truly envied aren't trying to keep up with anybody because they are simply doing what they love to do.

To be that kind of person requires a lot of luck. Not only do you need to have loving parents who interacted with you in a way that made you part of the family without imposing their ambitions on you, but you also need a relatively placid passage through childhood and adolescence. Scorn is the greatest enemy of enthusiasm. If someone reaches school cherishing various activities, ideas and possessions and the other children laugh and point because they think those things are ridiculous, it takes a strong character to prevent their being spoiled. When what children love is spoiled they are humiliated, and they sometimes try to get over it by beating the opposition, but more often by joining it.

Conformity is another big enemy of enthusiasm and meaning. Children form groups because they enjoy one another, because they need to differentiate from their families, and they need each other's support, and for many other good reasons. But in the wear and tear of daily life everyone is shamed at least occasionally. The natural thing to do then is to try to figure out what the group accepts, and to do and be that. It's a vicious circle. As everyone tries to embody the group's values, everyone is anxious that he or she hasn't done it well and tries to make up for it by showing that at least his or her effort was better than someone else's. Competition to be included and to exclude others makes everyone miserable, tightens the limits of what conforms and increases the need to prove that one fits in. The group becomes a collection of false selves falsifying themselves more and more. Their cohesion is usually organized around loyalty to ideas, activities, heroes and other symbols that are shibboleths, not loved extensions of the self.

For good or bad, groups define themselves with symbols that are important to them: beliefs, customs, gods, saints, crosses, stars, crescents, flags, songs, and so forth. These objects of veneration can have real meaning or can be mere proofs of membership. The people who were residents in psychiatry when I was almost all loved Otto Will, a visiting professor and an interpersonal analyst. Classes and, more importantly, informal socializing with him meant a lot to us. I knew him for the rest of his life and identification with him is an important part of my professional character. Admiring him was much more than a ticket of admission to the group.

Once Otto told us a story about his time as director of the Washington Psychoanalytic Institute. The American Psychoanalytic Association sent a delegation to visit Washington because they had received reports of unorthodox goings on. When the group from New York came to see Otto in his office, he noticed that one of them was looking around uncomfortably.

"Is there something wrong, doctor?" he asked.

"Dr. Will, do you see patients in this room?" the visitor asked. "Yes I do," Will replied.

"Where is your couch?" inquired the New Yorker.

"I don't have one," answered Will.

"Dr. Will, do you mean to say that you don't believe in the couch?" the visitor demanded, to which Will replied, "I wasn't aware that it was possible to believe in furniture."

People who knew Otto cherish memories of his stories, his brilliant ability to understand what was going on with his often uncommunicative patients, his complete honesty about himself, and his generosity. Our relationship with him strengthens our relationship with each other. Lots of us do have couches in our offices, but few of us believe in them as any more than furniture that is sometimes useful and sometimes not. That hasn't always been true of me. When I got my first couch, it reassured me that I had begun to arrive.

Among analysts there are many signs and symbols of group cohesion: a minimum of four hours a week for some, three for others, the analyst being silent, the names of our founders, leaders and schools of thought. Like the American flag, they can have real meaning for some people on some occasions, but often they are mostly the points we can rally around when we are anxious and need reassurance that we are okay because we belong to a worthy group and can prove that we are in good standing.

Real meaning expands and deepens our sense of life and connection to the world. On various occasions, alas mostly long ago, seeing the flag moved me, as I thought about how proud I was that the country had defeated Nazism, underwritten the economic recovery of Europe, fed hungry people and so on, but now I suspect that those who wear American flag buttons in their lapels are trying to prove that they are better than those who don't wear them. Symbols of the false self and the false group reassure us that we are somebody and not nobody, and they are used to differentiate ourselves from those who are nobody, or worse. People who don't believe in the couch, or four times a week, or the flag, are the ones we are better than, and we can unite against those who attack our emblems.

I was disheartened to learn that Senator Clinton was cosponsor of a bill outlawing flag burning. I doubt that she has any conviction that flag burners should be put in jail, and any flag waving and wearing she does seems to me to be probably a crude effort to stave off political attacks, but I don't think that it will work.

Going back to one of the last presidential candidates to have real meaning for me, Harry Truman radiated conviction and sincerity. I never met him and so I don't really know, but I believed then, and still do, that he really loved and hated everything he said he loved and hated. John Kerry opening his acceptance speech by saying he was reporting for duty was so obviously an attempt to forge membership in the false-self group of military veterans that it put off even those of us who really wanted him to win. It didn't mean anything except that he was trying to protect himself by putting on a false front. I heard him last year when he started a speech by saying, "I voted to authorize the war, and I was wrong." It sounded as if he had awakened from a spell he had put himself under to try to say things that research showed would be successful self-marketing. It would be a wonderful thing if people running for office could forget their polls and their focus groups and show us who they really are and what they really think.

Unfortunately, many people find it hard to know what they really think. They are so much driven by anxiety and so little by desire that they think what they imagine they should, according to the other psycho-analysts or Republicans or Baptists. Religions (of which psychoanalysis can be one) for some people have real meaning, but are mostly false-self groups. If they pray at the right times and places, eat the right things, wear the right clothes and so forth, they can feel and will sometimes be told that they are good and admirable.

When I was seven, a Catholic neighbor invited me to go to church with her. My mother explained to me what I would be seeing. The idea that I would be among people who were eating what they believed were pieces of the body of God appalled and excited me. I was eager to see how they would look when they did it. I was disappointed. They looked bored. Perhaps this is a cheap shot. I am sure that many Catholics have an abstract but meaningful interpretation of communion, but I think that probably more of them take communion because they want to re-main members of the group, and that is what their group does. The same can be said for keeping kosher, fasting during the Muslim Eid, or seeing analysands four times a week.

Routine, empty ritual, is bad enough, but the dogma that demands it can be even worse if it is used to justify the authority of those in charge and to suppress doubt, curiosity and innovation. I believe that religious life and many other forms of group life are marked by periodic conflicts between dogma and prophecy. Stodgy and sometimes immoral well-established hierarchies are overthrown by the vision of prophets who denounce what they see that is wrong and suggest new paths. The first followers of the prophet are scorned and sometimes persecuted by the conventional multitude and fight for what they see as vital and right. The early Christians, the first followers of Martin Luther (or Martin Luther King) or Sigmund Freud, were all filled with enthusiasm and zeal for the new truth that led them to fight majority opinion even to the point of martyrdom. No members of Freud's Wednesday evening group died for the cause as far as I know, but they apparently had an enthusiasm not often seen in analytic study groups these days when Freud's ideas have triumphed.

We can be thankful that the covers of national publications such as the *New York Review* or *Newsweek* still periodically announce that Freud was wrong, because the worst fate of prophecy is routine acceptance. The prophet and the first generation of followers often manage to throw the scoundrels out of the Temple, the Cathedral or whatever, but when the next generation of followers moves into the Temple offices, they ossify into bureaucrats and/or tyrants who enforce the new truth just the way their predecessors enforced the old. When the revolution succeeds, it establishes the secret police to detect and eradicate the next revolution. Yesterday's radicalism becomes today's empty practice.

I had the good fortune to be present when a revolutionary religious leader succeeded. David Clark, the president of the Native American Church of Navajoland, was sitting in my office in Window Rock, Arizona, when someone brought the news that the tribal council had just repealed the law against the religious use of peyote. David said quietly that this was the realization of the dream that had guided his life since he was four and that he had seen his parents, aunts, uncles and family friends arrested and taken to jail in the night for conducting religious services.

The religious and political struggle had lasted decades and had come to dominate Navajo politics. The Native American Church had largely supplanted traditional Navajo religion, which was too inflexible to meet the needs of the increasingly beleaguered and impoverished who were forced to live in a new kind of economy. The church, which was fairly old on other reservations, had arrived in the 1930s as a completely new force on Navajo, and it quickly gathered lots of adherents for whom it was exciting to the point of changing their whole lives. Having to practice in secret when the Council made them outlaws added to their enthusiasm and their conviction that they were doing something wonderful. Clark's triumph came when he was less than forty. I asked him what he would do next, and he was startled and perturbed by the question. Fortunately, a few weeks later he was arrested in Texas, where peyote grows, for possession of a controlled substance, and had a new fight on his hands. But decades later, with every battle won, the Native American Church in the Navajo Nation has become sadly routinized for many of its members.

More or less the same thing happened to psychoanalysis. Freud was pretty intolerant of those that disagreed with him and kicked some of them out of the club, but in many ways he was much more flexible and tolerant than some of the bureaucrats who came into office after his death. His way of practicing included such things as his giving breakfast to the Rat Man, consulting Theodore Reik about literary references he wanted to put into his writings and otherwise collaborating with him in between stints of analyzing him, and accepting gifts from analysands, for example his beloved chow dogs from Marie Bonaparte. His idea of technical neutrality was far from the puritanical set of rules it became later, especially in this country. He was also ready to accept all sorts of people as eligible for training. In this country, the local chapter of Freud's International Society restricted its training to psychiatrists for rather a while.

When I was first a candidate, in the sixties, theory was taught dogmatically and foreign dogmas were denounced, but gradually in the next decade or two the dogmatists were worn down by the appeal of useful new ideas coming from within and without the organization. By the eighties, it wasn't possible any more to prove we were members of the true faith by our adherence to dogmatic theory, and something had to replace it. I think the replacement for dogmatic theory was dogmatic practice as epitomized in the works of Robert Langs, who proved that Freud was a poor analyst because he did not adhere to the frame. Langs also published a book to help consumers of psychotherapy distinguish between good therapists who honored the holy frame, and quacks who didn't.

I once had dinner with Joseph Sandler, who was visiting the Seattle Psychoanalytic Society and Institute. He was laughing about something that had happened in the case conference with the candidates he had presided over in the afternoon. The analyst who was presenting had told of an hour when he was free a minute or two before the hour was to begin and saw the analysand in the waiting room. Rather than starting, he went into his office and closed the door for a minute so as to preserve the frame by starting the hour at exactly the scheduled time. "Only in America," Sandler said.

When I was a senior in medical school, I once worked up a patient who, I discovered on physical exam, had severe hemorrhoids. He hadn't complained about them, but I asked if he didn't want to consider treatment for them. "No," he said. "They're useful in my work." I asked how that could be and he explained that he worked on weekends for his brother-in-law, the undertaker. He said that it was his job to stand in the lobby and ask visitors, "What name?" and then to refer them to parlor A, B, C, or D, where the dead person they wanted to see was on view. "Sometimes," he told me, "The situation will strike me as kind of funny and I'll have a hard time maintaining the appropriate expression, but after I've been standing there for a few minutes these things just make it a sure thing that I have the right look on my face."

I often think of that man when I look around at some of us because it seems to me that we try to keep that expression. Sometimes it seems as if psychoanalysis is such a serious business that laughter and enthusiasm are not allowed. Anyhow, when I reveal various of my clinical heresies I get definitely hemorrhoidal looks.

I think we are often a self-reassuring group honoring the symbols of our false selves. It makes life a lot less lively for us than it ought to be, and it does our customers more harm than good. We can't be a blank slate, and when we try we are likely to be a black slate or, to vary the metaphor, a wet blanket. I think we should often respond with enthusiasm and we should help our people develop their own capacity for enthusiasm and meaning by letting bits of experience and ways of speaking become funny and/or highly idiosyncratic experiences that are special to our particular partnership. For example, one of my customers and I often refer to certain kinds of actions as "stepping out of the telescope line." It has a number of appeals to us, one of which is that we know exactly what it means and other people wouldn't.

Another person told me of a patient of his who had attempted suicide by shutting herself in a bathroom with a running gas-powered lawn mower. I was amazed and said, "I thought I'd heard everything in this business." Several weeks later, he remarked that my pleasure in his story was one of the most useful things I've done in a long time. Another customer said that one of the best things in the world is when two people who have been talking conventionally suddenly manage to open up and talk about what is real.

An atmosphere of freedom and play may be the most important tool we have for helping our people find meaning in their experience, but we also have to help them to see the ways in which they fear exposing their real selves to our lack of understanding or, worse yet, to our lack of response. Often that can't be done until we have actually done poorly, but a readiness to hear that we have made a mistake, to acknowledge it without defensiveness and, most importantly, to show that we learn and do better afterward can sometimes do more than any interpretation of how the customer's mind works. While I was writing this paper, several pages ago, I got a phone call informing me that E was in the hospital. I went to see her and asked about the emergency that got her there. In telling about it, she said, "Four of the cutest firemen came to my apartment!"

Up to this point I have been trying to finesse the difficult philosophical question of what the word *meaning* means, by implying the attitude of Justice Potter Stewart toward another important concept: "I shall not today attempt further to define the kinds of material I understand to be embraced by the term obscenity, but I know it when I see it."

Having specified conditions that interfere with meaning, I feel somewhat prepared to speculate about how to define it psychologically. What interferes with meaning is disconnection between people, or false connection. If we attempt to identify with one another through hollow portrayals of ourselves, we feel that the relationship, and perhaps we ourselves, are meaningless. I think that meaning is connection.

If all goes more or less well, we are most connected at the beginning of life and just after giving birth. I think that we rely all our lives on the residue of that experience as the essential ingredient in our making sense of ourselves and the world. As we grow up, the sense of connection can be transformed into an infinite variety of forms, including membership in family and society and the possession of treasured goals and purposes. But even in solitude, at fortunate moments we can connect to the world or all of creation as we once related to the mother who nursed us. At such moments, we are sure that life has meaning. Yet there is unfairness in the way that many people cannot feel that they, and life in general, are meaningful because they were poorly received in the world when they entered it. Nevertheless, I believe that no matter how poorly people are received, if their reception is just barely good enough that they survive infancy, there remains in them some spark of meaning, deeply buried. It's our job to help them find it.

Injury and Bitterness

I hurt people all the time. It's part of our business. Experiencing the many reactions to that pain, and my reactions to those reactions, has led me to think about the way people in general, and I in particular, can treasure hurt. Giving a talk on injury and bitterness to an organization that has been so good to me seemed like an act of considerable ingratitude, but I did it anyway.

I ONCE KNEW A SURGEON WHO SAID THAT HE AND HIS colleagues were divided between the screamers and the moaners. The screamers, he said, yelled "Fix the goddamn light!" and the moaners murmured "Why do I always have to operate in darkness?" This paper is about the moaners. The strategy and tactics of moaning are stereotyped commonplaces of psychoanalytic life, like their foremost practitioner, the controlling, martyred mother, but like that mother they get more attention in jokes than in serious consideration. Indeed, it seems to me that I have learned more about them from non-analysts.

A lawyer, like the surgeon, was another authority whose words I have thought about for decades. He told me that it is a principle of law that you can't increase damages. If you get hit by a car and don't go to the hospital you can't collect for the suffering and disability caused by your neglect. And yet we all try to. When I was twelve, a friend and I were set upon by five other boys who wanted to steal his new football. We fought them off until adults intervened, and the would-be thieves ran away. My friend's house was closer than mine. His mother suggested I wash the blood off my face and offered a clean shirt to replace my bloody one. I refused, not so politely, and at home again refused to give up the signs of my honorable suffering until my father came home and could see for himself. I thought that, without the blood, not only would my story lack vividness and credibility but it also would seem like boasting. It didn't occur to me that not getting cleaned up was like boasting.

Like so many other self-destructive acts, increasing or just maintaining damages depends in part on the notion of involuntariness and a resemblance to illness. I was on the ragged edge with my refusal to bathe and change my clothes, but at least I didn't have to avow my motive. No one else thought I wasn't showing off, but I more or less convinced myself they might.

My mean grandmother was in the habit of complaining loudly and angrily if someone bumped her chair in a restaurant, but her timid daughter, my aunt, instead of complaining would just as loudly yell "Ouch!" She would have blown her unassuming color if she hadn't represented her being offended as being physically hurt. If my grandmother received poor service, she would say, "I'm going to have that man fired," and she was so good at self-righteous indignation and self-importance that she sometimes did get someone fired, or at least in trouble.

My aunt restricted herself to being noticeably inconvenienced if not disabled. It was a strategy endorsed at the highest level of my family's moral authority, my cousin, the rabbi. He held kid religious services every Sunday morning (we were very Reformed), and most of his kid sermons featured stories about himself. He said, fairly often, that he had been consulted by a couple of suffering parents who were in agony because of their little girl. (His villains were almost always female.) This one spoke angry words to her parents. The rabbi suggested a plan. The child's favorite possession was a playhouse. Every time she said a harsh word, they took a hammer and drove a large ugly spike into that structure saying that her attacks were like spikes in their hearts. Soon the house was full of spikes and the girl cried, saying, "My beautiful playhouse is ruined!" The parents told her that every time she said a kind word, they would take one of the spikes out, and her conduct improved, but when all the spikes were out, she cried again and said, "Now my beautiful playhouse is full of holes!" The parents answered, with a line scripted by the rabbi, "In our hearts, too, the holes remain."

Speaking of hearts, he was very big on observing Mother's Day, and part of the annual celebration was a sermon featuring a story to demonstrate how completely self-sacrificingly mothers are devoted to their children. The hero of the story was a woman whose beloved son was lured away from her by a wicked woman. The wicked woman wanted ever grander proofs of the son's love, and finally asked that he bring her the heart of his mother. He didn't want to ask, but, bewitched as he was, what could he do, and he told his mother what he needed. She unhesitatingly bared her breast to his knife. As he was rushing back to the beloved with his trophy, the bloody heart spoke to him, "Be careful, my son, lest you fall and hurt yourself." I'm not making this sermon up.

What in the world is going on? As I claimed already, the appearance of involuntariness is crucial so that the question of selfish motive doesn't appear. The parents of the girl with the playhouse weren't demanding respect, they were the victims of the daughter's cruelty, and their trip to the rabbi's study was brought about by their pain. They weren't getting even; they were protecting themselves from getting more holes in their hearts, and they weren't cherishing the holes as evidence to be used against the girl. It was just a fact of life that the holes couldn't be healed. The rabbi told us of a world of perfect blame and blamelessness. Those who cause injury are blameworthy and those who suffer are blameless. If the mother of the lovelorn son had said, "What, are you crazy? When are you going to dump this bitch?" her son might have accused her of being possessive and standing in the way of his happiness. She would not have had an airtight case for being totally free of selfishness, and selfishness is a crime many of us can't stand to be accused of. My mean grandmother, who was an example par excellence of Freud's idea of the exceptions, gloried in her selfishness, but my aunt, who had been raised to be her unquestioning slave, couldn't bear to be thought to be selfish or demanding. Her alleged pain and cry of "Ouch!" was beyond her control, and her indignation with the person who had bumped her chair was perfectly justified by her having been hurt. We never know for sure what another person is conscious of, but I don't think my aunt let herself know what she was doing or why.

Of course, lots of the time we use injury as a tool quite consciously, but in general we can't make it work if we act as if we know what we're doing. One day long ago, I picked a can of Coors out of the refrigerator and heard an odd chink inside it. I thought perhaps the beer had frozen, but it didn't sound just like that. So I opened it and carefully poured it into a glass. I asked my children, "Do you know what this is?" "Looks like glass," my son said. "To me," I said, "It looks like a free case of Coors." I wrote the company on my University of New Mexico Medical School stationery, saying how dangerous it would have been if I had drunk the piece of glass and signing myself M.D. Sure enough, a few days later, a representative of the brewery brought me an abject apology and a case of beer. It might have worked if I had said, "I found glass, and you'd better give me something," but it would have been graceless and would have made life harder for everyone. The world of moaners is dominated by a blame, guilt and shame economy. A good injury is like money in the bank; it can be spent on causing another person to feel guilty and/or ashamed, which may in turn be cashed in on sympathy, beer or some other compensation. Even if the opponent won't take our money we may be able to get other people to, and they will punish, or at least dislike, the opponent. If even that doesn't work, we have the bitter satisfaction of knowing we are the good people and they are the bad. The game is zero-sum; that is, if one person wins, the other loses, even if we have to lose something else to win the moral game. I have the impression that these matters not only keep real money coming in to us therapists, but also support many lawyers. Lucrative personal injury cases are the obvious instance, but are not the only ones. The key words that catch my ear are, "It's the principle of the thing," especially when they are used as justification for retaining lawyers who won't take a case on a contingency basis because it is unlikely to be won. I have known a remarkable number of people who have got their brains beaten out in court repeatedly as proof, it seemed to me, that they were on the moral high ground, and that not only their opponents but even the whole system were far beneath them.

Some of the people who bring unsuccessful cases, in or out of court, seem to be just touchy and easily hurt or offended, but many suffer frequent harm that anyone would recognize as a reasonable cause for pain or worse. In some cases it's obvious how it happens, the most common being people, mostly but not exclusively women, who take up with abusive partners, collecting damages, or at least sympathy, and going back to them or others just like them. A long time ago, a friend of mine, who is a good friend if you're a man and a menace if you're a woman, was married to a woman who brought her troubles to a colleague, who saw her once a week. When the therapist was on vacation the woman happened to drop in at my house to visit at about the time she usually had her therapy. For several hours she recounted to my then-wife some of the awful things my friend had done and was doing to her. She also said that a couple of years earlier she had actually left him, and that a couple of friends were kind to her. They took her in, listened to her awful stories and found her a lawyer. They were so kind that she was surprised, she said, that they would never speak to her again after she decided to return to the marriage.

At the end of the afternoon, when they had moved to the kitchen, she asked, "So what do you think I should do?"

My former wife was cutting up vegetables and she said, "I think you should take a knife about this size and stab him in the heart. It's a big organ, pretty much in the center of the chest. Aim a little left of center and you can't miss. Don't worry about the point getting stuck in a rib. It'll glance off."

The visitor hastily thanked her for the chance to talk and left. In the next few days, she told people, "Edna Bergman is crazy."

It isn't immediately clear why people do that sort of thing unless one accepts labeling them with a diagnostic term to explain their behavior. I think there are a great variety of motives, some of which are pretty straightforward. Self inflicted, maintained or increased damages are strategies and tactics used for all kinds of reasons. While editing this, I had to get up to get something and, crossing the room, I tripped and fell. No one was around but you. I picked myself up, feeling grateful to be unhurt, but I was also a little sorry to be okay because it doesn't make much of a story without any injuries. There is a certain amount of inflation involved in giving accounts of one's triumphs and tragedies, or at least there is in mine. I fear that if I just say that I tripped and fell, you won't know that I was frightened as I was falling and aggrieved to have done it. If I put in an injury and you discount its seriousness, you will arrive at an impression of the misfortune pretty much like mine. In a small way, I am like someone who has been rear-ended at a traffic light and rushes to the chiropractor to get a bankable whiplash diagnosed. For a grander example, a criminal whose heartfelt primary goal is to get lots of money could use misfortune in order to promote some sort of scam. Mr. Peachum in "The Threepenny Opera," the king of the beggars, the poorest man in London, blackmailed the government by threatening to loose his horde of disfigured, disgusting panhandlers in the middle of the queen's coronation parade. Munchausen's syndrome and, much more horribly, Munchausen's syndrome by proxy, are rewarded with attention, sympathy, companionship and a well-defined role in life.

Even if people's reasons for suffering are unclear, at least you can often see how they're doing it. Some people are more mysterious. It's hard to see how they do it. Commonly they are incorrectly described as being like Al Capp's comic strip character, Joe Btfsplk. Actually, Joe did not constantly have terrible things happen to him; he had terrible things happen around him. He was the world's worst jinx, and it is as if some people are horribly jinxed. Their identity is stolen and the credit card companies insist they pay the bills. Their computers crash, and experts can't repair them. Their flights are cancelled when everyone else's get through, and (this is the oddest one in my experience) a roofing company mixes up the address of the house they're supposed to work on and rips off the roof of my customer's house instead.

Any of these things could happen to anyone, but there are some people to whom they happen all the time. A related Jewish joke is not only illustrative but also, I think, explanatory.

A man, who always tied on, went to minyan everyday, always walking there on Saturday, and never in his life ate tref, suffered one calamity after another. After his business failed and his wife ran off with another man, he went to see the rabbi—not my cousin.

"Rabbi," he said, "would you call me devout?"

"You are the most devout man I know."

"Then why does the Lord allow all these awful things to happen to me?"

"I don't know," the rabbi answered. "Let's ask the Almighty."

They knelt and asked. A great voice came forth saying, "Because you nudge me."

A lot of the seemingly godforsaken people are ever so high-prin-
cipled and ever so careful never to offend. The result is that to most of
us—I don't know about God—it feels as if they are nudging us. Or they
have compunctions against taking proper precautions. My grandfather
was a man who started out rich and ended up poor. A friend suggested
that they go into the mail order business. (This was about a century ago).
Each put up $10,000. Things went well for several years. Then some of
my grandfather's friends asked him if he were auditing the books. Alexander Bergman was aghast. "John is like a brother to me. Would you
audit your brother's books?" Yes, the friends all said, we would; but he
didn't, and soon his partner gave him the bad news that they had suffered
unexpected losses and were bankrupt. After the bankruptcy the former
partner reorganized the firm and went on quite successfully without my
grandfather. Several years later, the rabbi—an earlier one—heard the
story and asked the crook if he weren't ashamed of what he had done to
Alex Bergman. He said he was, and returned my grandfather's original
ten grand.

I never knew my grandfather, but I did know his wife and his children and, judging by their attitudes, I think he took his troubles with
quietly suffering nobility, which I think was his version of what I call
secondary ambition. I mean ambition to achieve a certain effect or semblance, and which proves that we are not nothing. I believe that lots of
the incidental use of injury and suffering as a tactic is in the service of
primary ambition—like Mr. Peachum—but I think that injury and suffering as a major part of one's way of life is usually part of a false-self secondary ambition like that of my schnook of a grandfather. If I am right
about him, his immigrant parents amassed a fortune by somewhat rough
and tumble means and wanted their son not only to be a real American,
but also a genteel one. He adopted their ambitions for him and created
his cultivated and somewhat vitiated persona in place of more vigorous and heartfelt versions of himself whose development was stunted
because my great-grandparents didn't respond to them. I imagine that
he got a quiet, sad but still ironically humorous satisfaction from telling people after the bankruptcy that he had not audited the books. My
father, who was pretty tough, still had a bit of that in him. He liked to
say that he hadn't lost all his money in the stock market crash of 1929

but that it had all been stolen by his criminal stockbroker (another awful cousin) two weeks before the fall. He said that by the time all his friends were crying about being broke, he could laugh at them because he was already used to it.

The pride my forebears took in being humble, and the equanimity with which they experienced defeat, I think, are typical of the way chronic sufferers use suffering: to maintain self-esteem or, to turn it the other way, to counteract shame. They, like many others, were able to feel pretty good about themselves because they believed that their representations of themselves were generally accepted, and they felt well attached to family and friends.

People who are less secure or who suffer humiliation also use injury to snatch some horrible satisfaction. In *Great Expectations*, Dickens describes Miss Havisham, who lived for decades in the petrified and tattered remains of her wedding banquet because the groom failed to attend. It never was eaten. She is more an object of horror and awe than of sympathy, and she seems to know it, but her limitless bitterness saves her from despair. Like that other fictional emblem of bitterness, Eeyore, in *Winnie-the-Pooh*, Miss Havisham knows she is better than most. For one thing, the grandeur of her reaction to losing out indicates the unusual depth of her feelings, maybe even of the strength of her jilted love. Just as the princess in "The Princess and the Pea" is proven to be genuine by her injury by the pea under all those mattresses, Miss Havisham is proven to have greater sensitivity and depth than some woman who would callously go on with her life after such mistreatment. Was she better off living her crazy life among the tatters than she would have been if she had killed herself because of unbearable shame? She thought so, and, as unpleasant as an embittered life may be, it is a life, a way of pulling oneself together after a single shattering event or severe continual defeat that allows for no other kind of coherent experience of self.

Unlike the wry smile of humorous self-deprecation, which welcomes and expects companionship in misery, the triumphant bitter smile pushes the other away and denies the possibility of companionship. I think we in the therapy business see that expression more than most. When we say something hurtful to a bitter person, we sometimes see a little smile that seems to say, "Yes, you've done it again; how clumsy, but it's what I've learned to expect from you." The awful victory it signifies is based on the very cold comfort of being right when we are wrong, on having successfully predicted our failure, on having been prepared for it by hundreds of previous blows, and so on. These are not only cold comforts, they are solitary ones. They are like straightforward grandiosity in depending on being unique, but different in that being the best is at least supposed to evoke admiration and envy, while being the most mistreated is supposed to evoke nothing; thus showing how callous and less human we are.

If we do claim to feel shame, guilt or remorse, a truly bitter person will dismiss the idea as bogus defensiveness. He or she knows that we have been proven inept and morally inadequate. Sometimes a bitter person will describe the sympathetic reaction of a better person than we. The comedian Elaine May long ago had a character, a mother whose son didn't call her often enough. When he did call, she told him that when her doctor heard how long it had been between calls, "That man turned pale, and he said, 'Mrs. Ginsberg I never heard of anyone so busy that he didn't have time to call his mother.'"

The sympathetic people are not only absent but they often are no longer available. The people like that we most often hear about are previous therapists who are dead or distant, or who for some reason have been replaced ever so inadequately by us.

The bitter smile, especially when accompanied by a quiet little laugh, is plainly furious, and we who are smiled at have no trouble detecting the rage, but I don't think that recognizing and interpreting the rage is much use. For one thing, if the person could bear to avow anger they would simply attack. Most bitter people believe that their claim to worth is their sense of superiority to those who attack, and being called angry is yet another calamitous insult. Being hurt and helpless is all the pride they have. Take that away and what's left?

I think that, in addition, that approach misses the point . I think that we are most useful when we find out how other people see things, not when we follow the vicissitudes of their instincts. It's true that anger, once aroused, tends to be discharged and can be displaced, but I think that anger is one of humanity's tools, not one of its motives. Our motives are to get what we need to survive and what we want to enjoy. Many people are so insecure that being told yet again that they are substandard threatens their psychological survival, and their anger, whatever its form, is a means to stave off annihilation.

It's a chicken and egg phenomenon. Many of you, whom I respect but with whom I disagree, see the situation as starting with envy and anger. The rage from that point of view is based on the need to destroy what they envy in us. The psychological annihilation they fear and sometimes experience is due to the rage being turned back on themselves. One of my problems is that I sometimes feel so defeated and attacked by a bitter customer that I think, "Gee, Maxine Anderson is right," referring to a colleague with a British Object Relations point of view. Maybe she, with her quiet, sympathetic way, can get good results by interpreting her customers' wish to defeat or destroy what is good in her, but I don't seem to be able to get anything that way except instantly making a bad situation worse. I can't claim that I make it instantly better, but sometimes over a long time the situation does improve, and what seems to work is the two of us somehow finding a way to talk about the feeling of helplessness, which we are sharing. That has its hazards too. For one thing, if I talk about my helplessness I may be condescending, because I feel helpless in my effort to be useful to the other, while he or she feels helpless most of the time—unable to defend not only against what are effectively attacks from me but also against constant attacks by the rest of the world.

I will return to questions of treatment, but for now I want to go on explicating my ideas of why people resort to the strategy of injury and bitterness. As usual, I would rather talk about interpersonal drama rather than about alleged inner beings, forces or structures, though I admit that much of the drama that matters is inner in the sense that it is imaginary. I mean the imaginary struggles we constantly dream up to evaluate how we are doing, how we did, or how we might do in the future. Those plots play out not only in the privacy of our thoughts but also as a constant accompaniment of interaction with others in moment-to-moment reality. They are the ghost images of folks we are with that are more convincing than what comes through our eyes and ears, and they are the ghostly audiences we generally play to, depending on our beliefs: God, posterity, our parents, public opinion or whoever.

I think what is most relevant in this context is the politics of dissatisfaction. When we lack something we want or fear something we might get, we will do something, suffer, or both. In deciding what to do, we weigh how it is we want to be regarded. If there's a choice, would we rather be liked, feared or pitied? Almost no one in present day America will avow wanting to be pitied, but what I am talking about is largely the way that we evoke pity without letting on—at least to ourselves—what we are up to.

It is also out of fashion, though not so completely, to want to be feared. When I was a minor federal bureaucrat I had an enemy who headed a rival bureau. He was a large former surgeon—definitely a screamer—who had a poster behind his desk. It showed an orangutan in its threatening posture and said, "If I want your opinion, I'll beat it out of you." Dr. Rabeau, the orangutan, thought more or less correctly that the ironic implication that he was unreasonable would save him from being disliked even if he was intimidating.

Many people feel they will be disliked if they ask for things unless they can prove that they have to ask, or if the request isn't really for them. One of the main things people worry about is being thought to be selfish. If we are at all insecure, we will fear that the other won't want to do what we want, and that is where the zero-sum idea comes in: if we get what we want we win and the other person loses, or vice versa. That belief is like the Illinois Traffic Code, or at least like the Code as it was a long time ago when I lived there. Since the laws are perfect, if there is an accident the police must cite someone for an infraction. Someone has to be to blame.

Secure people operate in a more than zero-sum universe. As a bureaucrat, I once called a meeting at headquarters, which was in a monstrous office building with only a giant parking lot. I needed to make parking reservations for those of us coming there, and I forgot. I thought we should try anyhow, and the bunch of us drove up in three government cars. I was driving the first, and when the attendant asked if I had a reservation, I admitted that I didn't and embarrassedly asked if we could come in anyway. We were turned away, had a long search for street parking and a long walk back to the office. When we got there, we found my friend, Jim Shore, and his passengers lounging around waiting for us.

He, the most secure person I know, had parked in the lot. "How did you do that?" I asked. "I said that we were with Dr. Bergman, and I was sure he had made a reservation." I had thought someone was to blame for the situation and that it was me. Jim didn't think anyone had to lose and that no one had to be blamed.

Humans vary a lot in how they feel blame and how they feel about blame. No one wants it, but some of us would rather accept it than risk being disliked. Screamers and moaners both assign it to others. The screamers would rather be right and impressive than liked, and so they would rather actively blame someone else than admit fault. They find it so natural and justifiable to keep some son of a bitch from harming them that they easily deny any responsibility for trouble. Some time back, a screamer friend of mine was telling a couple of us about something annoying that had just happened to her. There hadn't been much time between an appointment in the suburbs and one in town; it was rush hour, and, naturally, she had to drive in the high-occupancy lane. A state trooper, seeing her by herself in the car, stopped her and gave her a ticket. "That made me even later," she told us, "and it made me so mad, I peeled out of there, and the damn cop gave me another ticket."

She said all this with no humor and no shame, so that we were amazed not only by her not feeling guilty but also by her not knowing how the story sounded. A secure person would not have made the appointments so close together and would have assumed that a way could be found to reschedule one of them with no harm to anyone. A blame accepter would not have driven in the HOV lane and would have apologized for being late. A moaner might have driven in the HOV lane, have felt, like my friend, that he or she had to, and that the first ticket was an example of how impossible life is. There wouldn't have been a second ticket.

To well-established moaners, misfortune, a traffic ticket or whatever, serves as a way of getting even, a justification for getting their way, for failing, or generally for not being to blame. This claim may seem incorrect since many people who have continual trouble seem to blame themselves, but their supposed acceptance of responsibility is transparently false. If somebody says, "I'm just not attractive and smart enough, that's why I wasn't invited," everyone but the speaker knows that the non-inviters are being blamed.

People even represent threatened self-harm as beyond their responsibility. An armed robber who points the gun at his head and says, "Give me your wallet or I'll shoot," might have a hard time explaining his intention away, but lots of times people say things like, "Since you dumped me, I haven't been able to concentrate at all, but I'm okay, and I know you're very busy, so I wouldn't want you to worry about me." Transparently false statements are the hallmark of the vertical split, the disavowal of what I like to call secondary ambition.

Jim Shore's wish for a parking space was simple and primary. He wanted and expected to be liked, and to be well taken care of by people who like dealing with him. His behavior at the parking lot was in no way defensive. Neither was mine, but I was not to the manner born and I accepted being at fault. If I had said to my passengers, "There are so many regulations, I can't possibly remember them all, and it gives me headaches," it would have been from secondary ambition wish to be blameless.

I don't know many details of Jim's childhood, but I think that his parents enjoyed being with him from the time he was born and were good at collaborating with him in the complicated games of imitating expressions, vocalizations and gestures that make a newcomer welcome, happy and, in an essential way, proud of themselves. His primary ambition to be a great person was allowed to flourish and to be shrunk to reasonable size in its own time by the action of ordinary, unavoidable, but manageable disappointment. I think his parents also were secure people who accepted his seeing them as great without becoming anxious or overexcited. I think they didn't reject or promote his idealization of them and they were good-enough people that his inevitable disappointments in them were small enough to be withstood without damage and strengthened his ability to manage reality. Equally importantly, his parents probably were pleased rather than threatened by his assertions of independence around and after his second birthday. They managed to guide him without blaming or intimidating him and without allowing him to hurt or intimidate them.

By contrast, Ms. Y, a person I know better than I know Jim, was born into a family with an absent father and an overburdened, angry mother who was prone to feeling blamed and would never have any of it. She has told her daughter all her life that she was a bad baby, who cried all the time for no good reason, wanted to eat when it wasn't time and wouldn't eat at the right time. The mother says that fortunately by the time Ms. Y was two she had her pretty well shaped up.

The shaping continued more or less indefinitely. She interpreted any sign of the little girl's being unhappy as a bad mood and told her to get over it. She was quick to point out the deficiencies in whatever the child did. Her impressively successful father returned from the war, but had little to do with his daughter. In the evening, when he came home, he greeted the dog and played with him, not the children, and the mother told her that her father was so busy and important that she was not to bother him at all. The children were fed dinner early so that the parents could dine in privacy.

For as long as Ms. Y can remember she struggled mightily to do things right, but often failed, and tried somewhat more successfully to avoid ever disturbing her parents. She was afraid to go to the bathroom at night for fear of waking them, and she didn't even consider going to them for comfort on the many nights when she was afraid and couldn't sleep. As so often happens, she and her brother occupied different niches in the politics of the family. The boy, who is younger, was furiously re-bellious, but she never was, and only considered that her parents were less than ideal when she was well along in adulthood.

To this day, she feels that she is deficient and that only constant, im-mense effort to do her demanding work can possibly conceal her basic inadequacy. She also believes that if anyone is ever angry with her she has done something wrong. She tries hard never to disturb anyone. It is almost impossible for her to risk ever departing from these principles because to do so might alienate the people in her life, and she is in terror of separation, loss and loneliness. I believe that many of the people who live by strategies that lead to suffering are motivated by that same terror. Like Ms. Y, they have suffered awful loneliness when they were tiny and their parents gave them the conviction that they had to work hard to merit attachment.

As can be imagined, Ms. Y suffers a lot, but she doesn't complain, and through her superior intelligence and energy (her sense of inade-quacy is completely delusional) she accomplishes a lot, but seldom enjoys her success. Since she mustn't discommode anyone, she doesn't ask for anything, even by hinting, and as a result she loses many opportunities for pleasure, success and companionship. She is a gracious, generous person, but is surprised and bitterly disappointed, mostly in the privacy of her own thoughts, by the failure of others to be gracious and generous to her. Like many similar people, she hopes that by doing the right thing she will lead by example and that her friends will do right by her by reciprocity. I think that when they fail to do that it is partly because she doesn't ever ask for what she wants and partly because she is so anxious about causing trouble that she rejects help overtly and covertly. She never moans, except possibly to herself, but she suffers a lot.

With such a person, one of the main difficulties for a therapist is to notice when he has made a mistake or been out of touch, because Ms. Y doesn't want to be a bother and will often hide her distress. It seems to me that, much more commonly, people whose way of life promotes suffering will make it more than clear when I screw up, and my screw-ups are frequent. Most people whose parents were at all like Ms. Y's de-idealized them pretty early but were defeated in their attempts to defy them. (People who defeat their parents early in life are likely to be screamers.)

Bitter customers are more difficult to work with than simply angry ones. I'm the one who's likely to get angry, especially when I say something and the other person smiles a little to himself and laughs slightly at how predictable it is that I have yet again got it wrong. I think there are a number of reasons I find that so irritating. I feel excluded. The other person has gone into a private domain where another useful, trustworthy person could possibly exist, but it surely isn't me. Since it's clear that this is how things always go, there is no hope for our ever getting anywhere, and since it is a reminder of how much of the time I get things wrong, I feel as if everything I have ever tried has gone wrong.

I often think of Harry Truman's infamous obscene letter to the *Washington Post* critic who panned his daughter's concert. The president said to friends as he mailed it, "That son of a bitch didn't even like the paint on the pianner!" There have been many more times than I like to think about that I have indeed gotten mad and said something along the lines of, "There's no satisfying you. You have to destroy everything."

I wouldn't mind my having done it a few times, but I am ashamed of its being many because it never helps—at least not when I do it.

There are lots of times when I get mad and it does help a little, but those are times when I get mad for the people and not at them; but there are problems with that strategy too. For one thing, I sometimes feel like a fool and imagine all of you being pityingly amused with me for giving in to pressure to make a self-defeating lifestyle seem to work, and anyhow I may get carried away and say, or imply, that my customers should be more assertive, and they feel they've got things wrong again. Ms. Y's husband fairly often says things like, "Don't let them do that to you," and she thinks he is seriously dissatisfied with her and it panics her. She commonly describes his or my doing that as our "jumping down her throat."

My former wife's murderous advice may have worked a little. The woman didn't stab my friend, but she did—a long time later—actually divorce him, and Edna's medicine may have made a small, slow contribution to that desirable outcome. One of the good things about it was that it didn't shame the wife. She thought it was Edna who was crazy, not she whose throat was being jumped down for being a wimp.

But, as I was saying, pointing out the way that the other person's rage wrecks everything doesn't seem to help. It can sometimes seem to. Some people are so good at being run down and dominated that they will join in the attack on themselves, which can also be pretty irritating. The man who was my first control case got to the point where he would say, "Oh! I'm being compliant again; I'm sorry." The cause of being assertive can become a quasi-religion and a new false self. Not only does the basic sense of emptiness and dissatisfaction remain, but the convert can identify with the aggressor and become a clone who digs out the hidden rage in people around them—and if the clones are in our business, they dig it out of the people who come to them for help.

Maybe the reason my complaining that my people are wrecking our time together doesn't help is that I don't stick with it, but I don't think so. I think that what helps, even though it often takes a very long time in developing, is a give-and-take relationship with the real person inside the secondary ambition false self that protects the real person by such costly means. Still, it's hard to keep from getting embroiled in conflict directly with the other person because many people will themselves bring us back to our relationship all the time by their complaints about it. To the extent that I can stand never getting things right, and try to figure out with the other person what it was I did that hurt and why it was hurtful, we both profit. Since the real person is horribly fragile and can be damaged many ways, I unfortunately hurt them fairly often. I try to understand what I did to cause the damage and as a result learn all kinds of subtle—or at least they seem subtle to me—ways that I can be doing something harmful without meaning to, or at least that I have fooled myself into thinking I didn't mean to. If I can manage not being defensive, at least most of the time, the other person can avow not just the vertically split-off rageful maneuvers, but also how lonely and frightened he or she is.

Recently, a person whose analysis I hear about came to such a moment. For a long time he has been involved with an alcoholic, abusive woman, and for years before that he was married to another. He has often broken off and then almost immediately resumed the friendship. He did it again lately, while his analyst was on a brief vacation. In one of the first analytic hours back, he said. "I realized that I couldn't stand the loneliness, and I thought only a person like that would have me."

I like to follow the example of the late Lou Shapiro, the highly esteemed Chicago analyst, who used to say, "Every day the character comes in, and I talk with the character, and then some day the person comes in without the character and that's a wonderful day."